Bringing Value,
Solving Problems
and
Leaving a Legacy

To Phil.

From Paul J. M

I wish for you a life of wealth, health, and happiness; a life in which you give to yourself the gift of patience, the virtue of reason, the value of knowledge, and the influence of faith in your own ability to dream about and to achieve worthy rewards.

– Jim Rohn

Good luck! ☺

See P. 70.

Published by
Kyle Wilson International
KyleWilson.com

Distributed by
Kyle Wilson International
P.O. Box 93927
Southlake, TX 76092
info@kylewilson.com

ISBN-13: 9798513562870

Printed in the United States of America.

PRAISE FOR BRINGING VALUE, SOLVING PROBLEMS AND LEAVING A LEGACY

Bringing Value, Solving Problems and Leaving a Legacy *shows you how to increase your sales and profitability, dominate your market, and position yourself against the competition almost overnight. These proven strategies will give you the winning edge from the first day.*

— **Brian Tracy, Author, Speaker, Consultant**

Kyle Wilson is a constant hive of motivational creativity and it shows in his newly published book Bringing Value, Solving Problems and Leaving a Legacy. *Kyle remains as calm and superbly motivated as the first day we met. I am honored to call him a dear friend and look forward to all that is yet to come.*

— **Phil Collen, Author, Songwriter, and Guitarist of Def Leppard**

If you're ready for more success, prosperity, joy, and big value, read, absorb, digest, and use this book from my friend Kyle Wilson and his world-class contributors.

— **Mark Victor Hansen, World's Bestselling Author, Co-Creator of *Chicken Soup for the Soul* and *ASK!***

In Bringing Value, Solving Problems and Leaving a Legacy, *Kyle brings together an amazing collection of thought leaders and experts who provide insight and knowledge that will benefit any reader. The magic comes from the humility and vulnerability of the authors who share their lives to help readers grow and take the next steps to transform their own.*

— **Dr. Amy Novotny, Founder of PABR® Institute, Breathing and Pain Specialist, 2x Amazon Bestselling Author**

In our world of fast-paced change and challenge, Kyle Wilson and his fellow authors' new book Bringing Value, Solving Problems and Leaving a Legacy *provides us immense wisdom gained from the real life experiences of its world-class authors. I greatly appreciate Kyle's previous books, as each has provided me with a wealth of valued wisdom and insight, as well as thought-provoking perspectives. I'm confident this aptly-titled book will be the best yet.*

— **Tim Cole, Colonel USMC Ret**

Kyle hit the highlight real with this book on how to win as an entrepreneur and a human being. This book entices you to lean into your best self. You will NOT be able to put it down without feeling like getting up!

— **Rock Thomas, Bestselling Author, Amazon Music #1 R&B Hit**

When you read these pages, you are getting an incredible combination of the things that help us grow: stories from those who did it and how they did it, inspiration from their journey, new ideas to immediately insert into our lives, and the challenge of all successful people—putting the lessons to action. Kyle has some of the best of the best in their fields letting you inside their minds as they share their wisdom.

— **Kevin Eastman, Former NBA World Champion Coach, Speaker, Author**

Any opportunity to grab wisdom from Kyle Wilson and his fellow writers shouldn't be ignored. Their collective wisdom is backed by their experiences and efforts that have produced results and success far beyond what you might think possible. It could literally change your life.

— **Mike Muhney, Co-Inventor of *ACT!* Software, Author, and Speaker**

In Bringing Value, Solving Problems and Leaving a Legacy, *Kyle combines the magic of storytelling from some of the most successful thought leaders and "real talk" that reminds the reader to keep showing up and building the legacy. The authenticity of the stories combined with humor and life-changing lessons make this book a true gift to anyone open to growth!*

— **Olenka Cullinan, Founder, iStartFirst, Speaker, Women's Coach**

We learn from experience. We grow as we learn. Kyle Wilson has brought us dozens of successful individuals who selflessly share their experiences, giving us the opportunity to blossom as individuals, family members, and entrepreneurs. Take advantage of this gift!

— **Dr. Tom Burns, Author of *Why Doctors Don't Get Rich***

Kyle is dedicated to elevating lives by bringing together the stories of heart-centered individuals who have endured and overcome the most difficult of life's challenges. These stories lead to self-discovery and healing and help us become better versions of ourselves and pay it forward to others. Don't just read the book, let it inspire you and share it through your life.

— **Kelli Calabrese, 34-Year Health Coach, Founder of Intentionally Fabulous**

My friend Kyle Wilson has a deep rolodex of very successful folks, some of them household names, who he brings together in this book to share their insights and wisdom with us. Study it and apply the wisdom shared with these authors to your life and go make an impact in your community.

— **Dave Zook, The Real Asset Investor & Investment Strategist**

I highly recommend this book. Since meeting Kyle Wilson, my business has grown exponentially. He's a wealth of knowledge and generously shares his marketing and branding secrets. He's brilliant, caring, and a genius in the field of marketing and creating a legacy.

— **Lisa Haisha, Film Producer, Humanitarian, Speaker, Author**

Bringing Value, Solving Problems
and
Leaving a Legacy

**Receive Special Bonuses When Buying
the *Bringing Value, Solving Problems and Leaving
a Legacy* Book**

To access bonus gifts and to send us your testimonials and
comments, please send an email to

gifts@bringingvaluebook.com

EXCERPTS FROM BRINGING VALUE, SOLVING PROBLEMS AND LEAVING A LEGACY

For me, a widow with a rose garden is as important as a politician, rock star, or superstar athlete. The sheer exhilaration of doing something excellent for its own merit—not to prove it to others, not to get the money, and not to get accolades—is its own reward.

— **Denis Waitley, Iconic Speaker and Author of *Seeds of Greatness***

For every dollar deposited, the bank can lend out nine dollars. That is called fractional reserve banking. Additionally, as loan repayments are made, they immediately lend that money again, often up to seven times during the course of a loan. That is known as the velocity of money. So why wouldn't you want to get into the banking business? It just so happens, dividend-paying whole life insurance is the perfect vehicle for doing so.

— **Eberhard Samlowski, Former Surgeon, Real Estate Investor, Infinite Banking Coach**

Change is good. Consider changing something in your life that allows you to prioritize a passion project. While happiness might feel elusive at times, a passion project will give you something that excites you and feeds your soul.

— **Brandy Wilson Edwards, Attorney, Speaker, The Self-Love Challenge**

In our aquaponics garden system, we feed the fish, the fish wastewater fertilizes the plants, the plants and their beneficial bacteria help to clean the water for the fish, and we're able to harvest fresh fruits, vegetables, and fish. All this takes place while using 90% less water than traditional soil gardening! This type of practice leaves behind a world worth inheriting and is something we can proudly stand behind as an ongoing business model.

— **Kurtis Drake and Ryan Pettitt, Real Estate Entrepreneurs, Permaculture Land Stewards**

Although I started making good money as a clinical nurse, I did not become a millionaire until I bought rental properties. That is when we achieved stability, and my net worth took off. I didn't want to keep doing the same thing over and over but instead work smarter.

— **Charles Vincent Kaluwasha, Founder CJ Investiment, Author, Marketer**

Instead of continuing to focus on what we were giving up or leaving behind, I decided to start focusing on the new journey ahead. I knew it would not be easy, but neither was sitting on a couch feeling paralyzed and sulking. Little did I know, the experiences I was about to gain would end up transforming all aspects of my life and career.

— **Michelle Oppelt, Serial Entrepreneur, Speaker, Humanitarian**

If you go through something terrible and it makes you a better person for doing it, then mission accomplished. Too many people don't want to pay attention to their mistakes. They think mistakes are bad when mistakes are actually the way we learn.

— **Robert Helms, Top Real Estate Podcast, Developer, Speaker**

I would never have guessed that my love for personal development, my curiosity about how the mind works, and my finally understanding who I was would lead me into building a successful home-based business with a team in six countries, a six-figure income, and the opportunity to speak on stages all over Canada.

— **Vanessa Canevaro, Author, Speaker, Mindset Coach**

I have learned to just keep pushing and good things are worth waiting for. I know the effect I have and will have on my family tree I may never fully see the fruit of. I look at my kids and other people who grew up like I did, or who just need encouragement, and I know it is all worth it.

— **Paul Aragon, Business Owner, Financial Coach, Speaker**

Doing something is better than doing nothing. Intentional progress every day will get you there. Keep people in your circle that see the best in you, cheer on your success, and pick you up when you fall.

— **Kerry Faix, Real Estate Syndicator, COO Stone Bay Holdings**

I think any problem can be solved if you bring the right people together to work as a team with respect, honesty, and open communication.

— **Mark Livingston, Corporate Executive, Alternative Investments**

Never underestimate your ability to redefine the limits of your comfort zone and accomplish something remarkable. By looking for opportunities to help others, you can solve problems, experience incredible personal growth, and change lives.

— **Dr. Lee Newton, Optometrist, Thought Leader, Real Estate Developer**

Everyone told me I was crazy and would never get hired. I chose not to listen. After all, I wouldn't have a chance if I didn't at least try.

— **Brandy Vega, Media Mogul, Speaker, Humanitarian**

I didn't consider myself "smart" because I wasn't the kind of smart that excelled at my academic high school. This narrow characterization of intelligence, combined with the upsets and losses I experienced, stripped me of confidence. As I matured, I came to realize that creating opportunities is its own type of intelligence.

— **Chad Hughes, Entrepreneurial Leader**

I've learned such an abundance of lessons financially, physically, and mentally. I say now that getting the hell kicked out of me by the pavement at 80 miles an hour was one of the greatest things that's ever happened in my life. The desperate day I spent looking for coins in the parking lot was the first and this was a second starting point in my life. The best that I can do is keep getting back up. I want my kids to be able to see that no matter what happens, you must stand back up.

— **Aaron Chapman, Author, *Breaker of Molds***

The accident shut many doors in what I thought was my perfect life. As those doors closed, other doors opened—doors I would never have previously considered. I became self-employed, building several businesses. Through one of those businesses, I made history.

— **Karen Newton, Coach, Author, Speaker, Multiple Income Streams**

Find something you are passionate about, surround yourself with people that encourage you, get mentors, and do not be afraid to change course when you need to.

— **Rocky McKay, Senior Living Expert, Speaker, Entrepreneur**

While the manner in which we achieve our pleasure goals and pursue happiness changes over the years, happiness and pleasure are our birthrights. We all need sleep, food, and exercise...and healthy sexuality. When we rewire our brains to access deeper levels of pleasure in our bodies, we tap into a wealth of vitality, one of the tenets of a flourishing life.

— **Wanda Santos-Haynes, Positive Relationships Coach, Intimacy Consultant**

You may be very good. You may be a star, but you may not be aware of it. As I say, "If you are not aware, you are nowhere!" It takes a genuine mentor to uncover your potential and unleash it to the world. For me, I will be leaving my legacy in books, radio shows, podcasts, and many other forms, thanks to my mentors.

— **Jeff McKee, Multifamily Apartment Sponsor, Real Estate Developer, Speaker**

How can someone who was born and raised in a third world country, who was condemned to a short life at birth, who was bullied at every level in school, and who was a super-ultra timid guy, become an 3x Amazon #1 bestselling author? Solving my continuous series of challenges created a new mindset within me. If there are always people present to help me, and if I have been helped along all throughout my life, then I should also be available to help others.

— **Ravin S. Papiah, Top Leadership Speaker, Trainer, Coach**

On July 15th of 2009, I decided that I was going to start doing a video a day, and I have not missed one day in over 11 years. There's a big difference between commitment and creativity. When you're committed, creativity is forced. If you wait for creativity before you're committed, it never happens.

— **Ray Higdon, Founder of RankMakers, Author, Speaker**

Time does not heal all, time teaches you to live with the pain and emptiness. Time creates different anger, when you can no longer remember what your loved one looks like without a picture, when you can no longer remember the way they laughed or the way their hugs felt. Even though this bad happened to me when I was young and I struggled, I learned from the mistakes I made through the process.

— **Jessica Cress, Realtor, Investor, Entrepreneur, Mentor**

I was a real estate investor. Commercial banks and lenders had this intimidating aura about them. But I knew, to grow my real estate portfolio, I needed larger and more flexible lenders who would lend on the cash flow from the investment properties (assets) we wanted to buy. So, I went in search of information and mentorship.

— **Billy Brown, Commercial Loan Strategist, Founder of The Golf Sanctuary**

With becoming a professional ballerina comes incredible struggles of resilience. There are strict rules of appearance, aesthetics, weight, body shape, and early training that shape the rest of your career. The casting of roles is a constant reflection of how you are being perceived, and if you aren't strong, it can have a serious impact on you. Aesthetically, I had nothing that it took to be a ballerina except passion and drive.

— **Nancy Paradis, Director, Choreographer, Founder of LA Dance Moves**

I love my career as a New York City (FDNY) firefighter. It is an honor and a privilege to serve others and to have a huge impact on people's lives. The path to real estate investing and working on financial independence was certainly not linear for me. Like so many others, it was only after I had realized that I was living my life with a scarcity mindset, a mindset that was engineered for safety and certainty, that I decided change was needed.

— **Timothy Lyons, NYC Firefighter, Real Estate Investor**

Moving from being employees to entrepreneurs was not easy, especially in this business because we are responsible for managing large investments for others. We have to constantly think and tune our approach as we both set processes to efficiently scale and stay prudent at the same time. The fruit of success is sweet, but it comes after a lot of hard work and patience.

— **Pancham Gupta, Syndicator, Podcaster, Bestselling Author, Entrepreneur and Rajan Gupta, Fintech Engineer, Syndicator, Asset Manager**

Even if I didn't succeed by some people's standards, I would succeed by mine because just in the process of trying, I would be learning things, meeting people, and moving farther along the road to being all I could be.

— **Mitzi Perdue, Family Business Expert, Speaker, Humanitarian**

From starting a family in college to early investing failures, life has been a journey of learning and perseverance. I learned you don't have to be the smartest. You just need to leverage other people's expertise, take consistent action, and persevere when things get tough. Do what others aren't willing to do, keep going, and you will achieve success.

— **Alan Stewart, Real Estate Investor, Leader, Entrepreneur**

One of the things I taught Professor Efimchik's students was that success can sometimes become a trap. You do something well and end up doing that something your whole life. Then, when it's too late, you realize that though you did that something well, it wasn't what you really wanted to do in the first place. It wasn't what you were put on Earth to do.

— **Dr. John R. Obenchain, Communicating Your Message Speaker and Teacher**

People see things differently, are wired differently, and express themselves differently. I tell myself to keep an open mind without being chained to my way of thinking, to take time to dig deep, to ask the same questions in multiple ways, and to explore my client's needs based on their background.

— **Lynn Yangchana, Commercial Real Estate CCIM, Realtor, Investor**

What do you want your grandchildren to remember about you when you are gone? Not all sheepdogs are a physical warrior like General George S. Patton or US Navy SEAL Chris Kyle. Many are warriors in their faith or determination for social justice, such as Mother Teresa, Billy Graham, Rosa Parks, Zig Ziglar, and many more. Search them out, follow their guidance, and as you learn from them, live accordingly.

— **Richard M. Morris, 10th Degree Black Belt, Speaker, Trainer, Coach**

Being lukewarm about anything doesn't have a very desirable end result, and it doesn't help us find our passion. To make a real difference and add the most value, we've got to find our purpose—the thing we were meant to do.

— **Cheri Perry, Leadership Expert, Author, Speaker**

I very often when faced with major decisions ask myself what is the worst-case scenario and plan for it. As soon as we can deal with the worst, the rest is upside!

— **Erik Mikkelson, Wealth Accumulation & Cash Flow Strategist**

The way you're going to earn a lot of money through your business is by first being genuinely focused on the other person and the immense value you're providing them. It comes down to understanding that "Money is an echo of value. It's the thunder to value's lightning." Thus, the money you receive is the natural result of the value you've given others.

— **Bob Burg, Speaker & Co-Author of** *The Go-Giver*

When experience meets passion and compassion, it helps us to discover our greater purpose: what we are uniquely made for and qualified to do with our lives. This purpose is not usually given to us, and it rarely becomes evident without years of trial and finding out what we are made of. Sometimes finding out what we are made of is necessary before we can truly know what we are made for.

— **Anna Kelley, Multifamily Operator, Impact Investor, Mentor**

Just get in the water, start swimming, put one arm in front of the other, and keep swimming until you get to France.

— **Paul Hopfensperger, Entrepreneur and 3x English Channel Swimmer**

How does someone go from a dead-end job, working 60 to 70 hours per week, to being financially free? I decided I was going to, and then I took massive action.

— **Chadd Naugle, Real Estate Investor, Syndicator, Entrepreneur**

I made the firm decision that nothing and nobody would ever stop me from moving towards my dream. I knew that stepping into new territory with no map would be scary at times. But if I wanted my life to have deeper and more satisfying meaning, I needed to embrace change and do something unusual!

— **Valérie Mostert, Transformational Coach, Writer, Author**

In your life, you are the actor, writer, director, and producer of your own movie. You are already writing the story of your character. Your strength is the realization that you have the ability to change whatever story you used to believe about yourself into whatever your heart desires. You are living your life every day, so why not write and act in an incredible movie and play the hero of that empowering story?

— **Rachele Brooke Smith, Actress, Filmmaker, Speaker, Entrepreneur**

I have consulted some of the biggest speakers in the world as well as 7, 8, and 9-figure entrepreneurs on the business model of The Wheel. It sounds simple, and it is, but The Wheel also has layers of strategic complexities and also provides a true north compass for creating a business model that supports your goals and intended lifestyle.

— **Kyle Wilson, Founder Jim Rohn International, Marketer, Speaker**

DISCLAIMER

The information in this book is not meant to replace the advice of a certified professional. Please consult a licensed advisor in matters relating to your personal and professional well-being including your mental, emotional and physical health, finances, business, legal matters, family planning, education, and spiritual practices. The views and opinions expressed throughout this book are those of the authors and do not necessarily reflect the views or opinions of all the authors or position of any other agency, organization, employer, publisher, or company.

Since we are critically-thinking human beings, the views of each of the authors are always subject to change or revision at any time. Please do not hold them or the publisher to them in perpetuity. Any references to past performance may not be indicative of future results. No warranties or guarantees are expressed or implied by the publisher's choice to include any of the content in this volume.

If you choose to attempt any of the methods mentioned in this book, the authors and publisher advise you to take full responsibility for your safety and know your limits. The authors and publisher are not liable for any damages or negative consequences from any treatment, action, application, or preparation to any person reading or following the information in this book.

This book is a personal collaboration between a number of authors and their experiences, beliefs, opinions, and advice. The authors and publisher make no representations as to accuracy, completeness, correctness, suitability, or validity of any information in the book, and neither the publisher nor the individual authors shall be liable for any physical, psychological, emotional, financial, or commercial damages, including, but not limited to, special, incidental, consequential, or other damages to the readers of this book.

TABLE OF CONTENTS

Dedication

To all the mentors and influences that have shaped the lives of each of our authors. To our families and loved ones who fan our flames and inspire us. To all those that read this book and are inspired to take action, apply the wisdom, and leave their own unique legacy.

Acknowledgments

A big thank you—

To Takara Sights, our writing coach, editor, and project manager extraordinaire, for your endless hours of work and passion in this book! Despite the complexities involved with a project like this, you keep the process a pleasure and always provide first-class results. A thousand praises! You are a rockstar!

To Joni McPherson who's been our go-to person for book formatting and cover design since day one for us. Your tireless hours and multiple cover revisions and interior galley corrections are greatly appreciated!

To Kathi Laughman, Adrian Sheppard, Dr. John R. Obenchain, Margo Duesterhaus, Vanessa Canevaro, Kelli Calabrese, Lynn Bodnar, and Heidi Wilson for being our second eyes and proofreading the manuscript as needed. We so appreciate it!

And to Phil Collen, Brian Tracy, Mark Victor Hansen, Dr. Amy Novotny, Kevin Eastman, Mike Muhney, Dave Zook, Dr. Tom Burns, Kelli Calabrese, Olenka Cullinan, Tim Cole, Rock Thomas, Lisa Haisha, and ALL the amazing mentors and world-class thought leaders who took the time to read this book's manuscript and give us their endorsements—thank you!

FOREWORD

by Tom Ziglar

"You can have everything in life you want if you will just help enough other people get what they want."
– Zig Ziglar

I'm honored to be asked by my long-time friend, Kyle Wilson, to write the foreword for this book. I love the title *Bringing Value, Solving Problems and Leaving a Legacy*!

I believe it all starts with the mindset of being a problem solver. Good news! If you are a problem solver, you have never had more opportunity than right now! My friend and mentor Rabbi Daniel Lapin says this: "God is never happier with his children than when they are solving the problems of his other children." When you solve a problem, the Creator of the universe smiles!

As you dig into this book, I want you to ask yourself the following questions as you read each chapter, so that you will be better equipped to bring value, solve problems, and leave a legacy.

Question #1: How can this chapter help me better understand what my customer or prospect is thinking and feeling?

You have in your hands the life experiences of more than 40 experts who have each dedicated years to solving the problems of their customers. Learn from this information, and as you build relationships with your prospects and customers, ask them questions that reveal how they are feeling about their situation which you can help them with. Are they worried about how much your solution will cost? Concerned that you have the skills necessary to do the job? Afraid they will be taken advantage of? Once you have clarity on what is causing your prospect to hesitate, you are on your way to helping solve the problem.

Question #2: What is this chapter teaching me about what people really want?

Many times, our ultimate goal when serving others and solving problems in the business world is to get fantastic referrals and five-star reviews. In the process of doing this, we sometimes get confused and forget to deliver both what people need and what they want. They may need our product or service, but what they want is a relationship they can trust.

Question #3: What is this chapter teaching me about the value and values I must demonstrate to my prospect so that they move from a skeptical tire kicker to a raving fan?

It doesn't matter if you are a business owner, working in a business, a teacher, or a parent, we all have "prospects" that we are "selling." When you understand that selling is really serving and serving is delivering value with values, then you are on your way!

One final question. What do you want people to say about you behind your back?

I have asked this question to thousands of people. The words that come up are almost always the same: honest, kind, loving, hard working, integrous, dependable, passionate, respectful, trustworthy, etc. Now, take a few seconds to write in the margin the words you want to be known for. As you look at these words, realize that you have a choice right now to either build a legacy by chance, or by design. To build a legacy by design, simply focus on solving the problems of others by delivering value with the values you have written down. The more problems you solve this way, the bigger and better your legacy will be!

Tom Ziglar is a speaker, trainer, and the CEO of Ziglar. com, as well as the author of Choose to Win: Transform Your Life One Simple Choice at a Time. *He is the son of the legendary Zig Ziglar.*

INTRODUCTION

by Kyle Wilson

When asked to speak in front of groups or on podcasts, I often share four of the greatest lessons I learned from my 18-year friend, mentor, and business partner Jim Rohn!

And a few of those lessons led me to the title of this book.

At age 28, I heard Jim say, "If you want to become successful, learn to bring value to the marketplace."

He didn't say become a great networker. He said learn to bring value.

Jim also said, "Learn to be a problem solver. If you can solve problems, you will always be in demand."

And my mentor taught me, most importantly, to design a life that you will be proud of and set an example that will have a ripple effect, the smallest of which will still impact future generations.

Takara Sights, our editor and writing coach for this book, and I, as the publisher, are so honored to know and share the powerful lessons and stories from our authors in this book.

The process over the past year of conversations, interviews, and working and reworking the stories in this book has left an indelible impact on me. I get the unbelievable honor to learn and grow from these incredible people who share their stories in these pages, including long-time friends—the iconic Denis Waitley, someone I have known and worked with since 1996, Bob Burg the co-author of *The Go-Giver*, and Robert Helms the host of *The Real Estate Guys Radio Show* and podcast.

The advice Jim Rohn gave me 32 years ago remains true today as a roadmap to success. That roadmap comes alive in the examples shared in this book, *Bringing Value, Solving Problems and Leaving a Legacy*!

Kyle Wilson is a Publisher, Entrepreneur, Business & Marketing Strategist, Seminar Promoter, Speaker, and #1 Bestselling Author. Founder of KyleWilson.com, Jim Rohn International, YourSuccessStore, and LessonsFromExperts.com.

The greatest legacy anyone can leave behind is to positively impact the lives of others. Whenever you add value to other people's lives, you are unknowingly leaving footprints on the sands of time that live on, even after your passing.

– Emeasoba George

KYLE WILSON
The Day I Will Always Cherish

Kyle Wilson is an entrepreneur, business and marketing strategist, publisher, seminar promoter, and speaker. He is the founder of KyleWilson.com, Jim Rohn International, and LessonsFromExperts.com. Kyle hosts the Success Habits *podcast and the Kyle Wilson Inner Circle Mastermind and has published dozens of #1 bestselling books.*

How It All Started

People often ask how I was able to work with the legend Jim Rohn, launch Jim Rohn International, and call Jim my 18-year friend, mentor, and business partner. People also ask how I have worked so closely, then and now, with Brian Tracy, Les Brown, Denis Waitley, Mark Victor Hansen, Darren Hardy, Phil Collen, and so many others. It has happened through a whole series of serendipitous events, but at the core of each was a combination of bringing value and solving problems.

I was born and raised in a small town, Vernon, Texas. I wasn't a great student and found myself getting in trouble. That story is in a previous book. But I'd always been a hard worker and was ambitious, having a series of jobs going back to 8th grade.

After graduating high school, it never occurred to me to go to college. At age 19, I decided to start my own business, which eventually grew into 10 employees. Things were going well. But by age 26, I really wanted something different. I felt compelled to move away from the town I was raised in. I didn't have much of a plan. I just felt strongly the desire to move to a bigger metropolitan area. I ended up in Dallas-Fort Worth.

Getting Into the Seminar Business and Filling Large Rooms

After moving to Dallas, I attempted a couple of entrepreneurial ventures. Then 18 months after moving, I was serendipitously invited to attend a seminar. I met the promoter, Jerry Haines, and at the end of the seminar, Jerry said he was looking for sales reps to help him market his events.

The job entailed making 50-100 prospecting phone calls a day to book myself to speak at companies' weekly or monthly sales meetings.

The thought of getting up and speaking in front of a group was terrifying to me, but I really felt I was supposed to give it a shot.

"Opportunity always precedes personal development." **– Kyle Wilson**

This new opportunity got me excited. I started reading books on personal development and how to sell. I did everything Jerry told me to do. I made the phone calls. I followed up. I learned the presentation. I learned the close. And I went to work.

Little did I know, saying YES to Jerry and being pushed far beyond my comfort zone would lead me down a life-changing road.

In just one year, I became Jerry's #1 rep in the country. But there was one big challenge. I was hardly making any money. The commission model was broken, and I had no control over fixing it.

I decided I needed to go out on my own. I had a goal to do bigger events. I would ask myself 100 times a day, *How do I get 2000 paid attendees in a room?* After months of searching and hundreds of scribbled notes on a yellow pad, I finally had a plan.

I convinced my wife Heidi to leave her job, and we began to travel the country putting on events. We got really good at it, eventually getting 2000 plus people in each city. We would hire Jim Rohn, Brian Tracy, and Og Mandino to speak at our events.

We built a model that worked for us and were making great money, putting on events in places we wanted to live, working with amazing speakers, and building relationships across the country! We had broken the code.

Launching and Growing Jim Rohn International

In 1993, four years after getting into the seminar business, Jim Rohn and his business partner split up. I told Jim I really believed he was the best speaker in the world, and that I was a pretty good promoter, and asked him for exclusive rights to promote and market him and his products.

When considering another partner, Jim was reluctant. He had lost over a million dollars combined in two of his previous partnerships. So, I proposed the idea of it being my company. I would cover all the expenses and overhead, pay Jim's speaking fee off the top like a speakers bureau, plus give him royalties on all the products we would create and sell. That way, it was all profit for Jim with zero overhead and no risk of losing money. It also allowed me to build my company and team, have control, and create synergistic relationships with other speakers.

I made Jim an offer he couldn't refuse and he said yes. We did a handshake agreement which lasted for over 11 years until we finally put our agreement in writing in 2004.

It was an amazing partnership. Jim was the speaker and philosopher, while I was the marketer and agent and ran the company.

One of the main things Jim Rohn teaches is to bring value. And that was the goal we each had, to bring massive amounts of value to each other and the marketplace.

Game Changer, The Wheel

That first year, I took Jim from 20 speaking engagements at $4k each to 110 speaking engagements at $10k and then $25k each. Plus, I created multiple new products, including the *Excerpts From the Treasury of Quotes* that went on to be a viral marketing tool that moved over six million copies.

Jim did not have a customer list and had only a handful of products to offer. I needed to solve both.

The game-changer for me was a concept called The Wheel.

I remember sitting down and drawing on a piece of paper a big circle with a small center hub and multiple spokes—a wheel. Each spoke was an existing product or service Jim had, including a book, an audio series, one and two-day live seminars, plus his corporate and public speaking. The goal of The Wheel is, once someone gets on The Wheel, you then take them around it to experience other products and services you offer that may be a good fit for them. The key is to get more people on The Wheel, build a relationship with them and have GREAT products and services that they can benefit from!

I teach several criteria that any new spoke you are considering adding to your wheel should meet.

A new spoke on the wheel:

- needs to be synergistic to your core business

- focuses on your main customer avatar

- is built around your secret sauce (what makes you special)

- is strategic and something that will knock down the rest of the dominoes

- helps get new prospects and customers on the wheel

Being a wordsmith was part of Jim's secret sauce. He had the ability to take the complex and make it simple in a few words. So, for the first new spoke, I went through all of Jim's speeches and came up with almost 1000 Jim Rohn quotes. I selected 365 quotes and divided them into 60 categories.

That became a hardbound book, *The Jim Rohn Treasury of Quotes*. But, I really wanted a smaller gift booklet our customers and advocates could buy in multiples and give away. So I created a smaller version with 110 quotes, *The Jim Rohn Treasury of Quotes Excerpt Booklet*. The excerpt booklet had a page in the front with a special To and From and a place to write a personal note. It also had our product catalog in it with how to buy more booklets at a highly discounted rate. It checked every box and became a viral marketing tool we ended up moving millions of in large part by making it easy for our advocates to buy and give away.

Your Success Store and Online Marketing

After I would book Jim to speak at companies, and once someone bought all his products, then what? I found that once people discovered Jim Rohn and his message, they wanted more.

So I started another company called Your Success Store. In addition to Jim Rohn, I started booking other speakers—including Brian Tracy, Les Brown, Mark Victor Hansen, Denis Waitley, Bob Burg, and others—and selling their products to my customers. I also created quote booklets, similar to what I did for Jim, for Zig Ziglar, Brian Tracy, Mark Victor Hansen, and Denis Waitley.

I found each speaker and product would attract new people onto my wheel.

Then, six years later, in 1999, I dove headfirst into the internet and was one of the first people to build a 1,000,000 plus email list. By 2002, I had multiple publications and over 100 different products (including digital products) by Jim Rohn and other authors and speakers who I was marketing through my companies.

I have consulted some of the biggest speakers in the world as well as 7, 8, and 9-figure entrepreneurs on the business model of The Wheel. It sounds simple, and it is, but The Wheel also has layers of strategic complexities and also provides a true north compass for creating a business model that supports your goals and intended lifestyle.

I always say nothing changed in Jim's message. It was the business model and marketing that helped us reach millions more people.

Selling It All in 2007

In 2006, one of the few companies that I felt could steward Jim's message and also take the other speakers and authors I managed to the next level wanted to buy me. They were also in the process of buying *SUCCESS* magazine.

I had over 20 employees and I was representing several speakers. Things were going well, but I was tired and burnt out and my kids were growing up fast. I felt maybe the timing was right to hand it all off. I was able to negotiate a great deal allowing my team to stay on plus receive profit sharing on the sale of the company. It felt like it was a win/win for me, my team, the speakers, and the company wanting to buy me. So, in late 2007, I sold the companies. I stayed on for 12 months to help them transition.

The Making of the Jim Rohn Tribute Video

In 2008, at the age of 78, my mentor, friend, and business partner for so many years, Jim Rohn, had been diagnosed with pulmonary fibrosis and told he only had a year or two to live. Jim had taken great care of himself and believed he would live to be 100. Getting the news left him shocked. It was extremely hard for him.

With the help and support of Reed Bilbray and the new owner of SUCCESS and Jim Rohn International Stuart Johnson, I went to work on creating a very special gift for Jim and the world: a tribute video for Jim to see before he passed that would include Jim's closest friends, colleagues, and peers sharing their appreciation and love and the impact Jim had on their lives.

I was able to set up conversations and interviews with Brian Tracy, Zig and Tom Ziglar, Mark Victor Hansen, Denis Waitley, John Maxwell, Les Brown, and dozens more of Jim's peers, colleagues, and friends, all in preparation for the tribute video I wanted to share with Jim.

We had so many amazing stories, testimonials, and sentiments of love from this amazing group of people. But I knew we were still missing one, William E. Bailey!

Bill was in his 80s, had been sick, and was not able to travel. How could I put together this montage of amazing words of love and admiration from all these people in Jim's life, then sit and watch it with Jim, and not have one of his main mentors and friends?

I decided to fly to Lexington, Kentucky, and I rented a car and drove for a few hours east to Bill's family log cabin in eastern Kentucky.

I had known Bill for many years. In fact, I'd published his *Rhythms of Life* book several years prior and had booked him on many of my stages. I made the most of the trip and was honored to spend the day with this Horatio Alger winner, the founder of Bestline Products, and one of Jim's mentors.

After filming the tribute, Bill and I decided to go grab a late lunch.

I'll never forget that when we were talking he looked at me, and he said in a mentoring tone, "Kyle, you have a true genius about you. And your gifts have made room for themselves. There is no way you could've ever predicted meeting and working with Jim Rohn. How you arrived at what you do and your relationship with Jim is a byproduct of your calling and the hundreds and the thousands of things you did way before you ever met Jim. There's no way you could've ever predicted it."

After these almost prophetic words from Bill, we went back to our normal conversation.

Bill was right. I didn't even know who Jim Rohn was at age 27. There's no way I could have made it a goal of mine to get in the seminar business and eventually be the founder of Jim Rohn International, partnering and spending 18 years with this amazing man. That is why I often encourage others to keep showing up and bringing their best. We can't see or predict the future, but we can do our best today and trust that good things will unfold.

My Last Day With Jim

Time was of the essence. Now, we had to take 50+ conversations and interviews and edit them down to two hours of video. We did that, then edited a second version with highlights of each conversation that was 30 minutes. Jim could watch one or both.

In November of 2008, it was my great honor to deliver that video to Jim a month before he passed away. We sat down and watched it together. He was beyond touched and moved. He was able to hear the appreciation and love from over 50 people in his life.

As Jim and I watched together, the segments with two long-time friends who had worked with Jim for many years, really touched Jim in particular. In both cases, they had grown apart from Jim over the years. In their conversations with me, they both shared their love, their gratitude, and how much Jim had changed their lives. They both cried and were emotional.

I vividly remember Jim looking at me during their segments and saying "Wow!" Jim was moved! The video tribute was not only touching and overwhelming for Jim, it also provided healing.

After watching the tribute together, Jim and I had lunch and shared memories. We had one particular conversation about our faith that deeply moved me. After 20 years, we still had more to learn and discover about each other. It is a day I will never forget! My most cherished day with my friend and mentor.

The Passing of an Icon

Jim Rohn passed away December 5, 2009. I was honored to attend a private memorial with his family and close friends. He was beloved by all! It was a sad day. Seventy-nine years is a long, rich life, but we all thought we would have Jim for much longer.

In February 2010, *SUCCESS* put on an amazing public tribute for Jim. I was honored to speak along with Tony Robbins, Les Brown, Brian Tracy, Darren Hardy, and many others. People that were there still share with me how special it was for them to attend it and how much Jim Rohn impacted their lives.

Jim would always tell me he wanted to be the guy who impacted the few who impacted the many. Jim did both! His influence lives on today more than ever!

Meeting Jim in 1989, launching Jim Rohn International in 1993, and having Jim as a friend and mentor for 20 years, was one of the great honors of my life. Jim and his teachings and mentorship changed my life!

In the last year of his life, on February 9, 2008, Jim wrote in my journal, "Kyle, friendship is Wealth and you make me a Rich Man. Thank you for your friendship and partnership all these years. Love and Respect! – Jim Rohn"

That is one of my most cherished possessions.

Jim, thank you for your friendship, your mentorship, and forever changing my life. You are missed but not forgotten! Love and respect, my dear friend and mentor! – Kyle

To learn more about Kyle's Inner Circle Mastermind, his #1 Bestseller Book Program, or one-on-one consulting, send an email to info@kylewilson.com. To receive FREE 10 digital books and over a dozen interviews by Kyle with Darren Hardy, Les Brown, Brian Tracy, and more, send an email to access@ kylewilson.com with gifts in the subject. Follow Kyle on IG @kylewilsonjimrohn

Tweetable: "Opportunity always precedes personal development." – Kyle Wilson

AARON CHAPMAN
Getting Back Up

Aaron Chapman is a highly-productive real estate investment financier, author, real estate investor, and contrarian. His YouTube series, The QJO Initiative, highlights the pains that accompany success and shares stories of people who pick themselves up to face their next obstacles. He lives with his wife of 25 years and children in Arizona.

The 2008 Crashes

Blinking in an effort to focus my vision in the bright fluorescent light, I attempted to take in my surroundings. Vision still blurred, I could make out the figure of someone sitting in a chair next to me. A hoarse, labored "where am I" escaped my lips.

"The hospital. You have been in an accident," came the familiar voice of my wife Rizzo.

"What day is it?" I requested.

"August 8th, 2008," she explained. Going into greater detail, she explained that both my legs were shattered, plus I had road rash, burns, broken ribs, and a shattered clavicle, and I would need to get right with being in a wheelchair for a while. She'd been through this explanation with me a few times, but this time it began to stick.

That morning I left my home as an athletic person, with a paper net worth of over $3 million, taking three days on a Harley to get my head clear. An inattentive driver at 80+ MPH sent me skidding at 12:24 in the afternoon on a sunbaked Arizona freeway. Now, I laid in a bed, drugged up, with external fixators to position the bone fragments. I was facing multiple surgeries and extensive rehab, while the global market was teetering on a precipice.

Diaper Coupons and Loose Change

I come from an extremely blue collar background. My dad worked in all types of different things, mainly the mines and some cattle ranching in the '90s. After high school, I worked in the oil fields of Wyoming then in the mines in northern New Mexico with my dad. Underground hardrock mining was something I wanted to do since I was a kid. To enter the mine, you are lowered down a shaft a couple hundred feet. At your workspace, referred to as a heading, you drill multiple six foot deep holes in a specific pattern, load it full of explosives, blow it up, clean it all out, support the tunnel, then start the cycle all over again. I loved the job.

I got laid off when I was 23 years old and went hunting for a job. I was not finding one. I heard of an opening as a $10 an hour truck driver hauling landscape rock in Phoenix. I went to the landscape company thinking this had to be it, and it should be easy. I didn't want it, but I needed something. My wife and I were penniless, and we just had our first kid. Like every other job I applied for, they told me I was overqualified.

I remember going out to my truck shedding tears. I had to head to a grocery store with a coupon for free diapers. As I traveled to the grocery store, my gas light came on. I pulled up to the gas pump on the corner by the chosen store and ran my debit card. I got a decline because I was overdrawn. So, I started rifling through my truck looking for change. I found a few coins and then spent the next two hours wandering the parking lot to find more change.

I found enough to get two gallons of gas. Then I went into the store, found the corresponding diapers, and redeemed my coupon. As I was walking out, I ran face to face into a guy I used to work with running heavy equipment. He ran the office, and I was one of the equipment operators in charge of an excavation crew. He asked me how things were, and I explained my situation. He offered to take me to dinner. I told him I couldn't afford it, but he said he had a gift certificate for Red Lobster given to him by a client.

When he took my wife and I out to dinner the following night, he explained the mortgage industry, and he slid me the card for a mortgage broker branch manager. To meet with the potential employer, I cut a foot off my hair, shaved my beard, and dressed in some new clothes purchased by my mother so I looked somewhat professional. They started me as a telemarketer that December. It was absolutely miserable going from working in the mines to telemarketing, but within 10 days, I was able to create some good leads. Then, I convinced them to allow me to work as a trainee loan originator.

Rebuilding and Making Changes

Everybody took a beating in the 2008 crash. There were plenty of people out there who lost businesses or lost their houses. Some had loss so extensive they took their own lives. Me...I left that hospital a 6'1, 156 lb skeleton of my former self. The market shift and my crippled business pushed my net worth from $3 million in the black to in excess of $1.5 million in the red. In addition to the losses, the medical bills started to come in the mail. The first week alone was invoiced at $1.7 million. Because of the circumstances, I could negotiate with my creditors. I was blessed to be able to settle all of my debt, although I was forced to negotiate away these things from my wheelchair. I got out of it cleaner, in my opinion, than most people who were in similar circumstances who did not have a story of physical devastation to share and elicit compassion.

That nasty accident forced me to re-evaluate my chosen direction in life. I was back at square one again. For a second time, I was penniless. In this case, less than penniless. I had an extreme negative net worth. I couldn't stand on my own financially or physically. But that accident provided me with what I discovered was the divine gift of an accelerated education. With some highly concentrated effort, we worked our way out from under that debt. With more focused effort, I learned how to walk, and I started building myself up. By carrying a notepad with me to write down conversations, phone calls, and tasks to complete, I regained my short-term memory through tedious training.

I've learned such an abundance of lessons financially, physically, and mentally. I say now that getting the hell kicked out of me by the pavement at 80 miles an hour was one of the greatest things that's ever happened in my life. The desperate day I spent looking for coins in the parking lot was the first and this was a second starting point in my life. The best that I can do is keep getting back up. I want my kids to be able to see that no matter what happens, you must stand back up.

Defining Moments of Clarity

When you've got the noise of the world turned down and you're left to your own thoughts, you have the opportunity to decide if you like the person that you are and the direction you're going in life. This accident gave me the capability to be very open with folks and, critically, to focus on the most important task at the moment: to appreciate the people I enjoyed being with.

This focus personally led to my focus professionally. Coming back to the lending industry, I narrowed who I would seek as a client. That led me to the investors coming into Arizona and buying property at the bottom of the market because of the crash. I found the ability to align with them due to my newfound life experience. I was done putting on the show that most in my industry did—trying to dress, act, and speak in the way they believed the world expected them to. They would get the real, raw me. If they didn't like that, it was okay. Being myself allowed me to sort through masses quickly to those I could develop a relationship with. It wasn't long before those investors migrated from Arizona to Indiana, Texas, Tennessee, Missouri, and many other states. My business started spreading across the country. Now, I do business in 26 states and, in an industry of over 300,000 licensed individuals, I am ranked in the top 20 people for transactions closed.

Once you face your own death, you can face anything.

If You Want it...Write It

At a critical point in my career in the lending industry, I was tasked with providing my five year vision to the executives of a company I had been introduced to when interviewing with their firm. This is not something I had ever done before, yet I'd heard many talk about it. I had an interest in working with this firm, so I decided to play along and write this prediction of my future by addressing myself in a letter as if my future had already passed.

As I began to grow in the first couple of years following this exercise, some of the old adages and regurgitated statements from those encouraging goal setting and envisioning one's future began to have some new meaning. The mere exercise of trying it brought about the sense of setting my bearing towards a distant result and checking it often, if not every day.

Deciding that this long-term exercise needed to be condensed to a more short-term exercise, I determined February 4, 2017 to write down something similar but pointed it toward what I was to accomplish before the end of that year that would contribute to the overall vision I created years before in the five year exercise. The last week of December 2016, I had closed on two Ozark mountain lots in northern Arkansas. This came about through constantly looking at this area online after stumbling across the little Arkansas town and just plain marveling at the beauty of the photos.

Since I now owned property in the location I gave thought to consistently for so long, I started a short-term vision set in this landscape. Using the lesson I was gifted in the five year exercise, I created my short term hybrid.

It began with me sitting in a rocking chair on my porch, looking out over the landscape of the northern Ozark Mountains. I described what I saw and heard in detail. While sitting on that rocking chair, I was looking back over the year 2017 and my accomplishments. I had set a goal of 600 transactions in January 2017, so I used that goal as part of my list of completed items in this vision.

In addition to writing this down, I decided to incorporate daily disciplines. Humans are creatures of habit. All mankind become slaves to the habits they have formed over the years. I made the conscious decision to become a slave to good habits. I hated reading, writing, hell…thinking was a task I shrunk from. Concentration for any length of time was very hard!

I discovered many who have already done the researching, vetting, and deep thinking on innumerable subjects. If I were to form good habits, I would incorporate the study of much of their efforts. I began with the writings of Napoleon Hill. I devoured his writings and re-read, *Think and Grow Rich*, *Outwitting the Devil*, and *The Wisdom of Success* three times each. The message was impossible to ignore. In short order, my grasp of the points I had learned was to be tested.

I received a call from my regional manager asking how important the state of Missouri was to my business. Looking up the stats, it appeared to be 12% of my volume. This made it a pretty important state for my business. When I inquired as to why I was being asked, my regional manager explained that the company's license as well as my license were being put on inactive status because we were losing our brick and mortar, physical, location in that state due to the only licensed resident resigning.

Feeling significant pressure because of how much business I had in the state, I asked if I had latitude to "solve the problem myself." I made the call to Breanne, my younger sister, the moment I hung up from the previous call. When she answered, I immediately asked, "Hey, you wanna get licensed?"

"I haven't heard from you in six months, and this is the first thing you say to me...You wanna get licensed?" She replied.

"Yup" I confirmed. I then heard a crack in her voice as she began to tell me this was an answer to prayer. She and her husband Jim had discussed the very same thing the day before. She had been cleaning vacation rentals for some time, and it just wasn't working. They needed something else and this topic was discussed since she had worked with me before.

After hearing her story "Is that a yes?" was my reply, not pausing long enough to get the significance of what she told me.

The process of her getting licensed still required I secure commercial space in the state to meet specific regulations. While securing a location, we were directed to two older frontier style cabins covered in vegetation and somewhat run down. We called the number on the sign and waited for the agent to come open them up for us. Walking through them, Rizzo and I looked at each other and decided on the spot. We were going to buy them. The negotiations started immediately.

Some creative steps were taken to secure this seven acre property and a rehab was needed. Tickets were purchased and another trip was underway to meet a contractor to get started. I rented another vehicle in Springfield and drove back down to Branson. When I stepped out of the vehicle onto the deck that separated the two cabins, I looked over to the porch of the cabin that was to be the office, and there sat a rocking chair. The words that escaped my lips were "Hell yeah! I have a rocking chair!"

Taking large strides, I stepped up on the porch, sat down in the chair, and began to rock back and forth and look at the landscape of my new purchase. An immediate rush of realization forced the involuntary formation of goosebumps. I was sitting on my porch, in my rocking chair, overlooking the Ozark mountain landscape. Two months and two days prior, I described this scene in my notepad while envisioning my accomplishments for 2017.

My revelry was broken by the sound of my sister pulling up in her minivan with her head out the window screaming, "You weren't supposed to see that yet!"

"How did this get here?" I hollered back.

She walked down the railroad tie steps toward me and said, "Rizzo called me and insisted that a rocking chair be waiting for you on the porch when you get here. Jim knew a guy who handmakes them, and Jim talked him out of the first one he ever made."

Declaring my vision in writing, then sharing that vision with the one who was most important to me fulfilled the realization of it. I closed 676 transactions and found my place in the Ozarks. I may not have thought to place that chair there, but the collaborative effort of my closest friend— my Rizzo—and my little sis brought about the materialization of my mental picture. I learned another important lesson about sharing a thought or goal with others whom you care for and trust. What detail may be overlooked by us can be put in place by another. Choose wisely those who you trust with your future.

To contact Aaron Chapman, visit https://www.aaronbchapman.com/. Check out his YouTube series https://www.youtube.com/QuitJerkinOff and QJO Initiative *Book Series with all book sellers.*

Tweetable: The best example I can pass on to the coming generations is keep getting back up. A beating is coming for us all. The faster you jump back up, the further ahead of the others you get.

MICHELLE OPPELT

Avoiding the Practicality Trap

How to Push Past Fear and Do What You Love

Michelle Oppelt is a seasoned entrepreneur and founder of multiple businesses including Smartycat Kids, a STEM education company featured on CNBC, and Integrity Equity Group, a real estate investment company. Michelle is also co-founder of the Multifamily Women's Mastermind, empowering and encouraging women to achieve their financial and investing goals.

The Unexpected Trip

In the front passenger seat of our cramped SUV, with their noses smashed against the window, our two pups have lost all control. The barking is so loud that it almost drowns out the cackling coming from the back seats. As I grip the steering wheel, I cannot help but join in on the infectious laughter to the point where tears begin streaming down my face.

We slowly inch forward. The barking and laughter grow even louder as we creep closer and closer toward the line of furry giants parading ahead of us.

It is a crisp, sunny morning. We had woken up just after sunrise to hit the road, heading toward Yellowstone National Park for the day. We were all quite groggy before the dogs sounded their alarms, jolting us wide awake.

Outside of our vehicle, a group of massive creatures is enjoying a peaceful stroll down the side of the road. Inside of the vehicle, I am experiencing one of the loudest and most entertaining moments of my life.

None of us have seen bison up close before. Perhaps we may have seen some at a zoo in the past, but it is quite a different experience encountering them inches from our vehicle as they roam freely in this small town in Wyoming. The sound of my young son exclaiming from the backseat, "Mommy, look, their googly eyes are HUGE!" is one of my fondest memories from our trip.

I ended up traveling to 49 states during those two years. The trip was never intended to turn out this way. Life was never intended to turn out this way, but there we were—three kids, two dogs, and one mom traveling countless miles across the USA. The quote I had heard months before was still ringing in my head:

> *"You can fail at what you don't want, so you might as well take a chance on doing what you love."*

Fear Disguised

"So many of us choose our path out of fear disguised as practicality."
– Jim Carey

When I heard Jim Carey's commencement address from the 2014 MUM Graduation, I was sitting on my couch in a daze, scrolling through my phone, looking for any sort of inspiration to break me free from my mental paralysis. I felt as if my life had fallen apart.

I was recently divorced, and my ex-husband had just moved out of state. We had signed a lease on a house together, but that was four years prior, and the lease was soon coming to an end. I had no idea where the kids and I were going to move to next. I owned my own business running a children's education company and worked from my laptop, so I had ample flexibility. This flexibility, however, created an unlimited number of options to choose from, and I felt lost in the sea of possibilities.

I decided it was time to check out some new areas, hoping I would find one that might feel like home for us. I researched five or six cities in a handful of different states that I thought could possibly be a good fit. The problem was that the more I thought about it, the more it felt like throwing darts at a map and going wherever they happened to land. I didn't really feel compelled to go anywhere in particular, and I became frozen with indecision as it neared time to make our next move.

As I sat on the couch scrolling blindly, Jim Carey's commencement address came across my feed. He began to talk about the role that fear has in our lives.

"Fear is going to be a player in your life," he stated, "but you get to decide how much. So many of us choose our path out of fear disguised as practicality."

He had me intrigued.

In his speech, Jim talked about a valuable lesson he had learned from his father. He explained that his father could have been a great comedian, but he didn't believe that was possible for himself, so he chose a "safe job" as an accountant instead. Years later, when he was let go from that safe job, his family had to do whatever they could to survive.

Jim's father had chosen the safe, practical path, and yet it did not protect his family from hardship or struggle. At an early age, Jim witnessed firsthand the fact that even safe bets do not come with any guarantees.

"I learned many great lessons from my father," Jim recalled. "Not the least of which was that you can fail at what you don't want, so you might as well take a chance on doing what you love."

Jim's story hit me in a powerful way. It was exactly what I needed to hear at that moment in time. I was at a crossroads, and I had difficult decisions to make. What was my next move? Was I going to choose my next path out of fear and "practicality," or was I going to be bold and take a chance on doing something I loved?

His speech echoed in my mind for hours. I finally felt compelled to make some sort of plan for what was next. I started to think to myself—if we have to move on, why not turn this difficult time in our lives into something positive? Why not take a chance on doing the things that I loved: traveling, exploring, and creating memories with my children?

Instead of continuing to focus on what we were giving up or leaving behind, I decided to start focusing on the new journey ahead and what we could gain from this transitional time in our lives. I knew it would not be easy, but neither was sitting on a couch feeling paralyzed and sulking. Little did I know, the experiences I was about to gain would end up transforming all aspects of my life and career.

I sat down and poured over a map of the United States. I made the decision right then and there that instead of picking a handful of random cities to visit, we were going to do a giant road trip across all 48 states of the contiguous US. We were going to take this difficult time in our lives and turn it into a great adventure.

Three kids, two dogs, one mom, and the open road. That was the new plan.

Courage Is Not the Absence of Fear

I realized that it was going to take an incredible amount of courage for me to turn this crazy plan into a reality. It would involve selling almost everything we owned, moving out of the house we had called home for years, and living on the road for months at a time. I would be homeschooling my children and running a business, all while traveling across the USA. Every part of the plan was going to require courage, courage I was not sure I had.

Many people told me that they admired how brave I was during this time. While I appreciated that support very much, the problem was I didn't feel brave at all. I felt scared and lost. I had to remind myself constantly that courage is not the absence of fear. Courage is being afraid but moving forward anyway. This was an opportunity of a lifetime to experience something amazing with my children, and I could not allow fear to stop me.

This decision to push past my fears in such a massive way would forever change me. I was about to prove to myself what can be done. I learned to trust in myself more than I ever had before. I would soon experience the rewards that come from taking calculated risks and not only stepping, but leaping, outside of your comfort zone.

The Adventure of a Lifetime

Our trip ended up lasting just under two years. Each leg of the trip started from Tennessee, where we rented a small house to serve as our "home base." We would travel outward toward each corner of the US, circling back to Tennessee when we needed travel breaks. For most of the trip, we camped in our tent. Other times we splurged on a few nights at hotels. During one leg of the trip, I even slept on a mattress placed in the back of my SUV. We learned to quickly adapt as needed, a skill that came to serve me well in the years since, especially in business.

The adventures we experienced during those two years were truly incredible; from hiking in the Rockies of Colorado, to snowshoeing at Crater Lake National Park in Oregon, to visiting so many of the vast landscapes the USA has to offer. We explored rainforests, deserts, lakes, beaches, canyons, caves, and even climbed a giant volcanic dome. We watched manatees swim below our glass-bottom boat in Florida, and chased thousands of tiny crabs across marshy beaches in South Carolina. We saw mountain goats scale sheer rock walls in the canyons of Utah and watched wild horses race up the mountains in Arizona. We giggled at the sea lions playing in the waves of California and fed peanuts to curious prairie dogs outside of the Badlands of South Dakota. We visited countless National Parks but also enjoyed city stops where we rode roller coasters, watched a rocket launch, met Mickey, slept in a high rise, and marveled at the dancing fountains of the Bellagio.

When it was time for the kids to visit their father for the summer months, I continued the trip alone. I hiked various mountains throughout the northeast, meeting many fellow explorers along the way. I was even invited to join a backpacking trip in Hawaii, adding an unexpected leg to my trip. There I watched molten lava blast steam high into the sky as it flowed into the ocean. I swam with sea turtles, snorkeled alongside schools of tropical fish, rode horseback through a valley where Jurassic Park was filmed, and backpacked along the Napali Coast of Kauai. The intended forty-eight state trip had become forty-nine.

Had I let fear stop me and played things "safe," I would have missed out on two years of the most incredible memories I could have ever dreamt of. My children and I experienced more during those two years than most people get to see in a lifetime. I would not be the person or businesswoman I am today had it not been for that adventure. I would never be able to help others find their inner strength, encourage them to trust in themselves fully, or inspire them to become bold and courageous in their own lives and careers without first having learned how to do so myself.

Crossroads

It is important to note that throughout this trip, we never had a large budget. In fact, I was able to keep our monthly expenses lower during these two years of travel than they had been when we leased our previous home. We bootstrapped it many times and got creative when we needed to.

I was a single mom on a limited budget with three young children and two dogs in tow. This goes to show that with enough determination and courage, incredible things can be accomplished regardless of your current circumstances. A huge part of my mission today is to not only inspire others to overcome their fears but also to serve as proof that if you are willing to be adaptable, resilient, and resourceful enough, anything you desire truly can be accomplished.

We all experience crossroads in our lives, where we encounter difficult decisions and may have to choose a new path. I implore you to take a hard look at the path you are choosing. Are you choosing to do what you love or are you choosing fear disguised as practicality?

So many things that we desire are sitting on the other side of the practicality trap. Imagine where you could go in your life, career, or business if you did not allow fear to stop you. There is no guarantee that if you chase your dreams you will not encounter failures or possibly come up short. But as Jim reminded us, there is no guarantee those things won't happen anyway, even if you choose the safe, practical path that you don't really want.

As you make your way through your own journey in your life and career, perhaps it will be helpful to let Jim's words echo in your mind as they did in mine.

"You can fail at what you don't want, so you might as well take a chance on doing something you love."

Michelle Oppelt offers free 30-minute consultations to those who would like to discuss business strategy, getting "unstuck" in your life or career, or women's and youth empowerment. To schedule a call, visit: Calendly.com/MichelleOppelt/30min. To book Michelle for a speaking engagement or interview, email michelle@integrityequitygroup.com

Tweetable: Take the chance. Do what you love. It just might lead you to your next great adventure.

CHAD HUGHES

My Past Prepared Me for My Future as an Entrepreneur and People Builder

Chad Hughes is the CEO of LandSolutions, a company with a team of over 130 people across Canada and the US. He's an entrepreneurial leader, loves learning and growing, and is all about his family and making a difference to the people he leads.

In the Beginning

I grew up on a feedlot operation in Central Alberta, in rural Western Canada, where we raised cattle for beef by feeding and fattening them to their optimal weight. We raised and fed about 2000 head of cattle, which at that time, was quite a big operation. We also farmed about 2000 acres of land.

My dad was an intense entrepreneur, and in addition to running our family's large cattle operation, he had other business ventures keeping him busy. My dad's focus was often on the big picture. For my sister and me, this meant he couldn't always be hands-on with us.

We grew up surrounded by never-ending work and workers who were always willing to do more than what was asked. These people were like family and ensured my sister and I had the help we needed. We worked together, had meals together, and even had some fun together.

Physical wrecks like falling from horses or being run over by cattle and the emotional wrecks associated with the adult-like nature of my childhood were some of the difficult aspects of this life. But there were fun aspects too, like driving trucks and tractors without supervision or having miles and miles of land to ride dirt bikes and horses on. We had endless opportunities to create things and be resourceful.

It didn't occur to me until later in life that my upbringing was very different from most kids'. It took me even longer to realize what a benefit that turned out to be. Looking back, I see the deep respect these workers had for my dad and our family. I was observing forms of leadership early in life while learning to be resourceful, to forge quality relationships, and to rely on others.

Turmoil

In the 1980s, the farm crisis hit both Canada and the US. This was a period marked by high interest rates across North America. A glut in production depressed grain prices. This combination caused many farm families to struggle, leading to farm foreclosures, or forced farm sales.

Our family was among those affected. In addition to the farming challenges, there were challenges with the other businesses and the debts associated. We had to sell to satisfy the bank, and we started over. This was devastating for my parents. As teenagers, my sister and I faced our own challenges. For me, it was an experience where I felt very helpless.

I had this fear of moving as a kid. I went to the same school from kindergarten to grade nine. There were 100 kids in that country school and just ten in my class—two girls, eight boys. Any time someone new moved to the community, I remember thinking how hard that would be. Then it happened to me.

We moved 100 miles north to a town called Devon, Alberta, where my dad took on a job managing a ranch and feedlot for the Samson Cree Nation. Devon was different culturally from where I had been brought up. It was preppy, and I was a country kid. It was a very academic school, and I wasn't an academic kid. I was thrown into this new environment much like being thrown from a horse, but I didn't have the same support around me like I had on the feedlot.

It was the beginning of a lonely, lost time for me, and while I did manage to make some good friends and have some fun in those years, I wouldn't say I ever lived up to my full potential. In fact, I didn't even graduate and had to later attend night school to earn my diploma.

After high school, I took a job working as a sheet metal mechanic, or a "tin basher," as we called it. It wasn't my passion, to say the least. One day, we went to this gorgeous mansion to install some furnaces. I admired the house as my foreman and I pulled up to do the job. That day, I happened to see my foreman's pay stub in his lunchbox. He was earning $18.60 an hour, had seniority in the company, had three kids, and was the sole breadwinner for his family. This really struck me. I didn't know what I wanted to do, but I sure knew it wasn't installing furnaces in other peoples' mansions for $18 an hour.

A Career Launched in Land Acquisition

I found myself back working on the feedlot for my dad and the Samson Cree Nation. My parents encouraged me to go to college, and I knew this was an inevitable step for me, but I had no idea what to pursue.

Originally, I considered doing an environmental program as I had aspirations to someday farm on my own, and I thought that would support my plan. The problem was I didn't have the grades to be accepted into the environmental program. So, at the college's recommendation, I enrolled in the land program.

I had no idea how pivotal this "backup plan" would end up being to my later success.

This program started me down this path of being in the land business. When I got out of college, I worked for a consulting firm and lived out of a bag for three years while working across Western Canada, securing land access from farmers. I would go see these farmers and work out an agreement where an oil company could come on their land and drill a well, build a pipeline, or lease mineral rights.

I'm great at spotting opportunities to come to an agreement, inspiring myself and others to tackle these opportunities, and bringing ideas to fruition. That's part of why I enjoyed my new path in the land business. I was great at meeting and negotiating with farmers. I spoke their language. I could see deals from the perspective of all parties and look for outcomes that were wins for everyone involved.

I did that for three years until a client offered me a position to work in-house for an energy company. I took the position and developed important skills and experience but became bored. It occurred to me then that I needed to pursue opportunities that would allow me to leverage my own unique ways of doing things.

Here's the thing I have come to learn about myself: Autonomy is one of my core values. This means I thrive on developing my own opportunities and having a stake in the result.

In other words, I inherited my dad's intense entrepreneurship. For many years, I didn't even recognize it. I didn't consider myself "smart" because I wasn't the kind of smart that excelled at my academic high school. This narrow characterization of intelligence, combined with the upsets and losses I experienced, stripped me of confidence. As I matured, I came to realize that creating opportunities is its own type of intelligence. My drive to pursue this began to emerge.

My Own Path

I started thinking about doing my own thing, but I had only six years of experience. I worried that wasn't enough. Then I met Ron Vermeulen, who wanted to expand his existing company LandSolutions, into the type of land acquisition work I had been doing. He extended an opportunity for me to buy into the company. I was 26 and didn't have any money, but I knew it was the right path for me. My own path. So I borrowed through a line of credit, and I bought in.

I remember sitting at my kitchen table and sketching out ideas. I thought, if in ten years we had ten people, that would be quite an accomplishment. It seemed like a lofty goal. Five years later, LandSolutions employed 75 people.

This was the beginning of a new period for me, a period of expanding curiosity and growth. I began to regain confidence through the discovery of what brought me joy. The decision to join LandSolutions would be a life-defining moment, and it's an opportunity I am forever grateful for.

Today, LandSolutions has an international presence with offices across Canada and the US. In addition to specializing in securing access, we now also manage recurring obligations that result from access to land. We provide a variety of geospatial and data-driven solutions that complement our services. We have expanded the industries we support to include oil and gas development, renewable energy development, communication network expansions, public transportation and infrastructure development, and power transmission.

Our growth as a company has far exceeded what I first thought was possible, and my growth has far exceeded what I thought was possible for me. This is motivation for me. My desire is to solve more and bigger problems for our clients and to ensure we create an environment that presents others with an opportunity to surprise themselves with their own growth.

Connecting the Dots

At some point during the wandering period of my life between ages 15 to 30, I became more enlightened. The truth about my innate self started to emerge, and I became curious. I entered my thirties on fire for growth.

I built a lot of confidence, and to be honest, some of it was unfounded confidence. This led to some successes and some bumps and bruises as well. I often would joke that ignorance is bliss. Now, I say ignorance is bliss...until it isn't.

My curiosity led me back to school where I completed a two-year executive MBA program. I did this to prove to myself I could, because of my desire to learn and out of a sense of lost opportunity in my younger years. This experience led me to get involved with the Entrepreneur Organization and eventually to business coaching.

I have had some great coaches help me along the way. Right now, I work with two consistently. Dave LaRue is an entrepreneurial coach and Dietrich Desmarais is a neuroscience and EQ coach. I belong to Kyle Wilson's Inner Circle, where I have learned from Kyle as well as thought leaders like Denis Waitley, Brian Tracy, and Les Brown. I've got this thirst for learning, for being a better version of myself.

I have learned to surround myself with great people, inspired by the late Jim Rohn's "average of five" approach. I gain insight and inspiration from others who have wisdom and knowledge. This influence in my life is a non-negotiable. My desire is to have impact, and the extent to which I can help others elevate, will be limited by the extent to which I can elevate myself.

Bringing Value

I do my best to translate my experiences into value for the clients and people I serve, as well as into the corporate culture at LandSolutions. A big part of our success has been that internal culture. It has helped us grow, and it's how we've attracted and retained the kind of people who are sought after by our clients.

Right doesn't work in the access business—*relational* works. This goes back to the very first lessons I learned on the feedlot. The connections and culture that my dad, mom, and our employees fostered made it possible to get the work done and keep us all out of trouble.

When we go into a community to assist the developer in gaining some type of access or permission, there are multiple stakeholders that have an interest in what we're creating. These stakeholders include, of course, the landowners, but also towns, cities, counties, nearby residents, and Indigenous groups. Everyone has their own concerns, and sometimes these are conflicting concerns. There is no such thing as a "right" perspective because every one of these parties is right in their own minds. Of course they are. The outcome matters to them.

It can be difficult to get everyone on board with a plan. My team needs to be able to represent the client and forge successful relationships. Focusing on relationships with the people we're involved with by building rapport and trust leads to putting ink on paper. We've been able to marry that focus with local talent through effective recruitment, which is just something we've learned over time. By combining focus on relationships with the effective recruitment of local talent, we're able to integrate local resources into a process that works and is repeatable.

Looking back, I realize that my own relationship-building abilities come in no small part because of the experiences I had early in life. Whether I was asking for help on the family farm, trying to fit in at a new school, learning the ropes as a tin basher, or hitting the road as a land consultant, the ability to forge successful relationships has been a hallmark of my journey at every step. It's one of the ways I can bring value to almost any situation.

My experiences have enabled me to understand where I create value and what gives me energy. This has become a filter for how I spend my time and for the opportunities I pursue as well as an approach we take when we resource for our clients. Part of my desire is to impart this thinking and my experiences to others who have a desire to grow. I believe that helping others develop their own filters will bring them joy and energy.

My desire to help other people with their journey is about wanting to help people forge their own path and reach new heights while watching our business and the clients we serve realize the benefits. Continuing to grow is non-negotiable. The day we stop that is the day we start fading into the background—not while I'm here.

My coach Dietrich says that legacy is about finishing well. I think my journey has and continues to present opportunities for me to do so. I desire this for myself and others. It's what drives me to expand myself, to delight our customers, and to create environments where others can see their own path more readily. We learn from one another and with one another, and we finish well. That is legacy.

Chad Hughes is an entrepreneurial leader who loves developing opportunities. Chad is driven by a desire to grow, to help others with their growth, and to have a lasting impact. To learn more about the access business or how Chad might be able to support your growth, get in touch at chad@landsolutions.ca and tune into his podcast Elevated Access.

Tweetable: For entrepreneurs and business owners, your struggles are often the raw materials you use to build success. When you connect the dots, you can make life's challenges today's success.

BOB BURG

The Go-Giver Way of Business

Bob Burg is the author of numerous books on sales, marketing, and influence. His bestselling business parable The Go-Giver, *coauthored with John David Mann, has sold over 1,000,000 copies. He speaks for companies internationally, including those in financial services, real estate, and direct sales.*

Finding a System

I began as a sportscaster for my hometown radio station, eventually moving to the Midwest to work as a news reporter and then late-night news anchor for a very small ABC television affiliate.

Soon realizing that this was not going to be my life-long profession, I took a job in (or as I like to say, "graduated into") sales. Having no prior formal sales training and with none being provided by the company, I was really on my own. Indeed, I worked hard at it—knocked on a lot of doors, made a lot of calls, and told a lot of people about my products and services—and failed miserably. As Jim Rohn would have said, "I had the motivation, but not the information." Both are necessary.

After floundering for the first few months, one day while in a bookstore, I came across two books. One was by Zig Ziglar and the other by Tom Hopkins, two of the icons in the field of sales.

It was encouraging just seeing the titles. I had no idea that sales teaching even existed. I got those books and devoured them. Every day after getting home from work, and well into the night, I'd read, study, highlight, take notes, rehearse, and practice.

Within a few weeks, my sales improved dramatically. I now *had* the information. I had a methodology. I had a system.

I define a system as "the process of predictably achieving a goal based on a logical and specific set of 'how to' principles." The key is predictability. If it's been proven that by doing A you'll get the desired results of B, then you know all you need to do is A and continue to do A, and eventually, you'll get the desired results of B. That was truly inspiring to realize, and from there, sales became a fascination for me. I'd found my profession.

It also became obvious to me that a big part of sales involved personal development: building yourself on the inside so that success could manifest on the outside. This began my reading all the recommended classics like *How to*

Win Friends and Influence People, Think and Grow Rich, Psycho-Cybernetics, As a Man Thinketh, The Greatest Salesman in the World... and so on. I loved it! Several years later, I became sales manager of another company and eventually began a speaking business with a focus on sales and business development.

The Essence of Sales

Success in sales is about being focused on bringing immense value to others. We need to be inwardly motivated but outwardly focused. It's about them, not us. As I tell my audiences, "Nobody's going to buy from you because *you* have a quota to meet. Or because you need the money. Or just because you're a nice person. No. They're going to buy from you because they believe that *they* will be better off by doing so than by not doing so." Those salespeople and entrepreneurs who understand this are positioned to succeed.

Endless Referrals

My first major book, *Endless Referrals*, was written for the salesperson or entrepreneur who knew they had a great product or service, one that brought fantastic value to others, but either they didn't feel comfortable and confident going out into their community and building relationships, or they simply didn't know how. *Endless Referrals* was the "system." Its premise was that "All things being equal, people will do business with, and refer business to, those people they know, like, and trust." The book was a step-by-step guide on how to build these relationships so that people wanted to do business with them directly and refer them to others.

The Go-Giver

The Go-Giver is a business parable. Stories have a way of connecting with the reader on a deep, heart-to-heart level, making it easier for people to receive and embrace the message. So it seemed like a good idea to take the basic premise of *Endless Referrals*—shared in the previous paragraph—and write a book in that format.

That's when I called John David Mann, at that time known only within a specific niche (now co-author or ghostwriter of numerous bestselling books with a number of different co-authors) who is an absolutely brilliant writer and storyteller and asked him to co-author *The Go-Giver* with me. We wrote the book in a matter of just a few months. One year and 25 rejections later, we came across our perfect publishing partner, Portfolio, a division of Penguin Random House.

Interestingly, the initial adopters of the book were the very people who didn't need it. These were people who had built immensely successful businesses and organizations long before the book was ever published. John and I would often receive emails saying, "This is exactly how I built my business", "This is how I built my fortune", "This is how I built my company, but none of my people believe me." So they would then simply either recommend that their team members get the book (the power of "third-party credibility"), or they'd buy it for them. We had companies and leaders buying hundreds, sometimes even thousands, of copies. It's something we felt greatly honored by.

At heart, I believe *The Go-Giver* was a hit because it validated for people how they instinctively wanted to do business and receive abundance as a result. Most people truly want to bring value to the world. As human beings, we're built that way; we want to feel our lives have meaning and purpose. We want to know we have contributed and that we have made a difference. Salespeople and entrepreneurs do that through their products and services.

The way you're going to earn a lot of money through your business is by first being genuinely focused on the *other person* and the immense value you're providing them. It comes down to understanding that "Money is an echo of value. It's the thunder to value's lightning." Thus, the money you receive is the natural result of the value you've given others.

The Five Laws

There are five laws, or guiding principles, in *The Go-Giver*. They are the Laws of Value, Compensation, Influence, Authenticity, and Receptivity. The Law of Value says, "Your true worth is determined by how much more you give in value than you take in payment." This is really the foundational principle. It sounds counterintuitive at first. "Give more in value than I take in payment? Isn't that a recipe for bankruptcy?" Here it's important to understand the difference between price and value. Price is a dollar figure, a dollar amount. It's finite. Value, on the other hand, is the "relative worth or desirability of a thing to the beholder or end user."

In other words, what is it about this thing, this product, service, concept, idea, etc., that brings so much worth, or value, to another human being that they will willingly exchange their money for this value, and be very glad they did, while you make a very healthy profit?

A quick example would be hiring an accountant to do your taxes. Her fee, or price, is $1000. What value does she provide in exchange? Well, she saves you $5000 on your taxes, she saves you countless hours of time, and she provides you and your family with the security and peace of mind of knowing your taxes were done correctly. She gave you *well* over $5000 in value in exchange for a $1000 price. She gave you more in value than she took in payment. So you feel terrific about it, and she also made a very healthy profit.

After all, to her, it was worth it to exchange her time, expertise, and energy for that $1000 fee or price.

As the great Harry Browne used to say, "In any market-based exchange, there are always two profits: the buyer profits and the seller profits, because each of them comes away better off afterwards than they were beforehand."

It's also important to communicate value in a way that separates you from your competition. After all, if you're not able to distinguish yourself from your competition in the mind of your prospect, it's always going to come down to who has the lowest price. And that is not a productive, profitable, or sustainable way to conduct business. When you sell on low price, you're a commodity. When you sell on high value, you are a resource—a trusted resource.

The Law of Compensation says, "Your income is determined by how many people you serve, and how well you serve them. So while Law #1 is all about the exceptional value you provide, Law #2 is about *how many lives you impact* with that exceptional value. This is one major reason why building a referral-based business is so beneficial.

The Law of Influence says, "Your influence is determined by how abundantly you place other people's interests first." No, absolutely *not* in a way that is martyrish or self-sacrificial, but in a way that simply demonstrates your desire to make it all about them. Moving from an "I-focus" (or "me-focus") to an "other" focus is the fastest, most powerful, and most effective way to elicit the know, like, and trust feelings toward you that are so necessary for cultivating that powerful and desired relationship.

The Law of Authenticity says, "The most valuable gift you have to offer is yourself." All the skills in the world—sales skills, technical skills, people skills— as important as they are (and they are all very important) are also practically worthless if your words and actions aren't congruent with your true, authentic core. But when they are, it's a force multiplier for every other law.

The Law of Receptivity says, "The key to effective giving is to stay open to receiving." You breathe out, but you also must breathe in. It's the same with giving and receiving. And a big part of that is the *willingness* to receive. By following the first four laws, you've created the "benevolent context for your success." And you've earned the right to receive. Now you must be willing to do so comfortably and gratefully. From there, your world expands. You are in a position to give even more, and receive even more, and give even more, and on and on and on.

Selling The Go-Giver Way

While *Endless Referrals* can put people in front of you, you've then got to be able to communicate the value of your product or service in such a way that the other person understands and chooses to buy.

Defined, selling is simply "Discovering what the other person wants, needs, or desires…and helping them to get it." The most important part of the process is the discovery, which involves listening, deep listening, listening past the surface, and continuing to ask the right questions in order to understand the issues at their core.

Then, before moving on to the actual presentation, you must be sure to confirm that what you heard…is what they meant. Failure to do so will practically always come back to haunt the sales professional later, mainly in the number of "unnecessary objections."

Speaking of objections, it's so important to know that despite how often the following term is used, you cannot "overcome objections." Because to overcome is to *conquer*, and no prospect wants to be conquered. So, no, you cannot overcome objections. What you *can* do, however, is work correctly within the stated objection in order to—in partnership with your prospect—understand their actual concern, the true root cause of their objection, and from there effectively advance the sale forward.

The best thing about selling The Go-Giver Way is that when you get to the part where you ask for the sale, there is absolutely no pressure on either of you. You are simply asking them to take action on something they've already told you they want to take action on.

My Passions

I'm an advocate for the free enterprise system. I truly believe that the amount of money one makes is directly proportional to how many people they serve. Free market capitalism is the greatest economic system that humankind has ever had. Please understand that when I say "free market," I'm not talking about *cronyism,* where big businesses and other special interest groups, through their lobbyists, buy the influence of politicians in exchange for special favors that diminish competition and create an unfair advantage. That is *not* free-market capitalism. Again, that's cronyism. Unfortunately, many people don't understand the difference. This is something I wish would be taught in school. After all, how will people be able to distinguish between the two if never taught the difference? Free market capitalism, where people do business with one another voluntarily, has brought more people out of poverty than any other economic system by far. It's not even close! And to the degree it's permitted to operate, it's a beautiful thing.

I also have a passion for animals and am an unapologetic animal fanatic. I just love them, and I believe it's a shame the way we as humans have treated them over the past 12,000 years and continue to do so, and in so many ways. I work hard to do my part to educate the public about being kind and good to animals, who are always so good to us.

A Final Thought

If there's one last thought I'd like to leave you with, it's something taught to me 40-plus years ago by a wise, elderly man I hardly even knew. He said, "Burg, if you want to make a lot of money in sales, don't have making money as your target. Your target is serving others. When you hit the target, you'll get a reward, and that reward will come in the form of money. And you can do with that money whatever you want. But never forget, the money is simply the reward for hitting the target. It's not the target itself. Your target is serving others."

What I came to realize was that great salesmanship is never about the salesperson. It's never *about* the product. It's *about* the other person and how their life becomes better just as a result of you being part of it.

I believe that when we approach sales from that perspective, we're nine steps ahead of the game…in a 10-step game.

To read a sample chapter of The Go-Giver *and other books by Bob Burg, access lots of resources including his blog, podcast, and online video courses, or to schedule Bob to speak at your next event, visit burg.com.*

Tweetable: Selling is simply discovering what the other person wants, needs, or desires, and helping them to get it. — @BobBurg

KURTIS DRAKE AND RYAN PETTITT

Permaculture for the Permafuture

Cultivating a World Worth Inheriting Through Socially Conscious Investing

Kurtis Drake and Ryan Pettitt are seasoned real estate entrepreneurs and investors with a passion for teaching permaculture, farming, and agricultural principles through continuous improvement techniques. Their mission is cultivating impactful experiences and enriching lives through mutually beneficial solutions. Kurtis and Ryan are leaving a legacy by regenerating ecosystems in nature's image.

Life-Changing Moment

"You've got to be kidding me!" Kurtis exclaimed while rounding our fourth grocery store. "There are not even any dried beans. Do the majority of people even know how to cook dried beans? No toilet paper either!? Is the world coming to an end?"

We were smack dab in the middle of a total home renovation which included adding square footage to the lower level when COVID hit. A month prior, we moved all of our belongings out of the house and into storage with four weeks of travel plans. Our last planned stop was a small town along the Oregon coast, but we were receiving reports from the general contractor that they were behind schedule and would need another month to complete the project. The plan was to extend our time away and live in short-term rentals for a few weeks. It was early March of 2020, and suddenly, closures, cancelations, increased cases, and restrictions were being reported at alarming rates. Like the rest of the world, we were shocked and trying to figure out what this meant. A new state of normalcy had officially begun, which included masks in public, social distancing, limited-size gatherings, constant sanitizing, and virtual connectivity.

We decided to return to the Portland market to stay closer to the project. There were limitations on where we could book with three dogs, and several listings were removed due to fear of the unknown. Panic had left most of the shelves bare as we attempted to buy groceries for our shelter in place. Rumblings of supply chain disruptions suddenly became reality. We were in a dire situation with limited food on hand, no Amazon grocery deliveries available, the host threatening to charge $50 per missing toilet paper roll, and all of our rental houses were 100% occupied (usually not a bad thing, but timing caused a bit of a pickle). We found ourselves wildly unprepared for this type of scenario.

Thankfully, Kurtis' sister Tammy sent us what seemed like a truckload of dried beans, which helped to fill the pantry.

The renovation project was already delayed, and now the construction crew had new restrictions with some team members stating they would be unable to continue the job. We couldn't endure living the nomad life with a substantial increase in housing costs and lack of stability. Ryan, ever the level-headed and not-quite-so dramatic one, put his project management skills and negotiation tactics to the test as he worked with the contractor to get us back into the house. The proposal was to rotate spaces between the upper and lower levels while work was being completed in the opposite area (reiterating the importance of health, safety, and observance of CDC recommendations). Fortunately, summer months were nearing, so many days we were able to work outside on the patio, separated from some of the construction noise between conference calls which did wonders for our summer glow.

Time for Change & Solving a Problem

Being afforded this gift of time after an abrupt upset to our day-to-day life, we spent the next several weeks reflecting, goal setting, and masterminding how to mitigate the impact of unexpected events and minimize the chances of finding ourselves in this predicament again.

We opened up our binder from The Real Estate Guys goals seminar just a few months earlier. Irony smacked us both in the face. Right there, plainly written out, was our goal of traveling less in 2020.

In 2019, we'd cumulatively stayed over 300 nights in hotels, had built up several million Hilton hotel points and Delta miles, and were running on all cylinders. Things were going well with the business, and we were meeting all kinds of great folks at networking events, but it was exhausting. Many times, we were only spending time with one another when we'd meet in Dallas, Los Angeles, Phoenix, San Pedro, Atlanta, etc. We'd spend a little focused time as a couple (usually updating each other on the business ongoings), and then it was off to the next event. We'd thoroughly enjoy the meeting and then head out to wherever our W-2 jobs had us that week. Rinse and repeat. Although fun in batches, it was chaotic, unhealthy, and not sustainable. In our 30s, both of us were constantly facing weight fluctuations, high blood pressure, and high cholesterol levels, which was a bit unnerving.

Ultimately, we felt disconnected and knew we were not living a life by design. This pause button was a blessing in disguise as it afforded us the opportunity to look at our lives and the business to assess what was going well, where we had opportunities, and how we could implement changes. Plus, we accomplished the goal of less travel, so that was fulfilling!

Over the course of the next few weeks while we were planning, we focused on the strategy for our primary residence. Through the remodel, our single family house was effectively made into two separate living units. We could rent one long-term or live in it ourselves and the other could be a short-term rental. No more being homeless and not having space in any of our own rentals during a global pandemic!

Reconnecting, Healing, and Sustainability

Simultaneously, we had the opportunity to reconnect as a couple, focus on health and fitness, and complete a ton of projects. This was the first time in our eight-year relationship that we had spent more than two weeks together consecutively. A majority of the time, we were out in the garden, with the chickens, or walking around the neighborhood.

Poultry has always been a part of Kurtis' life. In fact, his first segue into the entrepreneurial world growing up was when he would snag eggs from the family's pet goose nest, incubate and hatch them, raise the goslings, and then sell the yearlings in the local classifieds. He keenly remembers getting chased around the barnyard by an angry gander!

Gardens have always been a passion and a fun hobby for us, but the events of this year made it especially cathartic. This was also the perfect opportunity to start an aquaponics garden in our garage for increased production. (We'd been discussing it for years without implementation.) We enjoyed the yields, eating fresh spinach and kale while canning or dehydrating some of the excess tomatoes, cucumbers, and zucchini. Avocado toast with basil, chives, and cherry tomatoes became a daily occurrence. Our Airbnb guests also seemed to enjoy the garden and our feathered friends through several bookings due to our property offering a suburban farm setting. The lightbulb started to go off. By combining rental real estate with farming, we could pair two of our interests. It was a fascinating concept, and we were excited to take it to the next level!

One of the concepts we kept circling back to when strategizing our business model was the idea of sustainability. "Sustainability" is a buzzword, but at its simplest form, it is the ability to sustain. While we observed the supply chain disruptions and countless businesses close which were unable to sustain in the heart of the pandemic, protecting our business against these volatilities was critical. To date, our rental real estate is self-sufficient and has remained relatively unscathed (which we attribute to market selection, diversification, and excellent property management teams), but our land acquisitions and sales business has become more of a "churn and burn" type model where we continuously aim to sell more in order to increase revenue. As we've discussed with our manager Nola, this is not super fulfilling and doesn't convey the sustainability which we are seeking, so it was essential we pivot.

Bringing Value by Farming in Nature's Image

This led us to the practice of permaculture, also referred to as regenerative agriculture, which mimics real-world ecosystems to create farming in nature's image. The idea of this is Zen-like, where the farmer isn't degrading resources as time progresses and after each subsequent harvest, but instead, resources are replenished. All aspects of the ecosystem play an integral part and fit together in harmony. This can be observed in our aquaponics garden system: we feed the fish, the fish wastewater fertilizes the plants, the plants and their beneficial bacteria help to clean the water for the fish, and we're able to harvest fresh fruits, vegetables, and fish. All this takes place while using 90% less water than traditional soil gardening! This type of practice leaves behind a world worth inheriting and is something we can proudly stand behind as an ongoing business model. We were off to the races brainstorming what we could develop with a background in real estate, a passion for agriculture, and a desire to leave a legacy through impact.

A central theme for us has become how we can teach others to replicate the permaculture concepts as a step towards changing the world. Considering impact on future generations is especially important to us as we are preparing to adopt. We would love the opportunity to raise a child in an environment where they can witness positive change and experience nature as integral to our daily lives.

The Journey Begins

We were seeking the perfect place to embark on this new journey. After several weeks of searching for land which met our criteria, Zillow suggested a property in Eastern Washington located in a town called Walla Walla. In fact, this property was perfect with an existing home on site, a river and seasonal creek bordering the parcel, 18 acres full of rich soil not previously used for farming, a moderate climate, and an agriculture-mindset community. Now it was time to start putting our vision of sustainability and permaculture into practice.

We arrived at the property a few days prior to Labor Day. That week, the West Coast experienced detrimental wildfires in a variety of areas that caused hazardous air quality for over two weeks. Site preparations needed to continue, so we strapped on our hazmat masks and constructed a chicken coop so the girls would have a safe haven at night.

Many evenings were spent researching the best livestock options suited for grazing in our rotational pasture design. We selected Kunekune pigs, Scottish Highland cattle, and Southdown sheep, which all have a docile temperament and are not destructive. Our goal is to focus on heritage breeds used for traditional farming practices. Within three and a half months, we went from eleven chickens and three dogs to an additional 6 cows, 10 sheep, 11 pigs, 15 turkeys, 27 chickens, 14 ducks, and 9 geese plus another pup on the way! It's a good thing Kurtis grew up on a dairy goat farm and has an innate ability to care for farm animals. All of the animals will serve a purpose in the rotational pastures, which will create a complete ecosystem providing fertilization for the plants and in turn feeding the livestock. Our focus will be on perennials with elderberries, blueberries, currants, and huckleberries already in the ground and plans to plant hazelnut, apple, sugar maple, and pear trees in the coming spring as well as an assortment of other plants.

Everything is part of an incredible learning experience. For the business plan development, we completed a 10-week permaculture course using the property as our case study for design. With each animal, there is considerable time spent learning about care and creating a bond. There are numerous stories like transporting screaming piglets in a rental vehicle who left surprises in the hatchback, sheep escaping and herding them for 2.5 hours, calves charging us when they are not halter broken, and unexpected lambs born in the pasture. All of these things are part of the journey, and we are grateful.

Leaving a Legacy
The Walla Walla farm will become our flagship property for regenerative agriculture. We plan to incorporate an agritourism component with 10-15 yurts or cabins on site where people can visit and learn different aspects of permaculture. Whether it is harvesting honey, building an aquaponics system, setting up solar panels, managing pastures, designing a permaculture property, shearing sheep, making herbal tea, propagating plants, or countless other homestead activities, we'll have the ability to host people onsite to learn so they may incorporate the knowledge into their own lives.

Our vision is to have farm locations in markets where we have existing rentals or land, allowing us to leverage the teams and systems we have in place. The new business brand for our permaculture properties and products is Kaizen Roots. "Kaizen" is the Japanese term for "continuous improvement," thus we'll be grounded in continuous improvement practices in our business and agriculture ventures. Ultimately, the goal is to be 75% self-sustaining from farming outputs while also providing the community with locally sourced products from a boutique agriculture experience. This will help to circumvent potential supply chain disruptions in the future.

This last year has been a whirlwind of emotion and curveball experiences for us. Although everything hasn't turned out quite as planned, it has been extremely valuable and a needed lesson. We've learned to accept obstacles as teaching moments, appreciate the natural beauty around us, focus on gratitude, and follow our passion for greater life purpose. As the world and our lives continue to change, we will be reflecting on this experience often to ensure we remember these lessons.

This experience has gifted us with an appreciation for the important facets of life and has opened the door for stronger relationships with family (like Ryan's brother Matt) and friends throughout the country, albeit in a virtual environment. Ultimately, we feel more connected and grounded with a holistic approach to life, encompassing our minds, bodies, and souls. We are prepared and excited to cultivate a more self-reliant, sustainable, and regenerative future for our family and our investors.

Follow Kurtis Drake and Ryan Pettitt's agriculture journey on Kaizen Roots social media pages: Facebook (www.facebook.com/kaizenrootsfarm) or Instagram (www.instagram.com/kaizenrootsfarm). For a free report with 25 ideas for household permaculture projects, send an email to info@kaizenroots.com.

Tweetable: Sometimes the journey isn't always linear and may require pivoting and fine-tuning. In the process of developing your legacy, focus on maintaining openness, enjoying your passions, and above all, approaching life experiences with an attitude of gratitude.

VALÉRIE MOSTERT

How Backpacking Around the World Turned My Mess Into a Message

Valérie Mostert is a transformational coach, author of five books, and founder of Vision in Mind. She helps women connect to their mind, heart, body, and soul so they can find their uniqueness and be their best versions. In 2017, she was awarded "Person of the Year" by the We're Smart World Association.

Between Worlds

"You're a dreamer!" said my father when I told him about my plan to travel the world with my backpack and no road to follow! I was 22, studying literature, linguistics, and philosophy on weekdays and going back to my small village of 300 people on weekends. I was constantly switching from one world to another.

My upbringing was a world of emotional struggle. As a teenager, I was often feeling empty, sad, depressed, and without any purpose or meaning in my life.

After spending my childhood on my grandparents' remote farm, deeply connected with nature, my family moved. We ended up in a new house close to a main road where I started to feel disconnected from the wild nature, which had given me freedom and peace, and from my family. At that time, there was no communication at home: my father was very strict, my mother was working 24/7, my sister and I didn't have much to share, so I was spending most of my days alone in my bedroom. There was no room at home to express emotions or share thoughts, and I felt as if nature, my best companion in my early years, had abandoned me.

The uneasiness I was feeling at home created stories in my head. Just like any child, I was unconsciously absorbing the environment I was born into. One day, as I was silently doing my homework in the living room, my father said, "Valérie, do you know that you are an accident?" I was shocked, voiceless. Why did he say that to me? Why didn't he choose nicer words like, "Do you know that you are our lovely little surprise?" I only understood the power of language later on. But at that time, I felt useless, not worthy of love, and like a burden for my family.

For years, I woke up feeling desperate. My heart was suffering. I had low self-esteem and very disempowering thoughts.

A Whole New World

At the age of 18, I left home to go to university, and I discovered a whole new world. I met people who were uplifting and optimistic. They seemed to have life-enhancing thoughts and big dreams. I started to realize that my old stories didn't have to define me. I didn't have to mimic a lifestyle that didn't serve me. I could decide to live the life I was longing for.

So, I started to build up my first big dream: backpack and discover the world for a year. My parents had never left Belgium. Their only reality was work, and my father's limiting belief was that taking holidays is only for lazy people. So obviously, when I explained my dream to my parents, I didn't receive support. I was judged and labeled as "a dreamer!"

I realized something had to change, and I had to change it! I remember making a commitment to myself: "I won't wait until I'm old and full of regrets. The time to change is NOW!" I had to design my own life. If not, I would be sinking!

Building the Dream

The stories of Native Americans had inspired me during my literature classes, and the beautiful books from Virginia Woolf, Oscar Wilde, James Joyce, Maya Angelou, and others impacted me profoundly. I remember a quote from Oscar Wilde who said, "*To live is the rarest thing in the world. Most people exist, that's all,*" and "*Be yourself. Everyone else is already taken.*" Yes, I could be myself and yes, I was deserving of a great life!

I made the firm decision that nothing and nobody would ever stop me from moving towards my dream. I knew that stepping into new territory with no map would be scary at times. But if I wanted my life to have deeper and more satisfying meaning, I needed to embrace change and do something unusual! Instead of resigning myself to playing the victim, I decided to build the courage, grit, and trust to go forward and live one of my best years ever!

Every day I was obsessed with the idea of traveling the world. I made a plan of action: as I was still studying, I would go to classes in the daytime and work in the evening to save money. I spent most of my weekends finding sponsors as well as contacting newspapers and offering to write bi-monthly articles relating my story. I got in touch with travelers who gave me their support so I could build my new adventure. As I was nurturing these new ideas, magic happened. I started to feel new emotions and empowering thoughts! I began to be different, to be who I wanted to be!

A Year in South America

When I graduated, I left Belgium with a backpack, a budget of five dollars a day, and a big dream to discover the remotest parts of South America and volunteer in humanitarian projects. This year of discovery turned out to be the beginning of true and authentic self-discovery, the start of a new life.

Day after day, month after month, I started to "un-know" myself and "un-learn" what I had learned. The more I detached from my old patterns, the more freedom I could feel, and the better I was discovering my real self. The healing process had started.

Little by little, my negative emotions were replaced by positive emotions, the moments of depression by moments of gratitude. When I was in deep silence, I could feel this new life force and energy within me. My little voice was telling me it was okay if I had made mistakes in the past; it was okay if I had felt so much shame and sadness for the lack of connection with my own family. This was all part of who I was becoming. This was my journey, and there was nothing wrong about it. The only reality was now.

I also embarked on a journey of forgiveness. My parents did the best they could with the knowledge and tools they had at that time. Their childhoods had been much more complicated than mine, and the programming they received guided their behaviors. I forgave myself for the wrong perception I had all those years and for not honoring the sacred gift of life my parents had given me.

Releasing the pain and the burden of resentment gave me the most beautiful feeling of freedom. As long as I was allowing the pain to live with me, I felt stuck in the natural flow of life. After forgiving, a whole new world of possibilities and opportunities started to come my way! Ragnar Lothbrok said, "Don't waste your time looking back. You're not going that way." This was so true!

I was living most of the time with the Quechua communities in the Altiplano, and for the first time, I felt a deep sense of belonging. I was sometimes sleeping on the floor with the warmth of a wood fire and guinea pigs around. Living in those conditions pushed me to go deep inside and find something precious, which had always been there waiting. I was feeling so happy and grateful for my new life, the fantastic nature, and the beautiful people who had nothing but their smile, their strong sense of community, and their deep connection to the Pachamama (Mother Earth).

At that moment, I remember making a declaration that I would never feel the same again. Yes, I had suffered for years. Yes, I had been wounded. But I was not destroyed! On the contrary, I started to feel empowered, and I understood that every part of my life, even the most difficult moments, had been there to prepare me for my journey. That's when I realized that this year wouldn't be a year of escape but a year of transformation that would take place within myself! And I became aware that if I wanted to change the world, I first needed to change the way I think, feel, talk, and act!

A Life Journey

Of course, this self-discovery didn't happen once and for all! When I came back from this one-year trip, I still needed to improve my inner world. I made a lot of mistakes in my late twenties in all areas of my life! I experienced regret, remorse, nostalgia, and self-doubt. For a few years, I confused pleasure with happiness. From the outside, my life seemed satisfying and rewarding, but I was living according to society's values. I had a great job in a prestigious company, but I ended up feeling empty and disconnected from the real person I had discovered during my trip.

In my early 30s, I discovered books from Eckart Tolle, Deepak Chopra, Jiddu Krishnamurti, Thich Nhat Hanh, Napoleon Hill, Joseph Murphy, and many more. They all had a profound impact on me. I realized some of my beliefs still needed to come up for reprogramming; some of my unconscious patterns still required release. It took me a few years of trial and error to discover who I was meant to be, how I could serve best, and how I could live a life of significance in alignment with my true passions and values.

My Moonshot

After giving birth to my third child, I eventually made the leap to quit my job. I was longing to work from home, be present for my kids, and develop a business around healthy food and reconnection to nature. Taking care of myself, others, and Mother Earth had been a turning point in my life, and I was ready to raise awareness, give courses, and write books to share the best of my knowledge and experience.

Gardening became a mental, emotional, and spiritual practice that opened the doors to many new opportunities in my life. When I was nurturing the soil, I was nurturing my ideal life. I knew for my vegetables to grow, my soil needed to be as healthy as the seeds. Similarly, my dreams could not survive if they were planted in soil full of regret and resentment.

For 20 years, I studied many areas, including nutrition, energy medicine, epigenetics, quantum physics, cognitive psychology, neuroscience, and spirituality. I experienced, witnessed, and learned what happened in my own life. I both failed and succeeded. But whatever I was doing, I was doing it with more awareness and a deeper connection to myself, others, and life.

Every year, I reconnected to my first life-changing experience. I kept traveling to remote places around the world, with my life partner and our three amazing children, because I knew being in contact with local native populations would further push me to travel within myself. I am convinced that my stays with spiritual communities like the Kogis in Columbia, the Maasai in Kenya, the Himbas in Namibia, the Lolos in Vietnam, the yogis in India, the inhabitants of the longhouses in Borneo, the local families in Nepal and Laos, the nomads in Mauritania, and the shamans in Mexico, have contributed to my spiritual growth and to becoming the best version of myself.

Among those populations, I have discovered virtues of humility, integrity, authenticity, respect, resilience, and equanimity that seem to cross time and culture. Getting to know and experience our true self and meaning in life, or self-realization, is probably the most common point I have discovered among those communities. These people are fully alive because they live in alignment with who they are meant to be. Their behaviors reflect their inner values. They have found their inner source of power and life purpose. They live a life of significance.

With them, I experienced forgiveness, gratitude, self-love, worthiness, and appreciation of the beauty all around me, as well as hope, mindfulness, and spirituality. I discovered a new state of being, I found out my inner strength, I started to accept and love reality as it is, and I noticed I could find peace even in the most challenging situations.

For years, I asked myself, "Who am I? What makes me unique? How can I serve best? How can I move to the next stage of my life?" I listened to my intuition, and I realized my experience could serve women who are ready to find their purpose and live the amazing life they deserve!

An Epiphany

When I was visiting my oldest daughter who was volunteering for a year in Soweto, I met twin boys with grateful souls who, despite their harsh conditions, kept big smiles and a spark in their eyes. Today, I keep empowering their minds and awakening them to their true potentials by sending them audio messages, meditations, quotes, affirmations, and other self-help tools. They remind me of Nelson Mandela and Viktor Frankl, who kept their visions in mind and never gave up! I know that nothing will stop them from showing the best versions of themselves and creating masterpieces in their lives.

I believe if they can do it, everyone else can do it! This was a turning point in my decision to leave my comfort zone and redefine my life purpose.

My Ideal Life

Nowadays, the transformations I witness in the wonderful people I serve are so amazing that I feel I am exactly where I am meant to be. When you find meaningful work you are passionate about and you see how much it impacts and brings good, you realize you have to give your gifts away.

My new mission is to help women transform on a profound level so they can find solutions to their emotional, mental, physical, or spiritual challenges. My fuel is to connect them to their life forces within and to raise their consciousness so they can think better thoughts, have more life-enhancing beliefs, feel empowered, take better actions, and witness breakthroughs in their lives.

Everybody's life can make a big difference, and if we're here, we might as well dream and act big. So, I want to inspire them to become game-changers, so they can inspire others—their families, their friends, their communities—the world around them—in turn!

Lastly, I am motivated by the knowledge that now, after all my ups and downs, I am able to support the populations I wanted to help when I was 24. I just couldn't do it the way I had imagined then because it was not the right time for me. The person I needed to help first was myself. Now is the right time for me to help others.

Valérie Mostert offers an intense, transformational coaching program online as well as retreats and other self-help tools for women who want to write a new chapter in their lives. To get in touch with her, send an email to valerie@visioninmind.eu or visit www.visioninmind.eu/ facebook.com/visioninmind.eu

Tweetable: Your life is not determined by your past or present circumstances, nor is it by your genes. With the right mindset, mental skills, and habits, you CAN tap into your genius and create an extraordinary life!

TIMOTHY LYONS

A NYC Firefighter's Journey Towards Financial Freedom Using Multifamily Syndication

Tim Lyons is a lieutenant in the New York City Fire Dept (FDNY) and principal of Cityside Capital—a real estate private equity firm that focuses on building passive income for investors using high-quality multifamily assets. He has ownership in a $68 million real estate portfolio with 591 doors.

They Said

I remember hearing the same type of advice from the many adults that I looked up to when I was growing up. It sounded something like, "Study hard, get good grades, go to a good college, get a good job with a steady paycheck, max out your 401K, live below your means, buy a house—as it will be your best asset—and *someday* you will be set for life." Some of my early influences offered advice to "take as many civil service tests as you can. You will have a steady paycheck, a pension, and benefits for life."

I took all of this advice to heart, and for the most part, I have lived that life into adulthood. As a little kid, I can remember always wanting and craving more out of life. That burning desire has never left me, and I am acutely aware of its presence in my life.

It wasn't until I was well into my career and life that I examined my past, acknowledged my present state, and thought about wanting to more fully participate in creating a better life for myself and my family going forward.

I was married to my best friend, had two jobs that I loved, and three beautiful little girls that meant the world to me. But the burning desire to be, to do, and to have more was hotter than ever.

Education x Action

I realized that I was suffering from limiting beliefs, a scarcity mindset, and engineering my life to play small. I was a hard working, middle class, blue collar kind of guy, and I was surely proud of all that I had accomplished in life. Yet, that burning desire from childhood to be more, do more, and have more became more visceral as I moved through adulthood. I have gained enormous clarity after deciding that I wanted more out of life and committing to the process that will undoubtedly lead to success.

Everything changed when I took decisive action and found mentors and coaches to help along the way. One of my mentors is a successful entrepreneur and multifamily investor. It has been said that to be successful, you need to find the people that are successful at what you want to do, find out how they did it, and replicate it.

On a call, my mentor, Gino Barbaro, gave me the equation that has been guiding my real estate career ever since: Education x Action = Results. Simple enough, right?

That statement resonated with me in a huge way, and it continues to guide my career in multifamily investing. I am a 38-year-old father of three incredible little girls, a lieutenant in the New York City Fire Department, and now a multifamily investor. Until recently, I worked "on the side," like many firefighters do, as an ER nurse at a level one trauma center. I resigned from the hospital to focus more fully on my real estate investing career, and that has led to the creation of our real estate investing company, Cityside Capital.

The path to real estate investing and working on financial independence was certainly not linear for me. Like so many others, it was only after I had realized that I was living my life with a scarcity mindset, a mindset that was engineered for safety and certainty, that I decided change was needed.

I Love My Job

I love my career as a New York City (FDNY) firefighter. It is an honor and a privilege to serve others and to have a huge impact on people's lives. Let's face it, when people dial 911 on any given day, they are probably having one of the worst days of their life. The same goes for life in the emergency department of a Level 1 trauma center.

I have had tons of great days with lots of laughs and good times with co-workers, and unfortunately, I have had a smaller number of incredibly sad and soul-sucking days filled with tears, fear, doubt, regret, and anger. I have had days where my team and I brought someone back from the brink of death, fixed a problem, made someone's day better, and even rescued multiple people from burning buildings. I pride myself on "being in the room" when things are going bad because I can help make a difference. I've got so many stories of surreal experiences that my wife bought me a journal to start capturing some of these events.

As fulfilling as being a firefighter and ER nurse was, I knew that there was more that I should be (and could be) doing. I started to feel trapped in the W-2 grind. I found myself working 70, 80, and sometimes 90 hours a week.

My family was feeling it—and I was feeling it too. I thought I was **living the dream** by having a healthy family, two solid careers, a great marriage to my best friend, a solid social network, and bills that were getting paid on time with some savings leftover. I was having a positive impact on people's lives and I had a sense of fulfillment, but I just knew there was something more that I should be and could be doing.

I've always had my finger on the pulse of the markets by reading *The Wall Street Journal*, personal finance books and magazines, and talking with family and friends in finance and real estate. I started to listen to some podcasts about real estate investing and immediately felt hooked.

I'm Going to Be a Real Estate Investor

During the summer of 2019, I was on a family vacation in the Outer Banks, NC, and I ended up finally reading a book that had remained unread in my firehouse duffle bag for months. That book was *Rich Dad Poor Dad* by Robert Kiyosaki. Maybe you've heard of it?

I read that book in two days while sitting on the beach, building sandcastles with one hand and the book in the other. I couldn't put it down! When I finished it, I was sitting on the beach next to my lovely wife, Kristina. I closed the book, turned to her, and said, "Kris, I have something to tell you."

She responded politely, "Oh yeah, Tim, what's that?"

I continued, "I'm going to be a real estate investor!" I love Kristina, as she has been such a supportive and loving wife no matter what endeavor I've gotten into.

She looked across at me with a smirk and said, "Sure you are, Tim...."

That led to reading and listening to books about real estate, investing, mindset, selling, business, marketing, psychology, and more! I used every free minute during the day to listen or read a little bit more. Anytime I was driving, I turned my car into a "university on wheels" and would continue to consume content. Just four short months later, I took massive action and partnered on a three-unit apartment building with a friend of mine.

Getting Started

That first property was a thrilling experience! In such a short time, I had decided to pivot the direction of my financial future and undertook massive action to make it happen. I knew I didn't know it all, but I knew enough to jump in, and that made all the difference.

My partner and I didn't know about my mentor's motto of "buy right, manage right, and finance right," but we were well on our way to implementing such a plan. In short order, we put a new roof and siding on the exterior and renovated the vacant first floor unit. We did the interior work ourselves, and it took FOREVER. It was a great experience, and it provided a much-needed lesson. When at last, we were fully rented and were cash flowing nicely, it felt great to be a real estate investor!

From that experience, my wife and I had our much-needed *proof of concept*. We experienced what it was like to have monthly cash flow, and we even did better than expected on our tax return. In order for our family to commit more fully to real estate investing, it was important to me that Kristina be on board with the process, even though she did not want an active role in the business.

After only a few months of being a landlord, I realized that buying 100-year-old, wood framed, three-family properties was not really scalable. I had enough capital for maybe one more similar purchase, and then I'd be tapped out. I thought about it some more and came to the conclusion that it would be pretty difficult to raise private capital for such a project as well. That's when I turned my focus to multifamily investing and coaching.

Finding a Coach

Growing up in the greater NYC area, I have developed a healthy sense of skepticism—it's sort of built into our DNA! Realizing this fact, it was hard for me to come to terms with hiring a mentor or coach to learn how to invest in multifamily apartment buildings. During the early parts of this journey, I kept hearing the phrase, "Success leaves clues," on podcasts and other content. Acknowledging this phrase ultimately led me down the coaching path.

I had no idea how much coaching cost or what sort of ROI it would yield. I was all excited and pumped up, but nervous as anything, all at the same time. *Is this the right move? Should I really spend money on coaching? Is this a scam?* Oh, the limiting beliefs and little saboteurs in my head were having a field day!

I researched as much as I could on the internet about the different types of coaching and mentoring programs. They all seemed a touch different, so I went ahead and called each of them to find out how they worked.

I remember making that first phone call to a very well known syndicator and coach. I was listening to a podcast that he was a guest on, and he actually gave out his cell phone number at the end of the show! I immediately took out my phone and dialed the number. *What the heck am I doing?* I thought to myself.

We ended up having a great conversation as he was so amicable and easy to talk to. He was super encouraging, and our life stories had a lot in common. I felt so relieved that the phone call went so well. *What was I so nervous about before making that call?*

At this moment, I knew I was going to go forward with coaching—I just had to find the right fit. After dismissing a few other coaching programs, I got in contact with my eventual mentor's team. From the first minute of the first phone call—I felt as though I found exactly what I was looking for.

Putting It All Together

Being armed with the knowledge and having the confidence to take decisive action has made all the difference in the world to me. I had the proof of concept for myself, and I now wanted everyone in my ecosystem to have the opportunity to be involved. I am a firm believer in the saying that a rising tide lifts all boats.

In my first year in real estate, I went from having no real assets to having ownership in $68 million in multifamily. I have successfully partnered with more experienced operators in the space to leverage their knowledge and expertise. This has resulted in an increase in our monthly income and an increase in our net worth. Plus, there are immense tax benefits that serve to supercharge wealth building.

It feels amazing to be able to provide opportunities for my friends and family to participate in real estate using the syndication model. It is my new passion to help provide education and clarity to those that want more abundance in their lives and to experience what my mentor, Master Platinum Coach Trevor McGregor, refers to as the five freedoms that everyone should strive for.

Trevor, affectionately known as "Coach T," has been instrumental in supporting my outcomes, and he always says that anyone has the five freedoms available to them when they are *defiantly committed* to achieving them.

The Five Freedoms according to Master Platinum Coach Trevor McGregor:

1. **Financial Freedom** – to be engaged in impactful activities that you choose without worrying about finances

2. **Time Freedom** – to spend time with those who mean the most to you and to spend time doing what you want to do

3. **Geographical Freedom** – to be able to live where you want and on your own terms

4. **Freedom of Purpose** – to pursue what it is in life that you are passionate about

5. **Freedom of Relationships** – to be surrounded by people who lift you up and that you want to be close to

Commitment, Action, Impact

Though my initial goal was to become a successful and profitable real estate investor, I have found that my journey has taken me down a thousand different paths that have left me more fulfilled than I can imagine. The best part is, I am just getting started!

My passion is to provide a pathway for those who feel the way I did a few years ago. Maybe they feel stuck in their W-2 and want more, perhaps they crave more time with loved ones and want to establish passive income streams, or maybe they want to figure out where they belong in real estate.

I welcome the opportunity to speak with anyone who fits the preceding descriptions. Sometimes all it takes is that one phone call, like the initial call I made to a prospective mentor, to set your pathway to be more, do more, and become more.

Connect with Tim Lyons to find out more about how you can get started investing in real estate passively and build out multiple streams of passive income. He can be reached at tim@citysidecap.com – on Facebook and LinkedIn – or on his website www.citysidecap.com.

Tweetable: It feels amazing to be able to provide opportunities for my friends and family to participate in real estate using the syndication model. It is my new passion to help provide education and clarity to those that want more abundance in their lives.

PAUL HOPFENSPERGER

Just Keep Swimming Until You Get to France!

Paul Hopfensperger is CEO of Body and Mind Studio International Ltd in the UK. As a John Maxwell Team Certified Coach and Speaker specialising in mindset and goal setting, he values people and continually strives to add value to people. He is a naturopathic health coach, author, musician, and politician of 18 years.

Humble Beginnings

More people have climbed Mount Everest, the world's tallest mountain, than have swum The English Channel. More than five hundred cargo ships and tankers pass through the channel each day. Around thirty-five cross channel ferries sail diagonally through the shipping lanes each day. The water temperature in the height of summer is around 15°C (59°F). Swimming across it, from England to France, averages between 12 and 15 hours continuous swimming in the frigid water. Despite these overwhelming statistics, and at age 43, I was about to tell my wife Beccy that I was going to swim the channel.

Since childhood, my parents drove us from the UK to my dad's home city of Regensburg in Germany for our annual family holiday, and this necessitated an overnight trip on the ferry across the channel. I absolutely loved it! Arriving at the port to see the mighty ocean glistening in the moonlight and smelling the fragrant, heavy ocean air was always the start of our 2000-mile adventure.

I loved the sea and adored swimming. My dad first took me swimming in The Corporation Baths, an outdoor pool in Bury St Edmunds, when I was four years old. He was, in fact, my adopted dad, as I had been abandoned into a Roman Catholic children's home by my birth mother, Eileen Currid, a waitress, formerly of Sligo in Ireland, but then of Corby in England. My birth father was listed on my birth certificate as Jesse Adcock, a USAF serviceman stationed in England.

So the first six months of my life were spent alone in a cot in a children's home, being attended to by nuns, with no motherly affection, until Johann and Vera Hopfensperger rescued me. They were, without doubt, the best parents anyone could ask for. They brought me up with Christian values: to be honest, not tell lies, respect others, work hard, have integrity in everything I do, open the door for ladies and give up my seat if they didn't have one. It's how I was raised and how I've tried to live my life. I loved them more than I can possibly say, but I knew that one day, I had to trace my roots.

My mum signed me up as a member of the Bury St. Edmunds Swimming Club when I was five years old, and I am eternally grateful to her for doing so, as swimming became my life. I represented my town and county, became club captain, county champion, and county record holder. Having retired due to injury in 1994, on July 2, 2006, I reflected on the past 12 years and realised I had barely swum at all. I was now about to walk into our kitchen and break the news to my wife, the Mayor of Bury St. Edmunds, that I was going to raise money for her charities by swimming over 33 kilometers across the busiest shipping lane in the world. If I could do that, swimming the channel would be no problem!

Trembling nervously, I announced to her, "I'm going to swim The English Channel."

Her response to this potentially life-changing announcement was, "What would you like for your evening meal?" I kid you not! It's a moment I will never forget.

I replied, "No, honestly," staring into her eyes. She stared back at me in silence and, having known me for 11 years, knew I was serious. We ate our evening meal, then set out to solve the immense problem of how I was going to swim the channel, something I had wanted to do since I first met Mike Read "King of The Channel" when I was 17 years old.

Solving Problems

On July 25, 1987, good fortune came my way. Having got involved in the diet and nutrition industry, I flew to Chicago and met my first mentor, "Billion Dollar Man" Larry Thompson, who was speaking on stage with a gentleman named Jim Rohn. That was the day that changed my life forever. I found out that Jim was hailed for being "America's Foremost Business Philosopher" and the training and type of thinking I was introduced to that day blew me away. He said things like, "If you will change, everything will change for you" and "Don't wish it were easier, wish you were better. Don't wish for less problems, wish for more skills." Wow! I spent 12 years at school and six years at college, and no one ever told me this before! It was the first of many trainings I had with Jim and Larry over the next three years. By 2006, Jim's teachings had become a massive influence in my life. He taught me that anything was possible if I just changed my philosophy, focused my mind on my goals, and learned the skills required to achieve the particular challenge I wanted to undertake.

So, how does someone get from not having swum for 12 years to spending 14 or more hours in 15°C water, swimming through the busiest shipping lane in the world? I had absolutely no idea! All I knew was, I was going to swim the channel and I had a burning desire to achieve this goal which I had first set myself in 1980. Along with representing my country at swimming, it was my dream, and I was not going to negotiate with my dream.

I decided that I was simply going to get in the pool, start from where I was with my swimming capabilities, and see where this journey would lead me. Whatever goal you want to achieve in life, you can only start from where you are right now.

An initial thought which came to mind as I set off on my journey was Jim's teachings on setting goals. He said the reason to achieve a goal is more about the person you become by achieving it, rather than achieving the goal itself, and that struck a chord with me. What would I become by achieving this goal?

Having booked my channel swim for July 10, 2007, on August 19, 2006, I entered Culford School Pool and completed thirty-two lengths (800 metres) in an hour. I was shattered at the end but now had my starting point. Session two, I completed thirty-six lengths, then 42, 50, 52, 54, 56, 60, 64, and in just a few weeks, I completed 120 lengths (3,000 metres) in an hour. Now, how did I do that? Easy. A few simple disciplines repeated every day meant that I got better. Now, who can get better at anything they choose to do? Answer—anybody. If you try.

I was getting fitter and stronger, but the next big challenge was an essential part of the journey. A swimming pool is warm and has no waves, no jellyfish or sea creatures, and no ships. I had to get into the sea.

The North Sea in December

On December 26, 2006, my wife and I headed to Felixstowe in Suffolk to take part in a Boxing Day "Charity Dip" in The North Sea. Before leaving home for the 40-minute drive, I checked the water temperature online. It was 6°C (42.8°F). Everyone was going in for a "dip," but I planned to swim from the beach near the "Fludyers Arms" public house to the pier. It didn't look too far on the map, but I had never swum in 6°C water before, and I was terrified about getting hypothermia.

As I stood on the beach with just a pair of skimpy swimming trunks, cap, and goggles for protection, I stepped cautiously into the water alongside multi-channel swimmer Mike Read who had inspired me to get to this point when I met him in 1980. As I looked at the pier, I now realised that this was going to take a Herculean effort to complete. It would be a one-mile swim, in 6°C water, against the tide. The "charity dippers," ran in, screamed, and ran out again. Mike and I were up to our trunks in the frigid water, and I was already gasping for breath. It was freezing. I looked nervously at Mike for reassurance that this would be okay, but he appeared to be struggling also. I just had to get my head under the water and start swimming.

I had never felt so traumatised! As I plunged my face, then head into the water, it was as if an elephant had stood on it while my body had been violently thrust naked into a bath of ice. I struggled to get my bearings or bodily senses to function. I had read a book by extreme cold-water swimmer Lynne Cox. In it, she explained that when hypothermia is setting in, you will know as you experience disorientation and confusion and your fingers separate widely, which means that your central nervous system is starting to shut down. I was determined to complete this swim as BBC Radio Suffolk was on the promenade broadcasting live, while hundreds of people were watching and cheering me on. I was, after all, a Suffolk County Councillor and the mayor's consort. There was to be no getting out!

I started swimming, and within five minutes, Mike Read had disappeared. I didn't care. I just needed to keep swimming. I was numb to the bone with cold, but I managed to get into a consistent front crawl rhythm. I repeated consistently:

> *1-2-3 are my fingers still together? Yes—no hypothermia, look to the left—oil tankers out at sea, breathe.*

> *1-2-3 are my fingers still together? Yes—no hypothermia, look to the right—people running along the promenade, breathe.*

This took my mind off the cold, and when you're in a situation like this, it's very important to take your mind off the cold! Thirty-five minutes later, frozen through, I touched the pier, swam to shore, and crawled out onto the stone beach. I had no time to think as Mike Read ran down to greet me. Mike said, "I got out as it was too cold. But if you can do that, you can swim the channel." As I shook profusely to get warm, I pondered Mike's inspirational words and knew immediately that next July I was going to become a channel swimmer.

Dover Harbour Training

In only 11 months of training, I had progressed from thirty-two lengths in the swimming pool to swimming for seven hours in Dover Harbour on a Saturday, followed by six hours on a Sunday in 12°C water (53.6°F). This is known as a split channel swim. In total, I was now swimming around 60,000 metres per week at 44 years of age while running my business, looking after my family, and being a local councillor. It was the ultimate challenge to balance everything.

On June 24, 2007, I had arranged to interview Alison Streeter who, as world record holder for the most channel swims, holds the title "Queen of The Channel." I wanted to find her secret for swimming it.

Leaning forward with my BBC radio microphone to broadcast to the nation, I said, "Alison, what's the secret to swimming The English Channel?"

Quite nonchalantly, she said:

Just get in the water, start swimming, put one arm in front of the other, and keep swimming until you get to France.

I eagerly awaited the more detailed explanation, but she turned and walked away. I shouted, "What else?"

She turned her head and replied, "That's it!" I was so disappointed! I spent the next few hours trying to fathom exactly what she meant. Then, suddenly, I got it. I GOT IT!

Many people have a dream to achieve something great. It could be anything from running a marathon or starting a new business to swimming the channel.

- We start on our journey to achieve our dream, and somebody says, "Boo!" and we quit.

- Somebody says, "Public speaking. You're no good at speaking," and we quit.

- Somebody says "Leadership. You're not a leader," and we quit.

- Somebody says "Sales, you're not going to get involved with sales. You're no salesperson," and we quit.

- Somebody says, "Starting your own business, what do you know about business?" and we quit.

But that one sentence from Alison, made me realise this:

Whatever goal you have in your life, whether it be in your business, personal, political, or sporting life—those simple words, when applied to whatever it is you are trying to achieve, will enable you to accomplish your goal.

This is what Alison meant:

- When you get in the channel, the water is going to be very cold—but just keep swimming until you get to France.

- When you are in the channel you are going to get very tired—but just keep swimming until you get to France.

- When you are in the channel you will probably get stung by jellyfish—but just keep swimming until you get to France.

- When you are in the channel, you are going to have self-doubts about whether you can keep going—but just keep swimming until you get to France.

Just keep swimming until you get to France—no matter what! That's what she meant.

Jim Rohn said it so simply, "How long should you try? Until." Until! Just keep trying, or swimming, or running, or building your business—until you succeed!

Whatever you are trying to achieve in your life, you are going to have to suffer pain of some sort. It will be one of two pains: the pain of discipline or the pain of regret. The difference is that the pain of discipline weighs ounces, but that of regret weighs tons. I was determined not to suffer the pain of regret.

Nothing great in life is easy. In Telford, England, it's written on the memorial to the first-ever conqueror of the channel Captain Matthew Webb who on August 24, 1875 swum from England to France in 21 hours and 40 minutes. Everything worthwhile in this life is an uphill struggle. The secret is to never give up.

Leaving a Legacy

On July 10, 2007, I swum from England to France in 13 hours and 52 minutes, becoming only the 873rd person in history to do so.

On July 13 and October 18, 2008, I became the oldest known person to represent Great Britain at swimming when I competed in two FINA World Cup Open Water Grand Prix in Serbia and Mexico, respectively.

On September 12, 2008, swimming through the night with no stars or moonlight, in the pouring rain, I swum from England to France in 13 hours and 3 minutes, becoming the 84th person in history to swim it twice.

On July 04, 2010, I was part of an international relay team, Team Iryna International, who successfully swum from England to France in 12 hours and 44 minutes.

On February 22, 2019, I flew to the USA to meet my birth mother, Eileen Currid, in Henry, Illinois. Unfortunately, it was two weeks too late as I ended up carrying her coffin at her funeral with my son, her grandson. I hope she was proud that we made it.

To date, I have told my story to people across the world, raised tens of thousands of pounds for charity, appeared in the press on TV and radio, and helped many others achieve their goals using this simple philosophy. Importantly, I have achieved most of the goals I have set myself in my life, the biggest so far being swimming the channel. How did I manage to do that not once but three times?

I simply got in the water, started swimming, put one arm in front of the other, and kept swimming until I got to France.

Whatever your goals may be, my advice is, *be the difference and just keep swimming*!

Contact Paul via PaulHopfensperger.com to learn more about Paul's consulting services and to book Paul to speak at your organisation.

Follow Paul on Instagram: @paulhopfensperger, Facebook: @PaulHopfensperger, LinkedIn: Paul Hopfensperger, Twitter: @phopfensperger and YouTube: youtube.paulhopfensperger.com

Tweetable: Whatever goals you have, NEVER negotiate with your dream! Setting goals that require problems to be solved, that will bring value to people, and for what you become by achieving them will leave a legacy which inspires others to do the same! #BeTheDifference #JustKeepSwimming

ANNA KELLEY

Investing for Meaningful Impact

Anna Kelley has active ownership in $160M of real estate and has invested in over 2700 doors. Anna invests in apartment buildings to make a meaningful impact for both her investors and her residents. She is a sought-after coach, speaker, and author, and enjoys changing lives through her real estate ventures.

Leaving a Legacy – Thinking Beyond Inheritance

When people speak of leaving a legacy, it usually involves leaving an inheritance of great sums of money to their family or a large financial gift to an organization whose mission resonates with their own. Legacy gifts are generally birthed by a desire to leave an impact AFTER we die! In reality, there is only a small percentage of people in this world who are ever able to leave a meaningful financial legacy which will outlive them. Most people, if we are honest, struggle to live the American dream and live paycheck to paycheck most of their lives. They do not consider leaving a financial legacy because they never develop the wealth necessary to bequeath one.

However, if we think beyond leaving a financial legacy and start to think of legacy as something we give that will make a meaningful impact in the lives of current and future generations, we can all begin to consider leaving our own legacy. Legacy may include leaving significant amounts of wealth, or it may not. Either way, each and every one of us has something special within us, uniquely formed from our experiences, relationships, passions, trials, and successes, which give us the wisdom and the heart to give exactly what someone else needs to receive from us.

A proverb in the Bible says, "The purpose in a man's heart is like deep water, but a man of understanding will draw it out." Another passage says that we are God's workmanship, created for good works He has prepared for us. And one of my favorite passages says that all of God's commandments are based on just two—to love God and to love others. What good works has God prepared you uniquely to do? In what areas have you gained the wisdom someone else needs to help them find their purpose? How can you spend some of your valuable time and resources to show love to others and make a meaningful impact on their lives today?

Understanding and embracing the important, unique responsibility and calling on our lives to leave this kind of legacy BEFORE we die results in what I call greater purpose living: investing our lives, our time, and our finances to make a meaningful impact on the lives of others. If we do it well, this impact will become our legacy and will inspire others to pass down the same legacy so that generations are invested in leaving those we meet better than they were before we met them!

Experience, Compassion & Passion Leads to Purpose

Having grown up in Section 8 housing, the oldest of six children, and a latchkey kid, my early years were focused on survival, protecting my mom from abusive relationships, and watching my siblings while my mom worked two jobs to make ends meet. While I cared about my family, I also knew that I needed to find a way out of the cycle of poverty, alcohol, and drugs that I grew up in. I used every waking moment dreaming of and pursuing ways to escape my life in the projects. I longed to find that thing that would give me self-esteem and purpose, that thing I could do better than anyone else, that would allow me to be recognized as special and hopefully lead to a scholarship to pay for college. I knew that if I could get a degree, I could make my own money, and I would never have to depend on a man to support me. Having seen my mom return to abusive men because she could not afford childcare while she worked, I vowed to become independent and self-reliant.

This gave me a drive and determination like no other person I knew from a very young age. I became resourceful. I bought and sold candy. I learned to crochet and went door-to-door selling my creations in all the neighboring apartments so that I would have enough money to buy name brand school clothes so other kids wouldn't laugh at my thrift store outfits. I was a sad little girl, with no resources, little guidance, few friends, and almost nothing beyond my hope that God would help me. My mother loved me and did the best she could to give me a better life. She told me I was special, brilliant, talented, and that she believed in me. She told me I had to go to college. She made sure we went to church and to Vacation Bible School ministries that came to our apartment complexes. She didn't want me to repeat her mistakes, and she wanted me to trust God to take care of us. This was her legacy sewn deep within my soul, for which I will always be grateful.

My mother also made sure that we spent time with my grandparents. They were our escape house during abusive nights, our babysitters, and our Sunday morning church takers, and they poured into me and showed me love and encouragement. They told me I was smart and kind and that I could do whatever I wanted to in life. They told me to stay strong and to trust God to take care of me. My grandmother shared with me stories of her life during the Great Depression, difficulties raising eight kids while taking care of her family financially as my grandfather suffered for years with bouts of PTSD from Iwo Jima that kept him from keeping good jobs. She showed me that life isn't easy, but that showing love and forgiveness and pouring into the lives of your children and grandchildren was the most important purpose in life. They had very little money, but they showed me how to make it go far and how to use it in small, inexpensive ways to enjoy life without very much. She taught me what it is to be resourceful, full of faith despite circumstances, and both gentle and strong. This is a legacy gift I am most grateful to have received.

At the age of 15, I made the difficult decision to leave my mom and siblings and moved in with my dad and step-mother. They taught me to have compassion and forgiveness for my mother and to become financially self-sufficient. My stepmother encouraged me to get a degree no matter what, and not to be distracted from that goal, so that I could forge a better, financially stable life. They taught me to use my network, to avoid debt, and to pay taxes! They paid for my college education. Most importantly, they took me to church and taught me to read the Bible and trust God to work all things together for my good if I lived my life to honor Him. I am grateful for the legacy they poured into my life, worth far more than any amount of money.

For as long as I can remember, I wanted to help others. God placed that desire deep within me. But I also had significant responsibilities at a young age and longed to be able to worry about only me and to have the kind of fun all my friends seemed to have at my age. I worked hard, got a college degree in three years while working full-time, and eventually landed a job as a financial relationship manager for Bank of America's Private Bank. It is there that I learned about finances, investments, and growing wealth. I had beat the odds of poverty, and I knew I wanted to give back. I began volunteering for Hope for Youth, an inner-city youth ministry that poured into the lives of at-risk youth living in drug-infested neighborhoods with very little guidance and the odds stacked against them. There was nothing more rewarding than helping other kids to see that there is hope for a better life! I still keep in touch with "my kids" and am so proud of the lives they built!

Eventually, I married and had a long, bumpy path to creating financial stability. We worked for years to pay off my husband's six-figure school loan, started a chiropractic business, and started investing in real estate to allow me to be home with our four kids. Having been a latchkey kid myself, I desired nothing more than to be home with my babies! Though it took many years of 80-hour workweeks, we dug out from the 2009 financial crisis and loss of most of my 401K. We methodically purchased enough rental real estate to allow me to replace my six-figure income and retire at age 44 from a 20-year career at AIG. Not only had I replaced my income but also we went from a negative net worth to a multimillion-dollar net worth. I know this is nothing short of miraculous! I now have active ownership in over $160M of multifamily apartments together with my partners.

My hard-fought journey to financial freedom was achieved through decades of blood, sweat, and tears, but I'm grateful I mustered the determination to relentlessly pursue creating a better life for myself and my family! I've learned to master money so that money doesn't master me. We have learned many valuable lessons, including how to weather the storms of life with strength, determination, grit, faith, love, and hope. My motto in life is this: Love God, love people, use money, and never give up! It is part of my legacy I hope to impart to my children and to all who know me.

Greater Purpose Living – Making a Meaningful Impact

Most of us begin our lives focused solely on ourselves. In the pursuit of independence, we tend to spend our early years, and even decades, trying to find self-worth and pursuing self-preservation, self-esteem, self-sufficiency, and our own self-interests. It is only as we go through life surrounded by others that we begin to truly discover the value, meaning, and joy that comes only from living our lives in such a way that considers and prioritizes the needs and interests of others. In giving our time, energy, money, and love for the benefit of others, we find far greater purpose for ourselves and leave a far greater impact on this world with our brief lives.

My understanding of and desire to pursue greater purpose living and to make a meaningful impact in the lives of others has become clearer, stronger, and deeper over the last few years. I have shifted from just surviving, to creating financial independence, to creating financial freedom for myself and my own children, to growing my real estate businesses in a way that is allowing me to impact many others with the experience, wisdom, time, and financial resources God has blessed me with.

I created both my speaking and coaching company REI Mom, LLC, and my multifamily apartment investment company, Greater Purpose Capital, LLC, to make a meaningful impact in the lives of others. I coach others to create financial freedom through investing in income-producing real estate, and I have a special place in my heart to help working and single moms to create a better life for their families. Through my multifamily investment company, I help my partners and investors create a financial legacy for their families through passive investing in projects where, in turn, they know their investment dollars are making an impact in the lives of the people living in the communities in which they invest. I am also developing programs, resources, and partnerships that will help our residents learn financial principles that will help them become financially stable, and that will give them hope and support to create a better tomorrow.

When experience meets passion and compassion, it helps us to discover our greater purpose: what we are uniquely made for and qualified to do with our lives. This purpose is not usually given to us, and it rarely becomes evident without years of trial and finding out what we are made of. Sometimes finding out what we are made of is necessary before we can truly know what we are made for. When we discover both what we are made of and what we are made for, our greater purpose becomes clear, and we are able to design our lives, investments, and businesses to serve that greater purpose and make a meaningful, lasting, legacy impact!

Greater Purpose Giving: My Legacy & Yours

By the grace of God, I have beaten the odds of persistent poverty. In doing so, I have found my greater purpose: to leave a legacy of grit, determination, integrity, money mastery, hope, and faith. I leave this legacy for single moms and young kids in poverty, for working moms who want to be home with their babies, and for investors who want to make a meaningful impact with their passive investment dollars while they pursue their own purpose. This is the heart, motivation, and purpose behind Greater Purpose Capital—investing not only for strong financial returns, but more importantly, for the eternal returns in the lives of the people in our communities. It is something I know I was made to be part of and a legacy I hope will last for generations!

My hope is that you will discover the joy of both greater purpose living and greater purpose giving, and in so doing, leave a meaningful legacy you were uniquely made for!

To learn more about Anna Kelley's multifamily investment opportunities, visit her website at www.greaterpurposecapital.com. For coaching, speaking, or other inquiries, email her at info@reimom.com. Follow her on Facebook and LinkedIn at Anna ReiMom Kelley and on Instagram at Anna ReiMom.

Tweetable: Understanding and embracing the important, unique responsibility and calling on our lives to leave a legacy before we die results in what I call greater purpose living: investing our lives, our time, and our finances to make a meaningful impact on the lives of others.

ERIK MIKKELSON
For Your Financial Future®

Erik Mikkelson is a family wealth advisor, active real estate investor, co-founder of Monona Docks and Monona Waterfront LLC, and founder of RMR Wealth Advisors LLC. As a Certified Financial Planner™ professional, Erik works to help others grow, utilize, preserve, and protect family assets to meet a family's lifetime and legacy dreams.

Gifts from My Grandparents

My grandparents grew up and lived through the Great Depression, and my grandfather worked at a young age for The Civilian Conservation Corps at a CCC camp in northern Minnesota to make ends meet. He eventually ended up becoming one of the first butchers in the state, which paved the way to my grandparents owning a Supervalu grocery store in Blue Earth, Minnesota. At a very young age, I was able to be around entrepreneurs and see how they treated their customers in a small, rural town. Looking back, the importance of providing great service and value was exemplified by how my grandparents conducted business and lived their lives. I believe those same values are at the heart of what makes so many businesses successful. I am blessed to have had such great role models to learn from.

Teach a Kid to Fish

Some of my best memories are of getting to go and stay with my grandparents every summer, during which we would often stay at their cabin on Bass Lake in southern Minnesota. I learned to operate the boat, and most importantly, to fish! Remember the saying, "give a man (or woman) a fish, and you feed him for a day, but teach a man to fish, and you feed him for a lifetime?" That concept applies to so much more than fishing.

I remember sitting with them in their sunroom most mornings. The newspaper would be out, and they would be looking at the stock market to see what happened the previous day. After viewing the paper, they would say, "Well, we can keep the lights on!" or "We might need to turn the lights off today," based on what Supervalu stock and other holdings of theirs had done. I was also taught through receiving my first stocks and bonds from my grandparents. That is when I started dipping my toe into learning about investing in publicly-traded companies based on profitable and viable businesses.

I also learned the importance of knowing the competition, as my grandfather would take me "undercover" (Everyone in town knew him!) into the nearby "Dirty Bird" (Red Owl grocery store) to check on pricing, produce, overall product displays, etc. I would get to buy a candy bar to see how I was treated by the checkout person. That was my pay for helping!

I began to learn about real estate ownership, although I don't think I realized it at the time. I remember, when they bought the actual Supervalu store building and parking lot. It was a huge deal for them. I remember them putting in a restaurant, the ownership of a residential rental home, the ownership of the cabin, as well as looking at properties they eventually decided to pass on. Looking back, all were based on utilization value, investment potential, and some form of lifestyle value. I have been a big believer in owning real estate ever since.

Starting to Fish

I studied economics at St. Olaf College with a minor in accounting and donated my knees to Division III college football. During my college years, I enjoyed one of my most fun and unique experiences at Lord Fletcher's on Lake Minnetonka in Minnesota working as a security guard (bouncer) and eventually the wharf manager with customers docking their boats for lunch, dinner, or just to grab some drinks and hang out. While I was working there, the owner allowed me, along with a great classmate Dave Sumners, the opportunity to complete my senior project for my economics degree on the feasibility of converting the downstairs bar into a restaurant and bar. Afterwards, that idea was found to be a good return on investment, and the downstairs restaurant was renamed Granddaddy's, which remained a key part of Lord Fletcher's for decades.

After graduating, I went into logistics management and manufacturing with Kimberly Clark and moved to Paris, Texas, a bit northeast of Dallas. The hours were long, but the experience of working in the consumer products industry was insightful. I soon was moved around to California and back to Texas and then switched companies to Newell Rubbermaid in Ohio at Anchor Hocking Glass. Eventually, I found my way back to Wisconsin, where I was born, working for Fiskars, a small publicly-traded company best known for the orange-handled scissors on desks across the country and a conglomerate of many small consumer product manufacturing and assembly companies. This proved to be one of my most drawn upon work experiences in corporate America before I entered the financial industry. As a member of and eventually a leader of the Fiskars corporate operations team, I would fly all around the US and Europe with my team to say, "Hi. I'm from corporate. I'm here to help," and hoped everyone did not run away. It turned out to be quite rewarding, and I was also able to gain some merger and acquisition experience as the operations lead for multiple projects.

From there, while flying to different locations, I found myself reading about estate planning, investing, and personal finance. I was finding my true passion.

Patience, Persistence, and Knowing When to Set the Hook!

On one trip, I went to a leadership center in Colorado with a group of colleagues, and during the exit interview, the leadership advisor asked me if I had ever considered being a financial professional. The line was cast!

We had some major changes going on in our corporate organization at the same time my first daughter was born, and it seemed traveling so much was not right for me anymore. So, armed with the notion of a career change, I called a great friend, which led me to have conversations with his network of coworkers in the mutual fund industry. Again, while taking some personal time, I was jumping on airplanes for a few more trips and took the opportunity to meet with and interview many industry leaders. I learned more about many aspects of the financial industry and found myself being a bit disgusted with commissions, yet drawn more and more to working with people, business owners, and their families and helping them with everything financial.

Around that time, my good friend and commercial real estate partner, Dr. Shawn McCue, and I were grilling burgers in the backyard, and he said, "When are you going to stop doing what you're doing and become a financial guy so you can manage my stuff?" And the hook was set!

I got into the finance industry and began assisting one of the earliest established RIAs (Registered Investment Advisors) and CFPs® in the state of Wisconsin just as the tech bubble was deflating, fast! He came to my desk and said, "Guess what? I need you to pay rent and become a full-blown financial advisor." So, I went from a paycheck to paying rent. I was spending money to get into the business and became a family wealth advisor. I studied to earn my CFP® designation and started finding people to help, or more like, they started finding me—thankfully!!

My goal became to work with a relatively small group of people as a fiduciary to help them enhance, utilize, preserve, and protect their family assets. I wanted to help people meet their family's financial and lifetime desires, retirement dreams, and wealth preservation and legacy wishes.

Becoming an Entrepreneur

After I personally witnessed a business owner and "planner" continue through his 70s without his own succession plan, I departed from my position to form my own firm and serve our clients. Prior to this, I was a big student of *The Millionaire Next Door* and the demographics it was based on. I had a vision of serving people with that mindset and lifestyle, much like my grandparents. I formed RMR Wealth Advisors, registered as an RIA, charging our clients fees for advice and service, not commissions. This path led me to develop what was a self-created job into a small business, much like as described in the book *Cashflow Quadrant.* I give both of those books, as well as the insight that comes from reading *Freakonomics,* a lot of credit for the foundation, values, and guiding principles we operate by. Today, just as I had envisioned, a lot of the clients we are fortunate to serve are self-made millionaires "next door," and you would never know it by running into them in public.

For the most part, they are fiscally responsible, meaning they have established the behaviors and habits to keep spending less than their resources, saving the difference, and in most cases, investing in the investment markets, in real estate, and in business, often becoming entrepreneurs themselves. Once again, my grandfather comes to mind, as he used to tell me to make sure I always took care of my own old man, meaning save for myself first for my future. Armed with that mindset and the power of compounding returns, I believe most can achieve a financially rewarding future.

Just Don't Panic

Unfortunately, a problem most of us face is that, as humans, we are behaviorally emotional, especially when it comes to our money and investments. For whatever reason, in the supermarket or anywhere we go shopping, when we find something we really want to buy is on sale, we are enthusiastic about buying it. However, when it comes to equity investments that go "on sale," we get scared, and often sell instead of buy. To have a successful investing strategy, one needs to have a system of saving and investing they believe in and adhere to through both good and bad, sometimes downright terrible, times. Having a process that guides one to have conviction to invest even more when times look the bleakest, often leads to long-term, above average performance. Indeed, to be able to rebalance or add to investments coming off lows is where you can get exponential growth. That is at the heart of our investment philosophy. Remember, patience, persistence, and knowing when to set the hook!

Weathering the Storms

It is our job to do thorough due diligence for investments, financial planning strategies, and cash flow management processes while also keeping it simple enough to understand. We have the math tell us when to rebalance to keep our emotions out of it. As people approach retirement, the most important thing they can do is have and trust in a well thought out lifetime cash flow strategy. Investments are important, but without a good cash flow strategy that holds up through both up and down markets, there is a risk of blowing up a person's retirement. I believe this is very misunderstood by many as they head into retirement and sadly even ignored or neglected by many advisors in the industry.

To help explain and manage investment portfolios and retirement cash flows, we have copyrighted *Capturing Profits and Preserving Wealth*© and service marked *3 Barrels and a Bucket*ˢᵐ. Our most aggressive barrel represents the larger risks and requires tolerance of volatility. Our most stable barrel is structured to preserve wealth and be the resource to draw cash flows from when needed throughout one's retirement. The Bucket is one's bank account(s), allowing the freedom to draw from as needed. This may seem like a lot, however, we have found that having 7 to 10 years of one's future cash flow needs invested in the stable holdings of Barrel 1ˢᵐ and their "bucket" provides the peace of mind and emotional stability one needs during such times as we experience during major downturns. There is nothing like the real-life stressful times of the 2008 and 2009 market crash to test a process. The resulting comfort and conviction in our process from not only surviving but also thriving following such a time is priceless.

Plan for the Worst and the Rest is Upside!

Throughout this process, we do not try to time the markets, ever. We do take advantage of different markets though, through this consistent, strategic, and thoughtful approach. It is really a matter of what does one want to accomplish, what can they afford to risk, and what are they willing to risk, and eventually what their desired cash flow needs are throughout their lifetime. We design a *3 Barrels and a Bucket*ˢᵐ approach specific to each family's circumstances and desires.

I very often when faced with major decisions ask myself what is the worst-case scenario and plan for it. As soon as we can deal with the worst, the rest is upside! That is part of our philosophy with financial planning and our *3 Barrels and a Bucket*ˢᵐ approach. It's really identifying one's worst-case scenarios and working to create acceptable contingency plans to solve for them should they occur. With those in place, it frees us to focus on achieving the upside!

Get Up and Get Doing it!

I was truly fortunate to get some one-on-one time with my grandfather when he was in his late 80s. We went fishing, of course! But we also just talked, remembered past times together and revisited old jokes. At one point, he stopped at the top of our stairs down to our dock on the lake. I had only seen him cry once before, at my grandma's funeral, but now he had a tear coming down a cheek. He said, "Dammit, dammit, Erik. We spent our whole life saving and investing, and all she wanted was a new dock and some things remodeled. What was I waiting for?!" I just gave him a hug, and we went fishing.

A few years later, in his 90s, I got to visit with him again, but this time we didn't go fishing. We were having coffee in the morning, while he was looking at the business section of the paper. I asked him, as he reflected on things, if he had any words of wisdom for me. He thought, and he said, "We did a lot, and there are things I still would like to do, and there are things I didn't get done. So, I think my best advice is, if there is anything in this world you would like to do, you had better get up and get doing it!"

Reflecting on the words of my grandfather while sitting quietly in the woods alone, as I enjoy finding time to do often, it occurred to me to pursue registering *For Your Financial Future®*, and I got it done! *For Your Financial Future®* guides my purpose, direction, and the actions of my firm while serving the families I am honored to have as clients.

To get in touch with Erik Mikkelson about anything related to your personal finances, business planning, succession planning, real estate due diligence, or to just start a conversation, you can email him at mikkerik@gmail.com, or call him at 608-436-0206. For more information, you can visit ForYourFinancialFuture.com

Tweetable: Get up and get doing it! For Your Financial Future®.

RICHARD M. MORRIS

A Warrior's Path – Becoming a Sheepdog

As a 42-year police veteran, 10th-degree black belt, chaplain, karate teacher, Zig Ziglar Certified speaker, and coach, Richard brings a unique set of skills. He is considered by many martial arts, military, and law enforcement leaders to be the world's leading authority on the science of fighting.

What Is a Sheepdog?

My good friend, Lt. Col. Dave Grossman, retired Army Ranger and West Point psychology professor, shares the following warrior maxim he gleaned from a Vietnam veteran, an old, retired colonel:

> *Most of the people in our society are sheep. Sheep account for about ninety-eight percent of our citizens. They are kind, gentle, productive, and generally hurt one another only by accident. About one percent of our citizens are the wolves, and the wolves feed on the sheep without mercy! Do you believe there are wolves in the land? You had better believe it! Then the final one percent of our citizens are the sheepdogs, who live to protect the flock and confront the wolf. If you have no capacity for violence, then you are a healthy, productive citizen—a sheep. If you have a capacity for violence and no empathy for your fellow citizens, then you have defined an aggressive sociopath—a wolf. But what if you have a capacity for violence and a deep love for your fellow citizens? Then you have a sheepdog, a warrior, someone who is walking the hero's path. The sheep generally do not like the sheepdog. He looks a lot like the wolf. He has fangs and the capacity for violence. The difference, though, is that the sheepdog must not, cannot, and will not harm the sheep. Still, the sheepdog disturbs the sheep. He is a constant reminder that there are wolves in the land.*

We are all born as sheep. As babies and small children, we are dependent upon others to survive. The role models we have can lead us to continue as sheep, become wolves, or become a sheepdog. Civilization would not exist like it does today without sheepdogs to protect the sheep and hunt the wolf.

My Journey as a Sheepdog

Dad was a remarkable man and a warrior—a sheepdog. He was a professional boxer before he entered WWII. During the war, Dad was a tank commander in the 759th Battalion for General Patton's Third Army. Dad drove the tank that Patton would often ride in, leading the charge. Dad also spent time in the

82nd Airborne and was at Pointe du Hoc at Normandy's Invasion. He was a celebrated war hero with many medals and commendations. Dad was also the kindest, most encouraging, and most humble man that I have ever known. While I began as a sheep, Dad raised me to become a sheepdog. When I was about five years old, Dad taught me how to box and some Jiu-Jitsu that he learned in the Army. He was training me in the way of the warrior—to be a sheepdog.

God has given me positive role models who were sheepdogs and godly men and women. Mom and dad were the first; they taught me with faith, hope, and love. They loved me unconditionally and had faith in me before I ever believed in myself. Dad had hope that I would one day become strong enough to protect others and myself. He told me that it is my responsibility to keep the Morris name honorable in all that I do. Dad taught me that I should protect the weak from bullies. This sacrificial love soon defined my role in society.

When I started taking karate in February 1971, I was the youngest in my classes. I was fourteen years old, stood 5'3" tall, and weighed 135 lbs. In my first karate lesson, Paul Smith asked me how far in karate I wanted to go.

I asked, "What is the highest belt?"

He responded, "Black belt."

I then asked him if there was a higher-ranking belt than a black belt, and he said, "Theoretically, 10th-degree black belt is the highest, but there are none of them today."

I told him, "Then I will be a 10th-degree black belt!" I saw him roll his eyes and smile. Paul was only a brown belt himself. I believe that I was willing to reach for the top because Dad taught me how to believe in myself. I went home that night with the belt test requirements up to the black belt level, and I marked the calendar with the soonest date I could test for each belt. Even then, I understood the importance of writing down my goals to achieve them.

It would take me three years if I were to test every time I was allowed. I practically lived at the karate studio. I cleaned the mat and bathrooms daily because I understood that it would build discipline and character. I missed my first belt test because we did not have the five dollars for the test fee. Belt tests were bi-monthly. That location closed in June, so I started training with Pat Burleson, the chief instructor, at his main location.

From Quitter to Teacher

On November 16, 1971, during sparring in the advanced adult karate class, I was beaten badly by an adult national champion black belt. Karate was much rougher then, but I was only a 15-year-old blue belt. That night, I drove my motorcycle home and told Dad that I wanted to quit karate. Dad listened to me intently as I told him what happened, and he could see that I had a broken nose, two black eyes, and bruised ribs. Dad said that he would talk to Pat Burleson the next day for allowing a grown man to fight me so hard.

As we walked in the next day, Mr. Burleson said, smiling, "Richard, I wondered what happened to you—you never miss helping me teach the kid's classes!"

I told him that I was quitting karate. He looked puzzled. Dad told Mr. Burleson that he needed to speak with him right away. Mr. Burleson looked at me and said, "Richard, if you will teach this class while I talk to your dad, I will get back with you in just a few minutes."

It was exciting to be teaching the kid's karate class by myself. About 30 minutes later, Mr. Burleson stepped outside of his office, stopped the class, and asked me, "Richard, how do you like teaching class?"

I said, "I love it!"

Mr. Burleson then asked the class, "Did you like Richard teaching this class?"

They all said, "Yes, sir!"

Mr. Burleson then looked at me and said, "Richard, would you like to be the new teacher for this class?"

I said, "Yes, sir!"

Mr. Burleson then told the class they would now address me as "Mr. Morris," as I was now their teacher. Somehow, I forgot about getting beat up. I became a teacher that day, and I have never missed a week of training or teaching since then. I learned perseverance and responsibility.

I was promoted to black belt three years and two months after starting karate— at least two years faster than most students who made black belt. Less than one in one thousand of the students who begin karate ever make it to black belt. My goal setting and determination did pay off!

For years, I wondered what Dad said to Mr. Burleson. After Dad died in 1992, Mr. Burleson told me what happened in his office that day: "Your dad sat in my office and drank coffee with me. He told me, 'I don't mind Richard fighting hard and know that injuries are part of being trained as a fighter, but the older black belts need more control until Richard gets older and stronger.' I told him that I agreed with him and would make sure it didn't happen again. After talking about unrelated things for some time, your dad told me, 'Mr. Burleson, I want you to make a man out of my son!'"

Dad wanted me to be a sheepdog.

Teaching Karate

As a shy teenager, Mr. Burleson would bring me to help with seminars until I was confident to lead seminars independently. Over the years, I have taught karate students, self-defense, and law enforcement seminars internationally to tens of thousands of people. On January 1, 2013, I became one of Pat Burleson's first students to promote to 10th-degree black belt in American Karate and 9th degree in Taekwondo, the highest rank in each. Karate was a significant, transforming process in my life.

From Bouncer to Police Officer

As an 18-year-old, I got a job as a bouncer in a popular hangout near TCU because I was a black belt, professional kickboxer, and full-contact fighter. There, I met many Fort Worth police officers that became my friends, and several became my students. I accompanied some of the officers on a ride-along and found it to be exhilarating. It gave me a chance to see how police officers can genuinely help people within the community. I also loved the warrior lifestyle! My role as a sheepdog continued to develop. I joined the Fort Worth Police Department and began the police academy in January 1978, just two months after getting married. I have since served in many roles, finally retiring in 2014 as the gang intelligence sergeant after 36 years of police work. As a retired sergeant, I continue volunteering as part of the police department's Critical Incident Stress Debriefing Team as well as the Peer Support Team and as a chaplain.

Meeting Zig Ziglar

In 1982, I opened my first karate studio and taught classes during my off-duty hours. My studio became successful, giving me the avenue to lead and motivate others. In 1984, a student of mine loaned me two Zig Ziglar cassette tapes. Within one month, I noticed that my attitude was more positive and my business more profitable! Soon, I met Zig at a seminar in Dallas.

Zig was humble, genuine, and thoughtful. He made me feel as if I were the only other person in the room. I met and befriended his son Tom in 1985. Tom invited me to give my Christian testimony during the Monday morning devotional time at the Ziglar Corporation when Zig would be there. Zig was such an encourager; he became my friend, karate student, personal mentor, and my "Dutch uncle."

International Recognition

I taught self-defense programs for children, women, senior citizens, and police officers throughout my police career. These endeavors brought me, and the Fort Worth Police Department, positive international media attention with Ted Koppel at ABC Nightline, Peter Jennings at World News Tonight, CNN, CBS, Fox, and many more news outlets.

Karate paved the way for me to become a police officer. I have taught self-defense and arrest control tactics to several thousand police officers, federal agents, and military personnel. I teach public seminars, private lessons, and I am a coach. I am a sheepdog who trains sheepdogs!

One of my friends noticed that the people I spend time with are sheepdogs, such as Lieutenant Colonel Dave Grossman, martial artists, police, military, and spiritual warrior friends. He said, "Richard, I have noticed that you collect warriors." He is right! I also train them to deepen their skills.

While not everyone aspires to be a sheepdog, few initially set out to become a wolf. But, if you want to move towards the warrior's path of becoming a sheepdog, this is my specialty.

To Become a Sheepdog

LOOK for successful sheepdogs to emulate instead of waiting for them to enter our life by chance. Decide to gravitate towards the positive role models to model our lives after and avoid the negative. We must seek and follow those who are wise, have good character, and inspire us to succeed. I continue to study and admire many.

> *"Surround yourself with the dreamers and the doers and thinkers,*
> *but, most of all, surround yourself with those who see greatness*
> *within you, even when you don't see it in yourself"*
>
> – Zig Ziglar

See yourself as successful and strong even when you feel weak. God instructs us to claim strength, even before there is evidence of that strength.

> *"...Let the weak say, 'I am a warrior'"*
>
> – Joel 3:10

LIVE as a sheepdog. Imitate your sheepdogs' behavior. Zig Ziglar said, "It is better to imitate excellence than to create mediocrity." After you identify righteous men and women, sheepdogs, study their positive qualities and embody them. Then train and mentor others to further develop your skills.

"True joy comes when you inspire, encourage, and guide someone else on a path that benefits him or her."

– Zig Ziglar

LEAVE a legacy. What do you want your grandchildren to remember about you when you are gone? Not all sheepdogs are a physical warrior like General George S. Patton or US Navy SEAL Chris Kyle. Many are warriors in their faith or determination for social justice, such as Mother Teresa, Billy Graham, Rosa Parks, Zig Ziglar, and many more. Search them out, follow their guidance, and as you learn from them, live accordingly. You will leave a sheepdog legacy that will far outlast your years on this earth!

Richard M. Morris has many private lesson clients, such as the late Zig Ziglar, Tom Ziglar, and Kyle Wilson. He also coaches individuals and groups, trains police departments, and has online and in-person training and speaking. You can connect with Richard at rm@richardmorristraining.com

Tweetable: The role models we have can lead us to continue as sheep, become wolves, or become a sheepdog. Civilization would not exist like it does today without sheepdogs to protect the sheep and hunt the wolf. Richard M. Morris trains people to become sheepdogs in all areas of life.

MITZI PERDUE

My Purpose Is to Increase Happiness and Decrease Misery in the World

Mitzi Perdue is a businesswoman, prolific bestselling author, and part of a legacy of household name family businesses. She was formerly president of the 40,000 member American Agri-Women and one of the US Delegates to the United Nations Conference on Women in Nairobi. She was a syndicated columnist for 22 years as well as a TV producer and interview show host.

Growing Up in a Business Family

I grew up in the Sheraton Hotel family. My father was the co-founder of the Sheraton Hotels, although we, the family, sold the business after my father's passing in 1967.

Even before Sheraton, our family had been in business since the founding of the Henderson Estate Company in 1840. I also married into a multi-generational family business. Perdue Farms began in the chicken business in 1920.

I am also a businesswoman. I've started multiple businesses, including the family wine grape business, now one of the larger suppliers of wine grapes in California.

Challenges Growing Up

Seeing me today, you would think I grew up as confident as they make them. But if you had met me 40 years ago, you wouldn't believe that I'm the same person. Until my mid-thirties, I was so shy that I found it difficult to enter a room or to use the telephone. If I had to talk to one of my kid's teachers, I would sit on the edge of my bed for half an hour trying to figure out how I could get past hello. It was a case of extreme shyness.

Part of the reason for my shyness was, I had a severe lisp. It was a lisp that you didn't just hear but could also see. People would confide in me after they knew me well that they had initially assumed I was stupid. If each time you meet somebody you assume they think you're stupid, it does not help develop loads of self-confidence. My lisp was a blight on my life.

Although I had a good education, my shyness coupled with fear of failure meant that by age 38 I wasn't doing a lot with my life. I did have an occupation; I grew rice in California. The great advantage of being a rice grower, if you're shy, is you do a lot of walking in the fields. You have some interaction with a few people, but otherwise, it's solitary. This suited me just fine because I didn't enjoy meetings and was scared of people. My shyness could have gone on forever, but there was a point where it changed.

A Lesson Learned From a Genius

In my rice fields, I had a tenant farmer who had an incredible, unusual gift. He had an IQ of over 200. In gratitude for this gift, he wanted to give back to the world. He wanted to glean, from all the world's wisdom, ideas that would benefit mankind. He even had a title for the great book he would write: *Life, An Owner's Manual.*

He spent a good bit of his life, when he wasn't being a tenant farmer, collecting more and more information for his book. Decade after decade went by, and he didn't start the book. He always felt there was more to learn before actually starting to write.

But, at age 68, something horrible happened to him. He was diagnosed with terminal heart disease. He couldn't walk across my office without crippling heart pain.

It was, for him, a death sentence. His doctors didn't think they could keep him alive long enough to go to the Mayo Clinic for quadruple bypass surgery.

You might think that nothing could be worse than a death sentence, but, there is something worse. Peter realized that his whole life had been working towards writing this great book, and now he'd never get to write it. The grief he felt was, I think, greater than what would happen with a death sentence.

However, things changed! I influenced him to visit the Pritikin Longevity Center, a spa that had (and still has) an extraordinary record for helping people with heart disease.

Their specialty was diet, exercise, meditation, and every other healthy lifestyle thing that you can think of. My genius friend spent a month there and lost 15 pounds. At the end of the month, miraculously—his heart revascularized. He was in great health when he returned!

I was so happy for him! I told him, "Peter, this is the most wonderful news in the world! Now you can write your book!"

To my surprise, he said, "Yes, I will write it. I just need to do a little bit more research, and I'll be ready." He lived to be 95 and never wrote his book.

I realized what was holding him back was fear of failure. When you spend thousands of hours walking rice paddies with a person, you get to know a lot about them. I knew that Peter was so afraid that he would not succeed at this goal of gifting the world with a spectacular book of wisdom, that he did the one thing that was guaranteed to cause failure: he didn't try.

I Started Thinking, What About Me?

I really wanted to be in communications. My dream had been television. What was holding me back?

I decided that I would turn my life around. If it was fear of failure that held my tenant back, I would redefine failure for myself. Failure would be not giving my all to whatever I wanted to accomplish. Failure would be not giving everything that I was capable of.

Even if I didn't succeed by some people's standards, I would succeed by mine because just in the process of trying, I would be learning things, meeting people, and moving farther along the road to being all I could be.

To start with, I knew I needed to get over my lisp. I went to the speech therapist, and she told me she didn't have the tools for helping somebody at my age to overcome a lisp. Because my new motto was "Try!", I went to another speech therapist and was told the same thing. I went to a third, and again, I was told there was no chance to help somebody with a lisp at my age or any age adult. This was the 1970s.

Redefining Failure

The third speech therapist told me, "I can't help you, but I'd love to take your money!"

That began nine months of practicing half an hour a day and getting absolutely nowhere. It was nine months, a lot of money and a two-hour round trip to the therapist each week with not even the slightest glimmer of progress. But somewhere around nine months, I began to hear when I was lisping.

When I could hear it, I could work on correcting it. By the end of the year, I was ready to audition for a television show. I fell on my face numerous times, but one day at an audition, the station manager happened to hear me and said, "You're natural for television. Would you like a show?" I went from somebody almost too shy to use the telephone to somebody who had a television show in the space of a year.

I had also always wanted to write, but I had never submitted anything. I began submitting stories about me as a rice farmer to the local newspaper, and soon, 20 newspapers were carrying them. Eventually, the Scripps Howard News Service, which at the time was one of the largest syndicators in the country, was carrying my work.

Before I had decided that I was going to redefine failure, I hadn't tried going for all of these things. It was not being afraid of failure that changed my life.

The biggest advice I'd give to anybody is if fear of failure is holding you back, redefine it. Every time you don't achieve your immediate goal, rejoice, because just the act of trying means that you've become a bigger person, you've increased your talent stack, and you've become more ready to take on the next challenge.

My Purpose in Life

I have a purpose in life! I would like to increase happiness and decrease misery. It seems to me that the more you develop your talent stack, the broader an impact you're able to have.

One of the rules that I set for myself when I decided to redefine failure was to not let a single year go by without taking a serious course in something — nuclear particle physics, drawing, humor, anything. I became an addict for self-improvement.

One of my mottos is success is measured not by what you can get, but by what you can give. If you keep working on self-improvement and your talent stack, you're able to give more and more. In my case, redefining failure and working to increase my talent stack brings me closer and closer to achieving what I want in life.

Ethical Will

As I get older, I care more about my legacy. I believe we all do. When we're gone, we would love to have something positive left after us.

I think the people who are most successful at leaving something positive behind are intentional about it. When it comes to family businesses, 70% won't make it to the next generation. That 70% didn't put the effort into creating a culture in which the young ones in their lives learn the important lessons such as:

- You can't always be right

- You're part of something bigger than yourself

- Stewardship is important

- Personal relationships are more important than money

If you don't teach the next generation that, after the patriarch or matriarch goes to his or her great reward, the selfishness genes come out. Children fight over the inheritance, and pretty soon the family's gone "poof."

I've seen that happen over and over again in the families that don't put conscious, intentional effort into creating a culture that will support them staying together as a strong family.

My husband Frank Perdue was extraordinarily intentional about those who came after him. Together, we wrote an ethical will composed of 10 values. He believed if those who came after him would follow these 10 values, they would have a chance of having a happier life.

One value was if you want to be happy, think what you can do for somebody else. On the other hand, if you want to be miserable, think what's owed to you.

I find this is true. Almost every time I'm really feeling down, I'm thinking, "Life is unfair!" or "This should have gone my way!"

But on the other hand, if I'm thinking of a charity, particularly my work to be a part of helping stop human trafficking, I feel good and that my life has meaning.

Frank Perdue's Ethical Will is sort of like a constitution for the Perdue family. Often, when there's an argument, we refer to it to determine our best course of action. I encourage all patriarchs and matriarchs to create their own version of what has become part of the "family glue" for the Perdues.

Frank Perdue's Ethical Will:

1. Be honest always.

2. Be a person whom others are justified in trusting.

3. If you say you will do something, do it.

4. You don't have to be the best, but you should be the best you can be.

5. Treat all people with courtesy and respect, no exceptions.

6. Remember that the way to be happy is to think of what you can do for others. The way to be miserable is to think about what people should be doing for you.

7. Be part of something bigger than your own self. That something can be family, pursuit of knowledge, the environment, or whatever you choose.

8. Remember that hard work is satisfying and fulfilling.

9. Nurture the ability to laugh and have fun.

10. Have respect for those who have gone before and learn from their weaknesses and build on their strengths.

Combating Human Trafficking

I want to spend the rest of my years combating human trafficking. One of the ways I'm doing that is through starting winthisfight.org, a 501(c)(3) charity.

If you're part of an anti-trafficking organization, you care a lot about awareness and funding. It occurred to me that I could help other anti-trafficking organizations by creating an auction that would enable people to convert high-value, tangible property into cash.

The idea for this occurred to me because I have a desk that I inherited that we believe is from the 1600s and belonged to a Di Medici Cardinal. It's a significant historical piece, and I thought if I put that up for auction, it might bring a lot of money and get a lot of attention in the press.

Then I thought, *Since I have something significant that I'd be willing to put up for auction, maybe other people would too!*

I began going around to some ultra-high net worth people who, as a speaker, I get to visit with. I got offers of things like one of the world's larger perfect emeralds, a set of 12 dinner plates that belonged to Tsar Alexander II of Russia, and a fantastic necklace that belonged to Marlene Dietrich, appraised at a million dollars. The best was a 69-karat ruby that belonged to a Qing Dynasty emperor.

The auction, as of early 2021, is on hold until COVID-19 is in the rear-view mirror and we can know that the economy will be in good condition. I don't want to have a high-end auction during an economic downturn when people are afraid to spend big money.

However, when the auction does take place, donors will receive incredible amounts of publicity because these items have fabulous stories behind them. This venture has had enough success that PBS has already done a half hour documentary on it.

So, why is it important to address the issue of human trafficking? I think it's the darkest thing that happens on the face of the earth. Imagine a 12-year-old girl who is forced to have sex with strangers 10 times or more a night. Or a guy who is forced to do illegal logging in a United Nations protected national forest, and after he's no longer useful to his trafficker, he's shot and buried in a shallow grave.

The evil equation that perpetuates human trafficking is spectacular profits plus almost no deterrence. If you're a human trafficker, your chances of doing jail time are less than one in 100. According to the United Nations, human trafficking is a $150 billion per year industry. That plus no deterrence equals explosive growth in human trafficking.

A year ago, the three largest sources of income for criminal enterprises were illegal drugs, illegal arms sales, and human trafficking. As COVID-19 swept the world, human trafficking became number two.

There are ways of addressing this. Traffickers succeed because they're capable of terrifying their victims, so their victims simply will never testify against them. Taiwan could be an example of how to counteract this for the rest of the world.

Taiwan has created safe houses where girls or boys who've been trafficked can be safe until they've testified against their traffickers in jail. 500 traffickers have been put behind bars. That's 500 people who aren't causing anguish. In Taiwan, if you traffic a girl or a boy, you are likely to spend 15 years in jail. As a result, trafficking in Taiwan has plummeted. That's attacking the evil equation.

Summary

I think most of us would like to look back on our lives and feel that we've made a contribution. The formula for getting there that I like is a) Don't be afraid of failure, b) Do everything you can to grow your talent stack, and c) Act on what Aristotle said 2300 years ago: "The only way to achieve true success in life is to express yourself in service to society."

Mitzi Perdue likes nothing better than to share insider tips and actionable advice for successful family businesses. To access Mitzi's books, blog, and podcast, and to engage Mitzi about speaking on family legacies and the end of human trafficking, visit mitziperdue.com.

Tweetable: If you want to be miserable, think what's owed to you. If you want to be happy, think what you can do for somebody else.

ALAN STEWART

Taking Care of My Family and Friends While Creating a Legacy

Alan Stewart is a Christian, family man, business leader, and 20-year consulting executive turned multifamily real estate syndicator and investor of over 3,300 units. Alan's mission is to help 10,000 families achieve financial freedom through investment in cash flowing real estate.

Sooner Than Planned

I had done what I was supposed to do.... I was involved at church, and I studied very hard and graduated third in my high school. I was accepted into the engineering honors program at Texas A&M University and was studying engineering as my "pre-med" degree with the goal of being a physician. I was the first-born, and my family and I had big dreams of me becoming a doctor.

One month into college, my girlfriend since high school, who was attending college three hours away near my hometown, was visiting for the weekend to go to an Aggie football game. We were pretty serious and had been talking about getting married after we finished college. Well, we didn't intend on getting pregnant at 19, but we did. We were scared. We were basically the first of our families to go to college. Everyone we knew expected more of us and had great things planned for us.

We told a few close people soon after we knew, and many were scared that we had thrown everything away and that my career dreams were over. We chose life, and our family began, just way sooner than we had originally planned.

Childhood

From an early age, I was driven. I always wanted to learn, ask why, and excel at anything I did.

My parents always worked hard, running a small automotive parts and repair business alongside my grandpa.

If I wanted something, I had to work and save up the money for it. My first jobs were mowing lawns. At 15, I worked in a farmer's market. It was all hard work, but I didn't mind and thought that was just how things were—work hard and trade time for money. Then, when I was in high school, I worked for my parents, delivering parts and as an auto mechanic. I learned to work hard and do something right the first time.

All along, I was studying hard in school with the intent of doing the best possible. A 100 on a test was the goal, or higher if bonus points were available.

College & Starting a Family

When my now wife and I got unexpectedly pregnant in my freshman year of college, our family started. We got married, and for the next three years, had an infant while we finished school.

We had to juggle our class schedules. One of us would be with our infant son while the other was in class, group projects, or student organization activities. Our son even attended a few lectures—one of my wife's professors commented that he was paying better attention than most of the other students. We learned the value of planning and being efficient with our time.

Halfway through college, I thought long and hard about being a physician and ultimately decided that wasn't the right path. Engineering, the backup plan, became the primary plan.

We had a great college experience at A&M. We were blessed to have many great friends in our Aggie family that helped us, like graciously babysitting so we could go to a football game.

We both did well in school and continued to excel at academics. That's what I understood I needed to do to get a top job and support my family. I graduated magna cum laude with engineering honors and was offered a job at Andersen Consulting, thus starting my management consulting career.

Corporate Life

Joining Andersen Consulting (now Accenture) was a natural fit for me. They were a bunch of smart, very driven, type A people that knew how to work hard, get things done, and deliver value. I learned a ton from many excellent colleagues and clients.

But, after almost a decade of being on the road, away from my family four to five days a week, it wasn't working anymore and something had to change.

I joined another consulting firm with a local approach that got me off the road. I managed big projects, took on more responsibility, and became an executive. I finished my corporate career as a managing partner at Gartner Consulting with responsibility for the Greater Texas portfolio of manufacturing and energy industry verticals.

Family Life

As a family, we regularly attended church and were actively involved in several ministries. Our faith life has brought so many blessings into our life, including knowing the love, peace, and mercy that our Lord and Savior Jesus Christ has for everyone. We've been through plenty of crises, triumphs, losses, and close calls as a family. Mercy and forgiveness has to be the most powerful gift. No one is perfect. We all make mistakes. Sometimes big ones. I know I have. Giving and receiving mercy, while not easy, is how you can reconcile yourself and another in any relationship. Jesus gives us that example. There is no way I would have the blessings I have today without my faith and family.

Despite working all the time and traveling a lot while the kids were younger, I was always heavily involved in their activities, in particular, with sports and building many years of fond memories outdoors in Indian Princess with my daughter and Boy Scouts with my son. I am so thankful we had that time together.

From Stock and 401K Investing to Real Estate

Three years into my consulting career, I was searching for an alternative way to make money rather than trading my time, a way out of the rat race. I was fascinated by the concept of investing, money making money, but didn't have much money to invest. I was pretty tapped out just supporting my family, but I budgeted and started investing some through my company 401K.

In 2001, I attended a conference in Dallas, TX, where Robert Kiyosaki spoke. Robert talked about his book *Rich Dad Poor Dad*, and the benefits of investing in rental real estate. He said, instead of working for money to pay bills, you need to buy assets that produce income to pay your bills for you. This was the beginning of my real financial education, the type of pragmatic financial education not taught in schools.

I knew I wanted to do rental real estate for cash flow but was afraid. The analysis paralysis started. I lost a good chunk in my 401K during the 2000-2001 recession, and I didn't have much money. I didn't want to fail again and didn't really know where to start. So between 2001-2005, I attended more investing conferences.

In 2006, I attended a conference in Dallas, TX, and one of the speakers was a successful single family investor. He said that rental houses were great, but single family wholesaling was a whole lot more fun. Even better, he offered a training program to help get you started. That's what I was looking for, a way to get started, and I signed up.

I started building my wholesaling business nights and weekends. I attended boot camps and training calls, bought lead lists, sent mailers, put out bandit signs, and talked with motivated sellers and potential buyers.

A few years later, I had basically created a second job for myself that wasn't making money and was costing me precious time. My corporate job paid way better. By early 2008, I had grown weary of wholesaling. I had been listening to a radio show about investing in rental real estate. This radio show brought me back to my original investing conference in 2001 where Robert Kiyosaki spoke, where the idea of building wealth through rental real estate first clicked for me. I needed to free up some cash to buy some rental houses, and the only way for me to do that was to liquidate my 401K, which was almost all the money I had in the world. I had left Accenture but kept my 401K invested in highly rated, professionally managed mutual funds.

Well, analysis paralysis continued, and I was busy at work. It was April 2008, and the stock market crashed. I started to see my 401K go down. I initially thought it would come back, but it kept going down until, in late 2008, it was down 60%. I had a big pit in my stomach. I'd "let" my professionally managed 401K be decimated from a stock market crash twice now.

I couldn't even think about cashing in my 401K after going down 60%, so I put my head back down at work and just focused on solving client problems.

I never stopped learning. I kept listening to real estate investment radio shows and feeding my mind what was possible. I wanted to be a real estate investor. This really seemed like the way out of the rat race, even though I'd been at it for many years with little success.

Breakthrough

In March 2012, a coworker invited me to a real estate investing meeting. It turned out, the meeting was with the same company that hosted the rental real estate radio show I'd been listening to for six years. It was great, a local Dallas-Fort Worth real estate investing company that offered mentoring for exactly what I wanted to do. I signed up that night. I was excited. A little bit of serendipity never hurt anyone—my 401K had also just gotten back to the same value it was four years ago before the 2008 crash.

There, I was first introduced to multifamily investing. I always thought some big company or rich person bought apartment complexes. It turns out, many are owned by small groups of individual investors just like you and me.

So, I liquidated my 401K and paid the tax. Lots of people thought I was crazy. It was an easy decision for me because that's what I had to do to get started. I had been in management consulting for 14 years and rose to executive. I was working long, hard weeks and saw real estate investing as my way out of the rat race.

The best financial decision I ever made was first investing in my financial education. The second best financial decision was to put my financial education to work and take action by re-allocating my investments from my 401K and into multifamily apartment buildings.

Final Victory

It took me six years of early mornings, late nights, and weekends while still bringing it every day at my complex consulting job, but we built a portfolio of over 3,300 units across 16 properties that I either syndicated or invested in, and I retired from my 20-year corporate career.

I believe in abundance and that over time, anyone can build, create, or achieve anything that they decide by taking consistent, small actions toward those goals every day. It is simply amazing what can be accomplished over time, especially in 5-10 years. I went from zero multifamily experience to "retired" from my corporate job in six years—special thanks to multifamily mentors Del Walmsley and Brad Sumrok.

Although I retired from my corporate job, I am very much just getting started. I am a life-long learner and strive to continue growing each day. I start out each workday listening to Darren Hardy on DarrenDaily.com. Darren is fantastic with simple, pragmatic, actionable advice.

My wife and I have now been married for more than 25 years. Our son graduated from college and is an engineer for a global semiconductor company in Dallas, and our daughter is in college, studying interior architecture and design.

My focus is on taking care of my family and friends and giving back in more meaningful ways to charitable organizations and causes we are passionate about.

Both of our kids have also been learning about real estate investing. When they were younger, they were sometimes "dragged" to conferences, and later they were going with me to properties to check on rehab projects and talk with onsite staff. They are both interested in investing in assets that produce cash flow, and we've discussed that someday they may join me in the business.

I've also gotten my parents involved in multifamily investing, including deals with me which doubled to tripled investors' money in two and a half to four years, which helped them retire. My brother also started investing in several multifamily deals and is on the path.

From starting a family in college to early investing failures, life has been a journey of learning and perseverance. I learned you don't have to be the smartest. You just need to leverage other people's expertise, take consistent action, and persevere when things get tough. Do what others aren't willing to do, keep going, and you will achieve success.

To make all this happen, I continue building my businesses and investment portfolio of cash flowing assets to not only create a legacy for my family but also to provide quality investment opportunities that will create a path for 10,000 other families to achieve financial freedom and create their own family legacies.

To learn more about real-life multifamily investing, listen to Alan's podcast at AlanStewart.com. To apply to be a part of upcoming friends and family passive income investment opportunities and start your journey to financial freedom, contact Alan at info@alanstewart.com or visit AlanStewart.com.

Tweetable: Decide to invest in your financial education, take consistent action, and financial freedom will follow. That's exactly how I retired from the corporate rat race in six years of apartment investing.

DR. JOHN R. OBENCHAIN
Finding the Fortune in Misfortune

Dr. John R. Obenchain is a respected professor and bestselling author. His approach to public speaking combines the detailed research skills he developed while earning his doctoral degree with the real-world experience he gained working with Fortune 500 corporations and Big Ten universities.

In the Wrong Place at the Wrong Time

Ever find yourself in the wrong place at the wrong time? I have. Boy, have I ever.

A very good friend of mine—Professor Efimchik—invited me to speak to her class of university seniors. I accepted because she'd been there for me at a critical moment in my life. She was there when I needed help finding a topic for my doctoral thesis. Had it not been for Professor Efimchik, I might not have graduated on time. I might not have graduated at all.

Later, when it was her turn to ask me for help, I couldn't let her down. This was how I found myself in a very uncomfortable situation—the wrong place at the wrong time, you might say.

Professor Efimchik's classroom was filled to capacity that evening. Every student was in attendance, eagerly anticipating what he or she was about to hear. Professor Efimchik stood at the head of her classroom. Seated beside her, in a neat row, were six of us—me and five others whom she had invited that evening. We were the "experts," the chosen few who had come to enlighten the students that evening as part of a career panel. Essentially, we would be sharing our career success stories with the students so that they could learn from our examples. Among us, there were doctors, professors, and representatives from the military as well as the corporate world.

Class began.

Professor Efimchik reminded everyone why we were there that evening and then asked us to each introduce ourselves.

One by one, my five colleagues introduced themselves, and then it was my turn to tell the room what I had learned by following my own career path.

The room was silent, so silent you could hear a distant buzz emanating from the rest of the building. I wasn't nervous. I was frustrated, even angry. Angry that I could no longer help my good friend. Angry that I could not meet the expectations of those young students sitting in the classroom before me.

Everyone was staring at me, expecting something—something I could not do. Not anymore.

Yet, in the midst of my anger, my frustration, I recalled the messages I'd been receiving from friends and colleagues. I thought about what they'd said about me. And then I thought that maybe, just maybe, I might still have something to offer.

One Year Earlier...

I'd worked hard all my life, even struggled. Why? Because I'd always been told that success followed hard work. And, eventually, I discovered that this wasn't just something people said to make you feel better. Indeed it was true, for I'd achieved a level of success unimaginable to me as a young boy growing up alongside the cornfields of Northern Indiana.

As the ink was still drying on my doctoral degree, I was hired by a global, Fortune 500 corporation for a senior-level position. Attached to this position was a healthy six-figure income—more money than I'd ever expected to make. There were also benefits: health benefits, retirement benefits, time-off benefits.

Career success was mine—finally mine—but it meant so much more for me. My success meant success for my family. It meant that I would be able to take very good care of my wife and two children. This was important for me, more important than many realized.

Family Needs

My wife had enjoyed her own success in her own time, but that time was over. Her success had been stolen from her by the misfortunes of ill-health. The many doctors cited many things. They tossed around terms like "fibromyalgia," "osteonecrosis," and "neuropathy." What it all meant, however, was that, early on, she reached a point where she lived in constant pain.

We searched for an answer, and though we did find treatments—some better, some worse—an outright cure eluded us.

When her employer found out about my wife's condition and began weighing the pros and cons of an employee working under constant pain, a decision was made to place her on disability. Then, that choice was reassessed, and the final decision was made to let her go—permanently. Health benefits and all.

While all of this was first becoming an issue, another challenge was added to our lives. Our daughter was born, and within the first hour, she was diagnosed with not one but two serious heart defects. She had a hypoplastic aortic arch and ventricular septal defects. In English, this meant that her aorta was too narrow to carry a sufficient volume of oxygenated blood to the rest of her body, and that the wall, or septum, separating the two ventricles of her heart, was perforated with multiple holes.

She underwent open-heart surgery a few days after birth, and the results surpassed our wildest hopes. Our baby girl would not only survive but also enjoy a normal childhood—with one important exception. We would have to closely monitor her heart, having it checked on a regular basis to make certain the surgeon's repair work was keeping pace with the rest of her body as she grew. This would require sonograms, ultrasounds, and the occasional heart procedure, such as the angioplasty she underwent after her second birthday.

Then, there was our boy, who enjoyed perfect health (thank goodness). He had his own dreams and his own ideas of success. All through elementary school and during junior high school, he was an excellent student who consistently made the honor roll. Unfortunately, our local high school couldn't meet his ever-expanding needs. As a result, he'd begun looking elsewhere for educational opportunities. During this period, he discovered the opportunity of a lifetime: high school in Japan.

Yes, to fulfill the goals he'd set for himself, our son had decided he would attend high school in Japan. He'd not only decided this, he'd worked very hard to make this dream a reality. He'd contacted the necessary people, filled out and submitted the required forms, provided the requested documentation, and most impressively, taught himself how to read and write Japanese. When he received his acceptance into the study abroad program, he only really had one request of me: that I pay for his opportunity.

Now that I was a doctor, now that I had the job of my dreams with an outstanding salary and excellent benefits, I could afford to send my son to Japan for high school. I could also afford to take good care of my wife and maintain our daughter's heart monitoring.

Having the ability to take good care of my family—is there any better definition of success?

A Terrible Blow

I'll never forget the day I got fired.

It came out of nowhere—a complete surprise. I was dumbfounded, utterly unable to argue my case or defend myself. I simply sat there—stunned at what was happening to me.

My head was still spinning as I drove away from the company site for the last time. There were no tears; there was simply an overwhelming feeling of disbelief.

I'd worked so hard. I'd worked such long hours. For what?!

My happy ending, well.... It had ended, swiftly and unexpectedly.

Moving Forward by Going Back

To say that I'd been completely unprepared to get fired would be an understatement. Despite having participated in Professor Efimchik's university career panel on several occasions, I had no current resume, no references or referrals, and no strategy for what to do next. Naively, I'd presumed that the job I'd held would be mine until I was ready for retirement.

I was very worried about money. The loss of my job obviously meant the loss of my paycheck, but it meant so much more for us. It meant the loss of my health benefits. While I did have some savings, I realized that the bills would not stop just because the money and benefits stopped. Indeed, the bills only seemed to multiply.

My first instinct was to make some deep cuts. Everything that wasn't absolutely necessary would have to go.

One by one, our family began crossing items off our wish list. Finally, we were left with just three things—three promises I'd made in good faith: my wife's pain treatments, our daughter's heart monitoring, and my son's school in Japan.

Though they remained on our list, I still wondered how I would pay for any of them, let alone all three, while still covering the basics like food and our mortgage.

Messages from Lost Friends

In the midst of it all, I began receiving unexpected yet welcome messages from former coworkers—people to whom, in the confusion of my last day, I'd never had a chance to say goodbye.

"John! I just heard what happened! I'm so sorry! Thank you for always being so kind & thoughtful!"

"Hi John - What the hell!???? I am truly shocked and I'm so sorry to hear something this crappy happen to such a good person."

"I know you'll get through this but you can never be prepared for a curveball like this. Please use me as a reference if needed. I have nothing but good things to say about you!"

"I'm sorry to hear this news. I hope that this opens up new and improved opportunities for you very soon."

As I read through these messages and many more, I began to realize that there were others besides myself who weren't happy about what had happened. I began to realize that there were many who felt that I'd been a good worker and a good colleague.

With this, my confidence began to reawaken. The kind words and encouragement of my colleagues helped me immensely. They helped me to realize that there would be other jobs, other paychecks, and other successes.

Back to the Beginning of This Story

About this time, I received an email from my good friend Professor Efimchik. She wanted me to participate in another career panel for her class of graduating seniors. With everything else going on, I seriously considered saying "no." In the end, however, I realized that I couldn't say "no." Not to her.

I attended her class, and as before, I took my seat at the head of the room with the other career advisors.

As the start of class approached, the students began filing into the room. Their expressions betrayed a mixture of emotions: anticipation, excitement, curiosity. There was a little talking as they took their seats, but mostly they busied themselves getting their notebooks and computers ready.

When it was time, Professor Efimchik began her class. She summarized what we would be doing over the next ninety minutes, and then asked the six of us sitting at the front to introduce ourselves.

My colleagues each spoke for a minute or two about themselves and the success they had experienced. Then it was my turn.

I decided to stand, something no one else had done. As I did so, I could sense all eyes following me.

"This class," I began, "is the most important class you'll ever take."

Glancing over, I saw that Professor Efinchik was smiling at what I'd just said.

"But—why is it important," I asked rhetorically. "It's important because, at some point in your career, you will be fired."

Suddenly, I commanded everyone's attention as no one else had that evening. Professor Efimchik stopped smiling. I'd broken the unwritten rule. I'd mentioned failure in a class that was supposed to focus on success strategies.

"Now, maybe a few of you will manage to hang onto your jobs," I continued. "The way things are going in the job market, however, chances are very good—excellent in fact—that most of you will get fired. You'll get fired at least once, and maybe several times. Even if you do everything right, even if you do everything you're told to do, it won't make any difference. There will be reorganizations. There will be mergers. There will be cutbacks. Sometimes valuable people will have to be gotten rid of—just because."

"You'll be told that it's nothing personal, that it's the business, not you, that costs have to be cut due to a global pandemic, that you're being 'separated' not 'fired,' but in the end, none of that will make any difference. Not really. Because the result will be the same: You will have to find another job. You will be in your thirties, your forties, your fifties, maybe even your sixties. Long gone will be the advantage of youth and your clean employment record. You'll have to try convincing a hiring manager to take a chance on you."

I turned and looked at the five experts who sat with me at the head of the room. Some were staring with mouths open. Others had clamped up tightly. Professor Efimchik was still staring at me, but there was something new in her eyes. I could tell that she was still uncomfortable, but there was now a spark of interest, and this spark compelled me to go on.

"My friends here," I said, gesturing towards the other five professionals, "they're going to tell you everything you need to know about getting hired these days. But getting hired is only half the story, and to survive in today's world, you're also going to have to know how to get fired. That's where I come in."

I resumed my seat, and the room was so quiet that I could hear my heart beating in my chest.

It's hard to discuss failure in a room full of people who have been conditioned to think about success. Several students did not seem very comfortable with what I'd said. Still, there was a core group who came right up to me, asked questions, listened to every word I said, and provided me with their contact information so that we could stay in touch after the class had ended.

And Professor Efimchik—she and I are still good friends. She's even asked me to come back for her career panel next semester.

One Year Later

Looking back now, I can say that things did work out for my family and for me.

My wife turned out to be a genius with medical insurance. She found a way to get the health coverage that both she and our daughter needed. This still cost money, but it wasn't as expensive as I'd feared.

The hard decision was whether to let our son attend high school in Japan. As I thought about his situation, I also thought about my own recent experience. I thought about all the hard work I'd done, only to be let go when I least expected it. I couldn't let this happen to our son—I wouldn't let this happen to him, not if I could help it. So, in the end, I kept my promise—as hard as it was—and our son left for Japan to enjoy the experience of a lifetime.

As for me, I took the lessons I'd shared with Professor Efimchik's students, those lessons on how to get fired, on how to fail, and I applied them to myself. And, guess what, before my son had been in Japan for a month, I was working again. I was also building up my savings so that I could afford my son's study abroad program as well as pay the mortgage on our home.

This time, however, things were different. For one thing, I wasn't working nearly as many hours as before, and this was intentional.

You see, one of the things I taught Professor Efimchik's students was that success can sometimes become a trap. You do something well and end up doing that something your whole life. Then, when it's too late, you realize that though you did that something well, it wasn't what you really wanted to do in the first place. It wasn't what you were put on Earth to do.

I'd encouraged Professor Efimchik's students to consider what it was they really wanted to do during their brief time on Earth and to use every opportunity to focus on that one thing.

This is what I've done myself. I've used my unexpected escape from success to find ways of doing something that I've always wanted to do.

As far back as I can remember, I've always wanted to be a published writer—and now I am. I always wanted to be a teacher, one who helps people understand something they'd never understood before—and now I am. I always wanted to be a professional public speaker so that I could share my message with as many people as possible—and now I am.

So, my friend, the day will come when you too are fired (if this hasn't already happened). The big question you'll need to ask won't be why it happened, but rather, what you're going to do about it. Are you going to feel sorry for yourself? Are you going to let someone else's decision defeat you—destroy you? Or, are you going to use it as an opportunity to find fortune in misfortune and do the thing you were always meant to do before success sent you off in the wrong direction?

Having trouble communicating your message? Want to be able to engage others and empower them to remember and apply your idea? Want to work with someone you can trust? Good.

Dr. Obenchain can be reached at jobench18@gmail.com

Tweetable: Reorganizations, mergers, cutbacks— You have a good chance of getting fired in today's market. You'll be told that it's nothing personal, but it makes no difference. To survive, you'll have to know how to get fired.

LYNN YANGCHANA

Focus on the Half Full
and Embrace the Half Empty

Lynn Yangchana specializes in commercial real estate in the Inland Empire of Southern California. She has been directly involved in 850+ transactions representing over $500 million of sales and leasing at MGR Real Estate since 2005. Lynn is involved with over 1.5 million square feet of office leasing portfolio. She is an active investor and the mother of twins.

From a Traditional Chinese Family Background

I came from a traditional Chinese family with great emphasis on cultural values, respect for the elderly, strong work ethic, entrepreneurship, and patriarchy. In the '60s, both my parents migrated from hardship in China to Myanmar. They later settled in Thailand, where I was born and where the rest of my extended family lives. Both my parents had little formal education but were business-minded. My father was a jade trader, and my mother was masterful in the relationship building part of my father's business. From hardship in their own upbringing and lack of decent family shelter, they both understood the value of real estate and put all their income from jade into real estate investment. That is where I got my real estate bug.

Patriarchy was the soul and shaping of my family path. Both my parents had prior relationships and children before they settled down together and formed our current nuclear family. From a total of eight siblings, that I know of, I'm the seventh one. Of the four children of both of my parents, I'm the third child, the youngest girl. Wishing for a boy to carry the patriarchal tradition, my parents were hoping for a boy after my two sisters ahead of me. When I was born, the third girl, they gave me a Chinese name Te-Lynn. "Te" has a meaning of brother in Chinese, with the hope that I would bring a boy next to carry on the family line. Their wish came true, and I was happy to have a younger brother.

My parents valued a good formal education for us children that they had lacked. And, for us girls, we needed to focus on our household skills to marry well in the future. I always felt like a black sheep in the family and wished to be more than a future housewife. I believe that was the seed of my lifelong aspiration to prove to my parents that I too can make a significant contribution to my family and my community and be financially independent.

Embracing Changes Starting at Six Years Old

Growing up in a big and active family, I constantly had to find ways to be noticed and heard. My parents were always busy with their business, and we were mostly raised and cared for by our nanny. When I was six years old, I did not perform well on the private school assessments and did not get admitted like my two older sisters. My parents decided to send me to Taiwan to live with my maternal grandparents to learn Chinese.

Moving to a different country, living away from the family, and learning a different language and culture at the age of six was difficult. No longer having the care around me that I had at home in Thailand, I had to learn to be on my own in Taiwan with my grandparents who I didn't know very well, and I grew up quickly. I had no concept of personal responsibility at that age. All I knew was that I had to keep getting myself ready for school every day, taking the school bus, and hopefully getting good grades so my parents would be happy to hear when they called. Although I did not remember showing much emotional drama to my parents about being homesick, I feared disappointing them and wanting to show them that I could do it and that I could be strong just like a boy.

In Change Lies Momentum, Progress, and Evolution of Life

An ancient Chinese philosopher Lao Tzu said, "New beginnings are often disguised as painful endings." Change can be a new beginning, new opportunity, new direction, and new you. I will be forever grateful to my parents for setting me on the path of welcoming changes.

After elementary school in Taiwan, I pleaded with my parents to move me back to Thailand to be with the family. They agreed, and from then to college, I felt a need for opportunities to change. I convinced my parents to let me travel to America for my master's degree. I was only an average student, but still, I made my way to graduating with a master's degree in advertising and communications from California State University, Fullerton.

Instead of going back to Thailand after my education like the rest of my siblings and friends, I found a job and started my career in marketing. Going through years of developing my marketing and communication skills, I still felt a void in entrepreneurial spirit, a spirit I felt was a part of me, coming from a business and real estate-oriented family.

The black sheep in my family, not only did I not follow the traditional path of a proper Asian daughter—honoring family tradition and marrying within the culture—I also fell in love with the Western culture, the independent spirit of America, the land of the explorer. Then I fulfilled my mother's greatest fear when I fell in love with my husband, an American Caucasian born in Thailand, and started my family here in America.

Making My Mark in Real Estate

From as far back as I can remember, all my parents talked about was their business and their real estate investments. Regardless of their limited formal education, they showed me how they successfully built their business with hard work, perseverance, risk tolerance, and entrepreneurial spirit. Their continuous investment in real estate from their business income endured through great challenges at various times in their lives, and ultimately, they created lifelong wealth and were able to put their kids through college without getting into debt.

After a few years of feeling the limitation on my income in my marketing career, I decided to follow the entrepreneurial spirit of my family roots and pursue real estate. I was fascinated with big buildings from a young age. It all started over a few summer breaks in my teenage years when my father took my younger brother and me along for his jade trading business trips to Hong Kong, the financial center of Asia with the highest number of skyscrapers in the world. During my father's daytime work, he arranged for his partner's wife to take me and my brother sightseeing around the city. In my fond memories of those summer trips, I am captivated by sky-high modern buildings and the fast-paced business environment that was overwhelming and a larger than life experience, drastically different from a slower pace of life in my hometown at the time.

With my desire to explore commercial real estate and the business environment, I found my mentor, who specializes in office leasing and investments, and began my real estate journey.

"Beyond the Tip of the Iceberg" Outlook in Business

Today, in my adulthood, I still count in Thai, do multiplication in Chinese, and then translate it into English. I gained trilingual skills through different stages of my learning from Thailand to Taiwan and to America. I have always felt knowing different languages provides me with multiple advantages. For one, I appreciate diversity. That is why I am so intrigued by all the business owners that I have the opportunity to meet and work with. Their entrepreneurial spirit, grit, and great conviction inspire me tremendously. Through years of honing my skills in matching business owners with new locations and investors with investments, I have learned to recognize the patterns of business. Certain business characters tend to be suitable for certain types of real estate. Meeting each investor in their walk of life and in their area of expertise is just like speaking a different language, and their mind is like a different location which allows me to explore, gain inspiration, and learn.

Over the years, there have been times when I failed to connect with the client's or investor's need, especially when I was first getting started. I learned to recognize that when a deal doesn't go as I planned, I might have misinterpreted the information the client gave me. I only saw the tip of the iceberg.

The mistake I made was making incorrect assumptions and overlooking their true desires. I have come to the realization that I'm a product of my own expectations and bias. If I'm not paying attention, I may overlook the core issues important to the client.

People see things differently, are wired differently, and express themselves differently. I tell myself to keep an open mind without being chained to my way of thinking, to take time to dig deep, to ask the same questions in multiple ways, and to explore my client's needs based on their background. This allows me to effectively solve problems and offer solutions based on a clear understanding of the elements beneath the surface. By not labeling people, events, or my own perception, I allow my mind to see the invisible, reflect on their needs, and offer advice and solutions that align with my client's background and requirements. This is the one lesson learned over the years that sets me apart and propels me forward in leadership in my career.

A Bend in the Road Is Not the End of the Road

The greatest fear I experienced in my early teens occurred on my first trip to Hong Kong with my father and younger brother. My father introduced us to the underground Mass Transit Railway, and it was so exciting to travel underground by subway. While getting pushed and shoved through a sea of commuters one morning, my father had my brother's hand and stepped into the train. Blocked by a few adults quickly sliding in between us, I was a few steps behind. Then the train doors closed, and suddenly, I was left alone with hundreds of other commuters on that section of platform for the next train. I saw vividly my father turning back for me from inside the train with a frightened look that we were separated. My heart dropped, and I froze for a few seconds, not knowing what to do in this foreign place with hundreds and thousands of strangers. I couldn't speak Cantonese, didn't remember the name of the hotel we were in, and had no idea where we were going that morning or the name of the destination stop. Being conditioned to face change from a young age, I refrained from crying. However, I was devastated and didn't know what to do.

A few minutes went by, and the next train arrived. As I was still standing at the front of the line, the train door slid open in front of me, and I felt another wave of people getting in the train. In those few seconds, the voice in my head told me to act and keep moving forward, to get on the train to find my father and brother in the next few stops the best I could. That full train ride by myself in a foreign country was the longest few minutes of my life. In a few seconds of clear thinking, I positioned myself to stand at the exit door and window to keep a lookout for my father and brother. When the train approached the next stop, my heart pounded, and I kept my eyes wide open, scanning through the huge crowd for my father and brother. To my pleasant surprise, I was able to spot my father in his tan suit with a distressed look on his face, standing at the elevated information kiosk talking to the subway personnel. As soon as the door opened, I ran as fast as I could shuffle through the sea of commuters. With happy tears on my face, I reunited with my father and brother.

That experience lit the fire in me and cemented a great lesson from a young age. Quickly, pick yourself up and keep moving forward when facing difficulties. In my adult life and real estate career, I constantly work through negative self-talk when confronting certain challenges. I learned to overcome my own thoughts and to tell myself that anything can happen and a positive outcome is achievable if I keep pushing forward, putting my mind to good use, and problem-solving. Like the quote from Robert Helms of *The Real Estate Guys Radio Show*, "A bend in the road is not the end of the road, unless you fail to make the turn." By being willing to take action, to make the turn, I conditioned myself to keep moving forward and go with the flow. Obstacles in a transaction are simply a bend in the road. It takes collaborative effort to accept and expect each bend in the road until we reach our destination or goal.

My Dream of Living a Legendary Life and Leaving a Legacy

I hear "legendary" daily from my twin boys playing video games at home. They always shout out, "That's legendary!" after struggling through different levels of the game to achieve the next win. As they go through each level, their characters evolve. It is the challenge and the struggle to overcome that keeps them in the game. The friends they persevere through the game with also give them purpose, excitement, and satisfaction, which are the real fun and the ultimate rewards of playing.

This led me to think that the real rewards in life lie in the adventurous journey with the people you care about. How you achieve life's goals by pushing each other to the next level is what is meaningful. My greatest wish is to live a legendary life with my family and people I care dearly about, to leave them gifts of knowledge, love, and encouragement, and to instill in them the love of learning, kindness, and compassion for others.

Reflecting on My Journey and Adapting to the Unknown

I would never have thought I would be able to survive and find my way to fit in, find love, and settle down to create a beautiful family in a different country away from my motherland, mother tongue (Thai), comfort zone, and culture. I also would have never imagined embarking in real estate, achieving success, and growing to multimillion dollar real estate transactions, complex investments, and becoming an active investor. Some of the best opportunities I have had came from times I took a wrong turn, faced challenges, or just sat down to think and absorb my surroundings.

The world of real estate allows me to play a direct role in the action and interact with many moving parts, places, and people. I'm grateful that I was given the opportunity to appreciate the experience of different cultures from a young age. It wasn't easy, but it gave me the foundation to build up my mental muscles and adapt easily to changes. Whenever I resist change or focus on the half empty—what I can't do or don't have—I find myself getting stuck in a rut, and it takes extra time and energy to overcome adversity and grow.

Focus on the half full and embrace the half empty. Focusing on improving what I have (my half full) and not fearing what I lack (my half empty) provides opportunities to achieve and motivation to grow. Winners are the ones who quickly pick themselves up and keep moving forward when facing difficulties and setbacks.

Instead of living the life preconceived for me by others, I go with the flow, maintain a broad mindset, and have deep gratitude for what I have already achieved. I believe that focusing on my passion for owning and operating real estate has drawn me to be open to seizing opportunities and to react positively to the unknown. I hope you do the same. Welcome changes, embrace your experiences, grow, and find joy in both work and play.

Contact Lynn Yangchana about office investments and leasing in Southern California or reach out to her at www.lynnyangchana.com.

Tweetable: Focus on the half full and embrace the half empty. Focusing on improving what I have, and not fearing what I lack, provides opportunities to achieve and motivation to grow. Winners are the ones who pick themselves up and keep moving forward when facing difficulties and setbacks.

CHERI PERRY

Find Your Passion:
The Secret to Adding Value

Finding your passion can transform your life and the lives of those around you. Business coach, motivational speaker, and successful entrepreneur Cheri Perry shares the stories, clues, and life lessons that led to finding her passion and developing the #1 workplace culture in the state of Washington (2020).

Never Be Lukewarm

So, because you are lukewarm—neither hot nor cold—I am about to spit you out of my mouth.

– Revelation 3:16

From a Biblical perspective, being "lukewarm" about anything doesn't have a very desirable end result; being spit out sounds like a bad deal! It's also hard to add much value to anyone's life when you are operating in a lukewarm fashion. But how do you find what you are supposed to be doing with your whole heart? Isn't that a question we have all wrestled with?

What's my WHY? What is my purpose and how will I know when I find it?

Looking back now, I realize that the various work experiences in my past played a major role in helping me find something I wanted to pour my heart into. I thank God that, throughout my journey, I was able to learn some valuable life lessons and find a way to turn my lukewarm existence into a passionate, on fire, difference-making life!

It is my hope that this walk down memory lane inspires you to reflect and find the stories, clues and life lessons in your own journey.

It's The PEOPLE!

My first job was working at a nursing home as a certified nursing assistant (CNA). My job was to clean up the rooms, clean up the people, and basically handle the day-to-day duties. I hated almost every part of that job except talking to the residents!

On more than one occasion, I was chastised for spending too much time talking with the residents or fixing someone's hair and not enough time working. You could say I was lukewarm about the tasks that were not directly related to interacting with the people: they call that a clue! When the people part of the job was minimized, my passion for the work declined as well. I fondly remember Ed, a refined older gentleman who sat in his rocking chair every day, making potholders out of yarn. Each day, I would go in, and we would talk while I took care of his room. He even made a special set of potholders just for me. Then one day, I went to Ed's room and he was gone. I asked a nurse where they moved Ed to, and without pause, she said coolly, "He died. They come and they go."

That was my last day as a CNA. I knew that the comments made by the nurse that day were not as cold as they seemed, but I also knew that I was not doing what I was meant to do. In order to add value, we have to find what it is we love about our work—even when we end up moving on to other opportunities.

We are all wired differently, and I believe that God has given each of us a special set of gifts. When we use those gifts to add value to others, we honor our creator! Making sure we listen to that "still small voice" will help us find the clues and eventually our path to our purpose.

Fired Over Potatoes

After my stint as a CNA, I moved into the fast-food industry. Because I grew up in a family where we were taught to give everything 100%, it wasn't long before I was on a management track. I felt important the day they gave me the keys to the door. It's funny how little things like that stick with you. It wouldn't be long before someone wanted those keys back!

As the night manager, it was my job to make sure the restaurant was cleaned and prepped for the next morning's shift. At the close of one shift, I noticed we had a large number of baked potatoes that hadn't been sold, so I placed them in a bag and gave them to a homeless person who frequently stopped by. Since everything had to be accounted for, I noted my closing paperwork about the gifted potatoes and locked up for the evening.

The next day, the manager placed a note on my time card asking to see me. I guess my youthfully righteous response to his "You're not supposed to give away the old food!" feedback did not go well. It was my last day as the keeper of the keys! When your heart is not "in" a job, obstacles become deal breakers. We do not give ourselves reasons to hang on and work through the feedback and growth opportunities.

Our internal wiring and the gifts we are blessed with seem to be designed to help us find our WHY/WAY. If we are distracted, however, and too focused on just getting by or earning revenue, we might miss the subtle clues. Seeing a need in another human being and adding value by filling it was second nature to me. That little clue would appear many times in my life before I actually grabbed hold of it!

I did not find my passion in fast food, but I did get further confirmation of my love of people!

Little People & More Clues

Elder care and fast food were obviously not going to be where I left my mark, so I decided to try my hand at taking care of children. As a nanny, you really NEED to be present. At least, you need to be paying attention all of the time!

The lady I worked for worked away from her home 8-10 hours per day, and she had two young children. It did not take long to fall in love with her babies. They loved playing, reading, and making messes for me to clean up! For several months, it was a dream job.

Then something happened—the same thing that had happened before (and that would happen again). Discontent began to set in, and pretty soon, I became an expert on how this mother should be raising her children. I found myself being judgmental and combative, just under the surface, of course. The once mutually respectful and beneficial relationship soon soured, and I made the decision to move on. It was one of the toughest decisions I'd ever made. I loved the children, but once again, I knew I was not in the right place.

When what you once loved turns into a chore, the way you show up in the job changes. You run the risk of moving from someone who adds value to someone who is judgmental and difficult to work with. Excellent communication and focusing in on my natural gifts could have made for a better ending to my nanny chapter. At the time, I was not open to hearing the feedback. Reflecting on the situation later definitely helped me to become a better employee and eventually a much better boss!

Keep Your Eye on the Future

There were many other jobs that ended for one reason or another: disc jockey, parts driver for a car dealership, retail sales clerk, fitness club manager, outside sales rep (multiple times), and a few others I am certain I've forgotten to include! The truth is, I had no idea what I was supposed to be doing. Other work experiences would look promising, but my true calling always seemed to be just out of reach.

I remember being so hurt and frustrated after a particular job experience. I felt as if I had given my all, only to lose another job.

I was a hostess at a busy restaurant. I LOVED the part of meeting and getting to know the guests, and they seemed to love me in return! Many times, people would wait to be able to sit in my section, which did not go over well with the other ladies I worked with.

Today, I could easily find a way to bridge the distance with my coworkers, but back then, I was an arrogant DOER who did not realize that getting along with my coworkers was a critical part of actually keeping my job! I remember the day I was fired like it was yesterday. The manager called me back to the office and said he was very upset over having to let me go because I was the hardest worker he had and the guests loved me. Fire ME?

It turns out that three of my coworkers had threatened to quit if he did not fire me. I let the manager know that I could do ALL of their jobs in addition to mine, so there was no need to fire me. Did I mention my arrogance? I was mad and crying when I called my dad, "I did everything you said. I showed up early, stayed late, worked my heart out, and I still got fired!" My father calmly said, "Sweetheart, maybe your future is not in food service." He was right.

There are clues in every chapter of our lives if we will spend the time to review the details, reconsider the circumstances, and take those lessons as the gifts they are! I loved the people I served. That was evident in all of the jobs I had worked. I was bossy, determined, and a bit stubborn and frankly did not concern myself with adding value to those I worked with. My future WAS calling. Perhaps with a little polishing, I could find a way to add value to everyone?

The People That God Gives You

The early "people" lessons of learning to add value to everyone I work for (and with) created a thirst and hunger for knowledge. I read every book I could find on developing myself and others, I joined Toastmasters, attended events from all of the top names in motivation. Meeting and developing a relationship with Zig Ziglar helped me further identify my passion for people and helped to save my marriage. In his book, Better Than Good, Zig was gracious enough to share a portion of our story. I did not know it then, but that encounter would have far-reaching impacts on my future and help me find my passion!

Eventually, I would end up owning several of my own businesses; some were successful and others taught me the lessons I needed to learn to become a strong business leader. Today, I still work with people! In fact, the experiences of those early jobs have molded and shaped the way I work with my team and the teams we are privileged to work with. As a business coach, speaker, and owner of Total Merchant Concepts (TMC), a national credit card processing company, I am blessed to be able to truly make a difference in the lives of everyone we touch.

Hard work, varied experiences, lessons learned, and a desire to help business owners resulted in early success with TMC. Our company grew steadily over 18 years, but I was worn out! I was experiencing issues with staffing and felt as if it was probably time to see what my next chapter might be. Remembering the lessons of my earlier jobs, I started asking some great questions to see if I could identify what I LOVED about what I was doing. During that time, I decided to become a Certified Ziglar Legacy Trainer & Coach. It seemed like a very natural transition considering my love of business and of people. Then a miracle occurred.

I was sitting in the back of the room, helping train the second class of Ziglar Certified Trainers, when Bob Beaudine took the stage. His book, *The Power of WHO*, was the topic, and as Bob made his way around the room, he paused at my table and asked the following question: "What are you doing with the people God gave you?" A chill ran down my spine because I knew in a moment that his question was meant specifically for my ears and my heart to hear that day. I left his training session knowing that I could do MORE with the people placed in my path.

Over the course of the following five years, my passion returned, and I fell in love with my people again. Zig Ziglar's words of wisdom, "You can have everything in life you want if you will just help enough other people get what they want," became my guiding principle. We started looking for the many ways we could add value to the lives of our team members, and a funny thing happened. Our team fell in love with their work and our clients, and we became a much closer work family. We were recognized by *Inc. Magazine* as one of the Top 400 Workplace Environments in 2019. We became the #1 company to work for in the state of Washington in 2020, and we have been blessed to see so many leaders emerge within our company. By finding my passion and developing a value-adding mindset in our company, the entire team thrived.

You Are Where You Are Supposed to Be

In 2020, our nation went through some of its toughest days. We saw many businesses fail, and my partner Dean and I experienced some hardships of our own. The true gift of a value-adding mindset is the sheer quantity of ideas and thoughts that rush to your assistance when they are most needed. I truly believe that if we were a less committed company with a weaker focus, we easily could have been "spit out" by our economy.

We have to look back at our life's journey with a certain amount of GRACE. Should haves and could haves have the ability to haunt our very being. "I should have done this sooner," or "I could have done better with my life," and other such comments do not honor the simple fact that we are where we are supposed to be! Just like me, your life experiences have prepared you for this moment! There are lots of people who need encouragement and inspiration. When you spend the time to find your passion, you have the greatest possibility of helping others find theirs.

Adding value and making a difference in the lives of other people does not take a special degree, a certain line of work, or a trouble-free past: thank goodness!

- It does take the courage to fail forward.
- It does take the tenacity to keep trying until you find the thing you were put on this planet to accomplish.
- It does take paying attention so you do not miss the clues to your passion.
- It does take an intentional effort to live your life with a VALUE ADDING mindset so you can reap the rewards.

Being lukewarm about anything doesn't have a very desirable end result, and it doesn't help us find our passion. To make a real difference and add the most value, we've got to find our purpose—the thing we were meant to do. If you are still unsure about your destiny or your passion, keep trying things on until you figure it out. If you are blessed to know what it is you are on the planet to do, then make the commitment to go ALL IN. People are waiting for you and your gifts.

As my mentor Zig Ziglar said, "You can have everything in life you want, if you will just help enough other people get what they want."

For access to a free 15 minute consultation and a copy of Delivering An Exceptional Service Experience Using G.R.A.C.E. plus information on business coaching, culture, or leadership training with Cheri Perry, please visit her website www.CheriPerry.com or email her Cheri@CheriPerry.com.

Tweetable: There are lots of people who need encouragement and inspiration. When you spend the time to find your passion, you have the greatest possibility of helping others find theirs.

CHADD NAUGLE

How Becoming a Dad Helped Me Find Financial Independence

Chadd Naugle is a real estate investor and syndicator who partners with experienced operators that have placed over $60 million of investor capital. He is passionate about helping others gain financial freedom and deploying accredited investors' capital in cash flowing, tax deductible assets.

Oh No... Not Again

We just got the news. This wasn't the first, but the second time we got the bad news. I still remember the look of pain, heartache, and desperation on my wife's face. We were running out of time.

The doctor said, "This just happens sometimes."

Something was wrong. It was time for a second opinion. It was our second miscarriage. This time it was twins. The roller coaster of emotions from the news of being pregnant to losing a child is unbearable. The agony, loss, and hopelessness were more painful each time. And we were running out of time to have a child at all.

My wife was closing in on 40 years old. We pushed for tests to be run, but the insurance companies would not pay for it since there was no evidence of a medical condition causing the miscarriages. We would have to finance what we could on our own. Since we did not have problems with conceiving, only the carrying part of the pregnancy, we started with blood tests. Luckily, it was quickly determined that my wife had Factor 5, which is a blood clotting disorder.

With the right medication, we could still have a baby. It was time for us to get to work. A year passed; nothing happened. The pressure was mounting, and time was running out. My wife was already considered advanced maternal age. We started to plan a life without a child.

Then, one fine day, a home pregnancy test confirmed it. We were pregnant.

We rushed to the doctor. We needed to mitigate the risk of a miscarriage caused by Factor 5 as soon as we got pregnant. As it turns out, my wife just needed a blood thinner. She had to take a shot in the stomach, EVERY DAY, for the entire pregnancy.

For the next eight months, we were on pins and needles. We never knew if the next time we walked in the office for a sonogram the baby would have a heartbeat. The third and fourth months were extremely tense. In the previous three pregnancies, the babies were lost during that time frame. We felt if we could just get past the fourth month, we might have a chance. We waited until after the fourth month passed uneventfully to tell anyone we were expecting. My mother and father-in-law were so overjoyed, you would have thought they won a $100 million lottery.

The Day My Life Changed

I will never forget that moment. The crown of his head was just about 1 ½ inches showing. The nurse said, "Do you want to touch it?"

I said, "Hell Yeah!" She further explained one or two more pushes and the baby would be out. Then before I knew it, BOOM. There he was.

On July 21st, 2012, Jax Elias Naugle was born. It was a glorious day. I felt a brief moment of relief. He made it. My wife made it. Both were healthy and doing fine.

We had a little baby boy! My feelings of excitement, relief, and thankfulness quickly turned to feelings of inadequacy and anxiety. Why? I didn't know how to be a dad. My parents were divorced when I was young. I saw my dad every other weekend at most. I didn't have a role model or father figure of what a dad should be. The one thing I knew was I needed to be around my son as much as possible and love him.

Through years of therapy, I learned experiences and messages we receive at a young age shape who we become. I struggled most of my life with feelings of low self-worth and self-esteem. I joined a fraternity in college, I joined the Army Reserve, I even joined an outlaw motorcycle club. It was an attempt to belong to something. I was trying to fill a void. I was desperately seeking to feel wanted or needed. In an attempt to feel better about myself, I turned to sex and alcohol as an escape. My relationships were empty. I never felt close to anyone, including my parents and girlfriends. I never let anyone "see" the real me. Part of it was shame, and I felt if someone saw who I really was, they wouldn't like or accept me. It was a horrible and lonely way to go through life. Through the grace of God, therapy, and a loving, supportive wife, I was shown that vulnerability and transparency deepen and grow relationships. This is something I practice every day in my personal and professional relationships.

How Was I Going to Be a Good Dad?

If I wanted to be there for my son, I needed to put myself in a position where I could get my son off the bus, coach his teams, participate in karate—be the dad that I wanted to be and could be for my son. I did not want my son to feel any of the things I felt growing up. My son was going to feel loved, wanted, and important just by being who he was. I was going to make sure of that.

When Jax was born, I was working as a distribution manager 10 to 12 hours a day. I had very little savings in a 401K and was only making 60K per year. I didn't have a college degree. Financially, we were making it, but just making it. I thought to myself, *There has to be a better way. There has to be something more out there.*

One day, I was watching a YouTube video when an ad popped up. The ads had just started running then. This was your typical ad, where the guy in the video showed this big house and fancy car, but then something in the video struck me. He panned over to his library of books, which were hundreds, and he said that was what he was most proud of. He further explained that those books were the single greatest reason for his wealth and success.

I didn't buy his program, but I did take his advice. I remember thinking, *I can read. I can certainly read a lot of books for the price of his program that he was selling.* So, I started reading everything I could get my hands on.

One of the first books I read was *Rich Dad Poor Dad* by Robert Kiyosaki. Two lessons I learned from this book shaped my future forever. First, don't trade time for money. Second, buy assets, don't buy liabilities. Assets make you money and liabilities cost you money.

With my newfound knowledge, I set out to start buying real estate. Oh yeah, but I had no money. I started researching how to buy houses with no money down. Yes, I thought it was a scam, but what if it wasn't? Other people seemed to be doing it. Why couldn't I?

Employee to Entrepreneur

I started spending all my free time learning about no money down strategies and going to real estate investor events. The lure of real estate investing was the promise that it would give you time freedom and financial freedom. I wasn't trying to get rich, just provide a living that would allow me to choose how to spend my time. I wanted to be there for my son.

I decided to focus on wholesaling. I did my first wholesale deal in the summer of 2016. I made $9000, and it took me about three hours of work. I knew right then and there what Robert was talking about. Don't trade time for money.

That $9000 would have cost me two months at my job. It wasn't the money I was looking at. It was the time. I didn't get $9000. I got two months of my life back. This was just the beginning. I quickly realized that it would only take five deals a year to replace an entire year's worth of income.

Two years later, in August 2018, I was wholesaling full time. I remember that month well. My wife, six-year-old son, and I were in Myrtle Beach on a few weeks vacation. I was closing deals while on vacation. As it turned out, I made more in that month at the beach than I did working a whole year at the job I hated.

Life was great, but there was one nagging problem. I had to go back to wholesaling when I returned. Don't get me wrong, I don't mind the work, but I was 47 at this point, and I needed to think about retirement. Having my own business helped me get the time freedom I was after, but it didn't help me escape the rat race. I was still a rat on a wheel, just a nicer wheel. I needed to create another income stream, one that was passive.

On the way home, I looked over at my wife and said, "We need to buy 50 houses to keep as rentals."

She laughed and said, "How are you going to do that?"

Time Freedom and Financial Independence

Within two months of that conversation, I closed on our first rental house. Within the next eight months, I purchased an additional 23 houses. I started with little money and actually did it with none of my own money. I didn't have the luxury of time. How did I do it?

While I was on that beach vacation, I was asked to speak at a real estate investors event scheduled for the day after I returned. I wouldn't have gone to this meeting unless I was asked to speak. That would have been my mistake! At the meeting, another presenter talked about how people had leftover funds sitting in 401K or self-directed IRA accounts. A traditional investment fund typically requires a $100K minimum or in $100K increments, so there is capital leftover to deploy. Often, that capital sits in the IRA doing nothing.

For example, if you have 267K in the IRA, you can only deploy 200K because of the investment criteria of 100K increments. So, there is 67K left over.

The presenter identified this as a problem. I immediately had a solution: my rental houses. These investors with money left over could be the bank for me. They would get a mortgage and note in return for the money to purchase the house. This is a great way to invest within a self-directed IRA because the income is more predictable and stable. If the investor were to purchase a rental house in the IRA, he would have expenses such as vacancy, turnovers, repairs, insurance, taxes, management fees, and other expenses associated with owning rental properties. For these reasons, his return on investment could vary greatly.

I set up a meeting with the presenter that following week. He had the problem, and I had the solution. This is often called the wealth pair approach. Identify what the investor is seeking or has a problem with and then pair an asset class or investment to help them reach their goal.

Leaving a Legacy and My Greatest Lesson Learned

This journey was never about me. I started down this path of entrepreneurship because I wanted to be there for my son. It quickly turned into providing financial security for my family, and eventually, something I could leave to my son. Legacy is something bigger than ourselves and more about what we can contribute to the world and how we can serve others.

How does someone go from a dead-end job, working 60 to 70 hours per week, to being financially free? I decided I was going to, and then I took massive action. The mind is very powerful, and you have the ability to program it. Once you start putting things in your mind you want to achieve, your subconscious mind starts to work on the how. This is why it is so important to dream big. Too many times, we cut ourselves short because we think we can't do something or don't know how we are going to achieve it. If you change your thoughts, you change your feelings, which changes your actions. Then you can become the person you want to become.

Want to grow your wealth fast? Get Chadd Naugle's free report to learn why rate of return is the most important factor in rapidly increasing wealth and cash flow at https://chaddnaugle.com. If you're serious, join the investors club.

To learn how to escape the rat race, email Chadd at chadd@chaddnaugle.com

Connect @chaddnaugle on LinkedIn, Facebook, Twitter, and Instagram.

Tweetable: If you change your thoughts, you change your feelings, which changes your actions. Then you can become the person you want to become.

131

JESSICA CRESS

Finding My Spark After Losing My Brother

Mother of three, real estate investor, and Realtor Jessica Cress teaches women how to create financial wealth through real estate. She has a passion for helping young women excel as entrepreneurs and investors. As a Realtor in Colorado, she also helps clients realize their dreams of being a homeowner.

Before The Knock

"You should really think about getting a good running back for your fantasy team. LaDainian Tomlinson is good, but Frank Gore is going to be a sleeper. Also, I have the perfect Christmas gift for mom. I will tell you about it tomorrow because I have to go."

"Talk to you later." I said my goodbye to my brother as if it wasn't the last time I would ever talk to him. I never did find out what that perfect Christmas gift was for my mom.

When we were little, my brother Ricky and I got along like siblings normally do. We fought with each other, laughed with each other, and schemed with each other. It wasn't until I got into high school that our friendship started to grow. Maybe it was because we were in high school together (he was a senior and I was a freshman) or maybe because we were growing up. Either way, it was great. We would talk to each other about our day and discuss each other's friends, girlfriend, or boyfriend. This is when we actually started to get to know each other and when my brother started to take on the role of my protector. He sheltered me from all the crazy things that can happen when you're a freshman in high school. Since I had a senior for a brother, I had the protection of him plus all his friends, so I never really got picked on, teased, or harassed in high school. I was instantly cool.

This was also when my brother became my cheerleader. It's unusual for a female to have a male figure in their life that genuinely wants her to do better than him. Ricky used to encourage me to do things that I wasn't confident in doing. He always believed in me and knew that I could accomplish anything. He gave me my positive self-image and helped me become the strong, confident, and independent woman I am.

Everyone always says they look up to their older siblings. I fall into that category, but not because Ricky was wiser, because he made a lot of bad choices, but because he was kind, loving, loyal, laid back, funny, and fun to be around. He would go out of his way to help anyone. I more than looked up to my brother—he was my best friend.

When I was around seven or eight, we went over to the field by our house on a cold winter day. The creek had frozen over, and we decided to walk on it for fun. My brother was in front of me, and when the ice began to break, he got off and told me to get off. I told him just one more step, and that last step sent me into freezing cold water. I began to panic, flailing my arms, and screaming. My brother kneeled on the bank and held out his hand. He looked at me and said, "Stop freaking out and just stand up."

I looked up at Ricky, and I stood up, grabbed his hand, and he pulled me out. Being so young, I thought I was going to die, but my brother was there with his hand out, telling me that it was okay and that he had me. There are countless stories like this. He was always there to protect me and tell me it was okay.

After The Knock

September 3rd was a nice and sunny day. I was in my parents' living room waiting for breakfast, and it was a strange atmosphere. I could cut the tension with a knife.

Ricky never came home, nor did he call my mom and say he was going to stay somewhere else that night. That's when we heard a knock on the door.

My father opened it, my mom at his heels. I was standing near the doorway.

My mom already knew before the female officer spoke. I could hear her crying when the officer asked if my parents were the parents of a Richard Allen Cress. Then the officer spoke again and said there was a car accident, and my brother did not survive his injuries.

I collapsed on the floor, happiness drained, hope gone, and the "it will never be okay" feeling hitting me, before I went numb. I don't remember much of the rest of the conversation.

I remember going with my parents to the coroner's office to identify my brother and set up the release to the cemetery. This is when his death became real and who I was ceased to exist.

I was not myself. I felt like someone else—totally a robot just going through the motions. I couldn't eat. I couldn't sleep. I did everything I could do to suppress my emotions to help my parents through the worst two weeks of our lives.

The funeral for my brother was on September 9th at the second oldest cemetery in Denver. The funeral area held a lot of people in general, but it was unreal how many people showed up, how many lives my brother touched. There were people at that funeral I hadn't seen in years: parents of childhood friends that my brother and I grew up with, old bosses of my brother's, neighbors, family, and friends. It was a standing room only funeral.

A few days later, on September 12th, it was supposed to be my brother's 29th birthday. My brother and I had talked about going out for his birthday and celebrating. Instead, I was sitting at the crash site, putting up flowers and a card by the tree he hit.

Hundreds of Bad Days

When I finally went back to work, I shut myself down and turned off my feelings. Working was weird. I couldn't focus. I acted like someone else to ignore the nightmare that was my life now. On the hour drive home every day, I would cry all the way home, not actually knowing how I got there because I was crying so much. The car was the only place I felt I could cry because I had to be strong for everybody else around me.

My behavior caused a lot of rifts in my relationships with others. I didn't have it in me emotionally to try, and some relationships weren't strong enough to weather my emotional shutdown. I just didn't want to be around anybody that knew me and began hanging out with people that didn't know me to keep my sanity.

I decided I needed a tattoo. At the time, it was more about me wanting a memorial of my brother, but as I lay there on the chair with the needle going into my back, the pain was surprisingly relieving. It was a welcomed, soothing escape from the real-world pain I felt inside, and for the first time, I understood why people would cut themselves.

A little over a month after returning to work, I was let go due to downsizing. And so, I thought my life was completely coming to an end. I had broken up with my boyfriend, lost my job, and lost my brother all within a two-month period. I was struggling a lot, and I was trying to figure out what was going on in my head along with trying to be strong and supportive to my parents. How was I ever going to bounce back?

Months had passed, and the difficulty of my situation wasn't getting any better. I was angry all the time, so I suppressed it and numbed my pain and anger with reckless behavior.

One night I went out with a bunch of people to a bar, and I drank way too much. I'm not sure how I got home that night. I was puking drunk and shouldn't have been driving, but I did. I drove all the way to my parents' house. I was in the bathroom puking, and I remember my mom on the floor of the bathroom holding my hair back and crying, telling me that she had already lost one child in a car accident and she didn't want to lose the other.

She wanted to help. She knew that I was lost. She even suggested a support group. I never did get outside help; my mom's words that night were the light I was looking for.

The Spark

As my actions started to sink in, I understood that the reckless behavior I was engaging in wouldn't have a good ending. I stopped hiding from my feelings, and I embraced the idea of living my life for my brother.

Time does not stop, lives go on, and people stop coming around or calling. Many don't understand the intimate bond between siblings. Only your sibling understands you perfectly. They understand the household you lived in and how you were raised. They know what you are thinking. They are a part of you and your identity. That was ripped from me. That part of my identity is gone, and that's what I struggle with the most.

Being awake was hard, but sleeping was the worst. Every night, I would be haunted by my dreams of my brother faking his death. I would be so angry with him for putting us through all this, and I would wake up so angry and sad. Those dreams still come, but not as often.

We all live with a certain amount of pain. My brother was my light. He lived every day like it was his last. So, to make sure his light doesn't go out, I live my life the way he would have wanted me to. It took the birth of my first son to get my spark back that my mother ignited years ago. I now understand how living for others can truly make you happy, and that is my why. Everything I do is to help better myself for my family, friends, and clients. Learning and growing personally has always been a foundation for my life and my passion.

Every opportunity I get, I help and guide my clients to their financial goals. Whether it is their first home or their 20th home either personal or investment. I create educational content to help those that are not ready to go out and explore, because education is a high priority for me. I also love to talk about what's holding them back from grabbing their dreams. I don't take these opportunities lightly. I cherish the bond created between my clients and myself while we are reaching their goals and learning together. If I am not vlogging about real estate, I am living it daily with my family. Having a better understanding of what real estate does for a person and a community makes everyone and every community stronger and better.

You Don't Get Over It, You Get Through It

Always being an optimist, positive and happy, I still struggle with the darkness and emptiness I feel. I made bad choices to get a quick pleasure high, but every time I came down, it was the same thing over again. I wasn't getting anywhere, and I wasn't happy. I still fight these demons every day. Time does not heal all, time teaches you to live with the pain and emptiness. Time creates different anger, when you can no longer remember what your loved one looks like without a picture, when you can no longer remember the way they laughed or the way their hugs felt. Even though this bad happened to me when I was young and I struggled, I learned from the mistakes I made through the process.

Knowing that time is our most valuable asset, I do not squander it with quick pleasure highs anymore. I love engaging with others about what I learned. Sharing my path with young people or others going through tough situations is a passion for me. There is good that comes from bad, and I am grateful for the memories I can share. I stumbled along the way but have found my way back better and stronger. Being able to share all of this with other people is my purpose, and I am grateful always.

To reach Jessica Cress for real estate transaction/ investment consultations or speaking engagements, contact her at jessicacress@yourcastle.com or 303-921-1084. Or reach out on social media: Real Estate with Jessica Cress on Facebook and LinkedIn, Real Estate with JRC on Instagram, and @JrcReal on Twitter.

Tweetable: In the blink of an eye it could all be taken away. Be grateful always.

BILLY BROWN

How to Get Loans Approved, Understanding the Commercial Lending Industry

Billy Brown is the founder of Investors Capital Group, a concierge commercial loan brokerage that educates, empowers, and amplifies wealth for real estate investors. He is also a real estate investor and founder of The Golf Sanctuary in Nashville.

The Lending Industry – A Complex, Perplexing Machine

In 2006, as we were heading into the great recession, I bought a home with a NINJA loan. Remember those? No Income, No Job or Assets. In hindsight, I should not have been approved for this loan. We kept the property for over a decade then sold it for a nice profit, but many other people who got into this type of loan did not fare as well.

In 2013, I was married and needed to buy a car. I went through my friend at his bank for a loan. I wanted a used car because I was taught all my life to never buy new. We had more than the amount of money I planned to borrow in the bank. I also had a good job in the mortgage industry, which was hard-won after my difficult transition out of my golf career. I thought for sure this loan was going to be an easy yes. I was shocked when they turned me down. I spoke to the loan officer in the consumer credit department to find out why and decided I needed to take steps to learn more about my financial picture.

I made an appointment with my banker friend to have him show me how to fill out this thing called a personal financial statement. I felt dumb when he said, "Well, you just fill it out." To say the least, I did not find this helpful.

I worked in residential lending, and in the industry at the time, everything was trending towards online applications. Today, you can get approved for a home, close, and have all the furnishings shipped to that new home from your smartphone! I was in disbelief that the bank had a paper form, and the boxes were so small I couldn't write out the answers to their questions.

I later found out the bank sent this document in without review to a place in West Tennessee so a junior processor could input the data to a computer program then make a decision based on their internal processes. That didn't seem right to me. Why was the system so arbitrary? I checked around with a few other banks and found out this was common, even with commercial real estate loans.

The Lender Makes or Breaks the Investor

In contrast to the process I had gone through to get the car loan, residential lending wasn't easy, but at least the industry was up to date on technology and proactive in educating potential borrowers. I had an insider's view of that. Outside of my work as a loan officer, I was a real estate investor. Commercial banks and lenders had this intimidating aura about them. But I knew, to grow my real estate portfolio, I needed larger and more flexible lenders who would lend on the cash flow from the investment properties (assets) we wanted to buy. So, I went in search of information and mentorship.

Fortunately, in Nashville, we have an active real estate investor community. One of the frequent presenters at a real estate investor event I regularly attended was not only an investor but also a former commercial lender—Yogi Dougher. He taught investing through the eyes of lenders.

It made sense to think of the lender's side of the story. The lender brings upwards of 70-80% of the money that goes into a deal. Often, without partnership with a lender, a real estate investor is stalled. You need money to make money, and the lender is in control. They are the decision-makers on the majority of the capital deployed in real estate investing.

I believed getting to know Yogi Dougher and learning more about commercial lending would compound my success in the lending industry and allow me to help other real estate investors. It just so happened, he was partnering with another gentleman on a commercial loan brokerage, and they needed someone with credibility and a database to help communicate and sell. They brought me on board.

Although I worked with them for only a few years, I learned a lot about the differences in lending, lender personalities, and why certain loans get approved and others get ignored.

As an investor, I still had big ambitions. We had a few rentals, but nothing substantial. So, we decided to syndicate an apartment complex. My intention was to buy a 100 unit apartment by June 30, 2019. We instead found a smaller 82 unit building, which we closed four days after my goal date. With momentum rolling, my wife and I then sold my first home, a little starter house, and did a like-kind, tax-free exchange into a large office building in my wife's hometown. That tenant is on a long lease where they are responsible for all property expenses, which makes it a nearly hands-off investment!

That year, we picked up nearly $5M in property and brought several investors along with us. The tax-advantaged cash flow from those properties now pays for all our family vacations and trips for my wife and I to be with other investors!

Global Shutdown

In the fall of 2019, I decided to go out on my own and form Investors Capital Group, a commercial brokerage that helps investors grow their wealth. Investors Capital Group started with a core principle: We work to invest. I borrowed this idea from Bigger Pockets co-founder, Brandon Turner, who advocates creating a business that serves your family's lifestyle, which for us includes investing in education, real estate, and time with family. We do this by consciously limiting the number of clients we work with at any given time to 20.

The momentum was building quickly for my new business. We maxed out on our clients in early 2020, and we projected we would make more profit in the first three months than my entire 2019 yearly salary!

As we celebrated, the news about COVID-19 began to spread. At first, we thought commercial lending was safe. Then, as businesses around the world closed to slow the spread, the institutions that buy commercial debt (commercial mortgage-backed securities) shut down, exposing a major flaw in our business plan. Without these institutions, we had no money to lend. If we don't have money to lend, we are out of business.

Fortunately, thanks to Kyle Wilson and The Real Estate Guys, I was surrounded by a great network of business leaders and investors. With their influence, I recognized an opportunity to create educational content around how to borrow money from commercial lenders. I often get invited to lunch by local real estate investors hoping to pick my brain. Now, still for the price of lunch, no matter where they are in the world, any investor can have access to our knowledge.

Most investors learn to borrow money for real estate projects through trial and error. Most investors have experienced the disappointment of empty promises of capital from lenders who eventually turn their request down, sometimes after months of suspense and delay. Depending on the investor's situation, this rejection can be more than disappointing. It can be downright financially devastating.

If there were a way to collapse timelines by learning from other's experience, rather than through trial and error, would that get you to your goals faster? If you could diminish the possibility of your loan request being rejected, would that save you time and hassle and get your return on investment into your pocket faster? If there were a way to negotiate better terms, wouldn't you want to know about it? In 30 days, we created over 25 short video modules and a free book guiding investors on who, when, where, why, and how of commercial lending.

The Golf Sanctuary

Like many people during the stay at home requests of the pandemic, I took some time to experiment and created a new business, one that is not dependent upon lending.

Since my daughter was born four years earlier, my career in competitive and recreational golf had ceased. Add in my commercial loan brokerage and investing, and the game I enjoyed was no longer accessible on a regular basis.

For around four years, I had been noodling on an idea for a business model using TrackMan Golf to create a virtual golf and social club in Nashville, but the timing wasn't right until early in 2020. The stars aligned when I realized there were more people moving to Nashville each day, but they were not making any more golf courses. In fact, all the private clubs were full with waiting lists, and three were about to undergo massive renovations.

A space was needed not only for golfers to play, practice, and compete without the uncertainty of weather and daylight, but also to be a replacement for the boring business lunch and a space for families to connect.

With my experience syndicating the apartment complex and office the previous year, along with the resources we have through being a sponsor of and contributor to The Real Estate Guys, we created a unique investment offering—The Golf Sanctuary. It's an investment that you can EXPERIENCE as every investor gets a membership at the club.

We now have our ideal location, a building large enough to have six full-size simulators, plus a putting green, bar, members lounge, and event space where we can host corporate events and connect business experts with golfers. In the same way I am able to connect lending to real estate investors, we will be able to bring in many incredible thought leaders like Nick Bradley and Kyle Wilson.

How Investors Capital Group Saves Investors Time and Money

The COVID-19 shutdown allowed me to dissect the commercial lending process. I asked key questions from my friends in the lending world. In my search, I met a community bank underwriter with insider knowledge on how most community banks make lending decisions, including what their motivations are, what trigger words on a loan application always get a quick no, and how to get past the bank gatekeepers to those that truly make decisions. He was more than willing to share his knowledge with us, and we brought him onto our team to serve the investors rather than the banks.

When our community bank underwriter explained to me the truth about how the industry really works, I was both enlightened and angry. I was angry at myself because, for years, we let down our clients by our ignorance. Most loans are declined due to incomplete documentation and miscommunication, mainly between the salesperson and the decision-maker.

The lightbulb went off. What if borrowers had a way to look at their financial situation and their loan request the way a community bank underwriter does BEFORE they apply for a loan? Wouldn't this help both the lender and the borrower?

What if they could take all the data in their financial paperwork and aggregate it in one easy to understand form? Information that would have taken a lender hours to comb through could be reviewed in 15 minutes. If both the lender and the underwriter were seeing the same information in the same form, wouldn't this eliminate many of the miscommunications that were occurring?

The answer is an overwhelming yes! We now see loan decisions sped up by 30-60 days and borrowers are able to save thousands in loan costs because they are in a strong position to negotiate. I am thrilled to provide this education and opportunity to investors through Investors Capital Group.

My growth—from being baffled by banking processes when I was trying to get a used car loan, to today, being a real estate investor, working as a commercial lender, and coaching others how to get capital for real estate investment deals faster and more reliably—has not been easy. But each curveball has provided me with opportunity. I am solving problems for investors, building communities, and working to contribute to the evolution of this complex industry for the better.

Email Billy Brown, founder of Investors Capital Group, at billy@billybrown.me to learn how to get capital for real estate investment deals 60 days faster and to receive a free copy of The Ultimate Guidebook on Commercial Lending for Real Estate Investors, How to Use THEIR Money to Explode YOUR Wealth. *TheInvestorsCapitalGroup.com*

Tweetable: When things don't go as planned, review your resources, and make a new plan.

NANCY PARADIS
From Ballerina to Healing Storyteller

Nancy Paradis is an inspiring educator, performer, artistic director, and storyteller. Her career has spanned over 40 years from principal ballerina to professor and entrepreneur. As founder of LA Dance Moves, she continues to bring light into the world in her unique way—through inspirational virtual performance art.

Early Life of an Aspiring Artist

I looked out over the rolling hills and slowly-turning-auburn leaves of the nearby forest. It was a beautiful sight, and not even remotely close to where or who I wanted to be.

At six years old, I took my first ballet class and knew this was the career I wanted with all the certainty in my heart. I loved the discipline and had a laser-like focus and even remember thinking "This is really odd for me to have this focus at six."

I come from a big, Italian, Catholic family. My father was a Marine and an artist. He was a multi-instrumentalist, arranger, composer, and conductor in the USMC wind ensemble. The styles ranged from big band and jazz to Dixie and swing. I was a little girl, but I remember how fun it was to hear the band. My mother is an arts lover, and she listened to both opera and John Denver. I have five older brothers who all loved classic rock n' roll, so our house was filled with a vast amount of music. While I was born into this world with an incredible amount of love from my parents and my brothers, our home was loud, chaotic, and fun, and I was shy. I didn't talk that much, and with so much going on, I was often talked over or just not heard.

At a pivotal time in my life, my parents decided to move from the hectic city of Woodbridge, Virginia to an area past historic Fredericksburg and into the country. Purchasing four acres of land, they built a house from the ground up. It was the solitude my father dreamed of. We were 45 minutes away from any town in either direction. As I was just entering middle school, it was a big shift and a lonely time for me.

Although I loved school and learning, it was difficult for me to connect to any typical teenage lifestyle. I was so focused on what I wanted to be in life. I played flute in middle and high school marching band, and that was the most connected I felt with my classmates.

Making It Happen

By 13, I was getting anxious about the daily training I knew I needed to become a professional ballerina. My mother drove me to my class once a week. Due to distance and our budget, that was all we could do... but I had to get to the next level in my training.

I started training at home, doing home workouts, cardio, strengthening, stretching, whatever I could do to push forward. I'll never forget the day I came home from school and went downstairs to do my workout, and my dad had surprised me with a home-made studio: dance floor, ballet barre, and a mirror. It was an incredible gift, and I worked harder than ever. I feel it was his way of saying, "I believe in you."

That summer, my mom and I started traveling an hour and a half once a week to get me to the best training possible. I helped her clean the local church to make extra money for these classes. I pulled the most I possibly could from each and every class, knowing this one had to last until next week.

The following summer, at 15, I auditioned for the Washington Ballet, DC, for their trainee program and was accepted.

At that moment... my career began.

"Everything Is Beautiful at the Ballet"

Although I was accepted, the real work was just beginning. The director told me I wouldn't perform in the upcoming performance that every company thrives on—The Nutcracker. I had over-developed my legs from my home training and didn't have the proper aesthetics nor enough turn out of the hips, which is imperative in ballet. But now, I finally had a daily company class, and I worked even harder to make up for lost years of training. Within two months, the director said to me, in front of the class, "It's really a miracle that you made these changes in your body and technique, and Nancy, you WILL perform with us."

I made continual growth performing and working with exceptional choreographers and a legendary artist director. It was a dream, but things were shifting in the program, and it felt I should move on. At 17, I auditioned at The Richmond Ballet in VA and was offered my first professional contract. Here is where I grew from an apprentice to a principal position in only four years. I know in my heart this was due to my hard work, the support of my family, and the nurturing company environment that groomed me into the artist I wanted to be.

Richmond Ballet was lovely to me, but I eventually came to realize that the ballet world is often cruel. It is about perfection, and the pursuit of perfection, all while making it look effortless. And when you can't get to that place, it plays with your head, your confidence, and your self-esteem. There are stories after stories of beautiful dancers destroyed by mental, physical, and emotional abuse and eating disorders. Although I had some difficult experiences, I'm so very grateful to have pushed through without long-lasting damage.

Working through these challenges makes you stronger and the reward even sweeter. It's the most surreal experience to stand on the stage in a principal role you envisioned your whole life. To have the warm lights on your skin, the orchestra playing for you, the dancers around you, and your partner behind you supporting you. It's a dream, reality, crazy, and awesome all at the same time.

Even with this success, after my fourth season, I felt it was again time to move on. I auditioned and moved to The Louisville Ballet, in KY. It was a different company culture than before, and I realized my talents as an artist were just not being utilized. That summer, I had the opportunity to drive with a friend cross country to visit Los Angeles, and I made a huge, game-changing decision to relocate here and leave the ballet world as I knew it behind.

A New Game

In LA, there was an amazing energy and passion from artists. There was a freedom and permission to be a little out of control while remaining in control. I had never experienced this before, and I wanted to be part of it! I retrained and refined my skills to work in the commercial dance world of film, television, video, and commercials. I worked on shows like *Beverly Hills 90210* and *Family Matters*, NBC commercials, Fox News, A&E Promo, Crunch Fitness, and the MTV Movie Awards. I danced on live Hollywood sound stages, the iconic Hollywood Bowl and traveled across the world to tour in Shanghai, China and Tokyo, Japan.

I trained with many teachers in LA, but one really drew me in. He was kind and energetic. He cared, loved people, and seemed to know everyone in the room. His name was Andre Paradis, and eventually, he became my husband.

We lived an amazing life separately as artists, touring the world and performing on incredible platforms. Then, one night, after I performed on a huge job for MTV, I came home feeling really great, smiled, and said to my husband, "Babe, I'm ready to start a family!" A year later, our son was born, and a little over two years later, our daughter was born.

As we grew our family, I continued to work and began teaching at local studios. I refined these skills to become a professor at universities and colleges, teaching, choreographing, and directing concerts. I also began my own personal growth and entrepreneurial journey.

My career that started at age 15 has spanned over 40 years, and I am still going.

The Fear of Wasting a Gift

My father passed on a tremendous gift to me through his artistry of creating joy with his music. I felt loved by him, but it was hard to connect with him. He was very introverted, and talking to him was awkward. He kept up with his musicianship after retiring by putting together a local community wind ensemble, in which I played flute for two summers. Being part of the ensemble and having my dad as my conductor was probably the closest I had ever felt to him. Somehow the music connected us, and it was a very special time in my life.

He passed away in 2009 from Alzheimer's, which was a difficult time for my family. I was honored when my mother handed me his conductor's score and said to me, "If anyone can do something with this, you will."

I worked for five years to find some way to have my dad's music restored and performed in an honorary concert for him. With the Moorpark College wind ensemble conductor and professor, we collaborated to recreate my father's music. I choreographed my dancers to perform on the stage with the musicians and had Marines representing Toys for Tots. It was a truly magical evening to honor my father, his music, and his life. This process began the creation of my own dance company, LA Dance Moves.

Slowly, through my company, I started creating works and giving dancers, musicians, and artists opportunities to perform on a digital media platform in film and video as opposed to live performance in a theater. I wanted to create something very different and very special, but I wasn't completely sure how.

Challenge or Opportunity?

As COVID-19 grew to a crisis and the world shut down, dancers' performances and income dwindled, and their way of staying in shape, their communities, and their sources of well-being dissolved.

It's very odd, but all this isn't new to me. I remember the isolation I felt living in the country and wanting my dream so badly. I remember doing home workouts to keep pushing forward and keeping my dream in sight.

As I picked all this back up, just to keep going in the COVID-19 world, I came to a realization. I feel a new inspiration and mission to get dancers back to dancing, to create a new form of virtual performance art honoring composers, dancers, and artists. To share stories of the human spirit to inspire the soul and warm the heart. And rather than filling a theater, we embrace technology and platforms that allow performances to be enjoyed anywhere in the world.

A Challenging Yet Guided Path

With becoming a professional ballerina comes incredible struggles of resilience. There are strict rules of appearance, aesthetics, weight, body shape, and early training that shape the rest of your career. The casting of roles is a constant reflection of how you are being perceived, and if you aren't strong, it can have a serious impact on you. Aesthetically, I had nothing that it took to be a ballerina except passion and drive. But people believed in me and my gifts, and I worked harder than ever because I knew I was going after my life!

I know that my path, with all its twists, has been guided, and I was lucky enough to listen to that guidance. It's unheard of for a ballerina to break a contract in the ballet world. But I listened, followed my heart, and moved to Los Angeles. I met my husband that same year and now have an amazing family. He serves the community as a relationship educator and coach, and I do what I can artistically to serve my community and bless the world. All the decisions I make come from a feeling of "knowing" in my heart.

Winning It All

Although having a career in the arts has been a vision of mine since I was six, what's been the most rewarding gift for me is finding the man of my dreams and having a family with two incredible children. There is no "all or nothing" to this story. I have done my very best to balance my life as an artist, a wife, a mom, and a woman with a dream. With over 40 years of performing, teaching, lecturing, choreographing, and directing, I am most passionate now about sharing my knowledge, my gifts, and my journey with the world.

I believe in the power of the performing arts, its impact on us, and the power it has to heal and inspire. I believe in creating a safe and kind environment where artists can be vulnerable and authentic and where those who've had a difficult career can heal and re-ignite the passion to be performers once again. Through creations of the human spirit, I have found my voice and my path to give light to the world.

Nancy Paradis welcomes opportunities to set choreography across the US, to guest lecture, and to inspire in her unique way. If you are interested in becoming a sponsor of LADanceMoves, viewing works, and learning more about Nancy's mission, go to www.ladancemoves.com. Contact Nancy at ladancemoves@gmail.com.

Tweetable: Embrace all that you have in your hands, and despite challenging conditions, make something magical happen and dance with it. #danceheals #ourlightwithin #bemoved

RAY HIGDON

Using Failure and Obstacles to Build a New Platform

Ray and Jessica Higdon are the founders of RankMakers, an Inc 5000 company which has helped network marketers enroll over 300,000 new customers, recruit 71,000 new reps, and achieve 14,000 rank advancements in the last three years. Their latest book with Hay House is called Time, Money, Freedom.

Overcoming a Challenging Childhood

My parents split when I was very young, and I lived with my dad and my step-mom up until the age of 12. Looking back, I think my step-mom struggled to make friends and probably wasn't treated very well at her job. She took it out on me. I was the punching bag. I remember almost every morning being woken up by being grabbed by my ankles, thrown against a closet, stomped on, and told how terrible I was. I remember going into kindergarten with bloody noses.

We've coached and worked with so many different people, and my story pales in comparison to some of the abuse I've heard about since, but it's something that you have to look back on without dwelling on it. It wasn't that I deserved it and it wasn't that I asked for it, but maybe that happening prevented me from being a certain way. I'm grateful that whatever happened in the past got me to where I am today because I love my life now.

Success, Failure, and Finding Mentors

I've never been super reliant on others. I've always been "I'll figure this out." My being willing to accept help is a newer development, and it came about in the last 10 years after I lost it all in real estate.

In Florida, from 2004-2005, everyone was making money in real estate. I didn't go to any of those guru workshops and didn't buy any coaching. I read my first real estate book in April 2004, and by July, a partner and I had three duplexes. I prided myself in being a go-getter and figuring things out myself, and that worked for me in a hot market. But when the market changed, I wasn't equipped to deal with it.

I got crushed. I went into foreclosure, was dead broke, a million dollars in debt, and depressed. I really didn't know what I was going to do. Now, I can say without a shadow of a doubt that I needed that humbling. It made me realize that I'm not bulletproof, I can learn from others, and I can have help. Ever since then, I've invested very heavily in my education and self-development with mentors and coaches.

When Everything Started to Change

I was dead broke, in personal foreclosure, a million dollars in debt, recently divorced, depressed, and drinking heavily, and someone on Facebook messaged me: "Hey, I'd like to pay for you to go through this program." I'm broke, and I think, "Oh, they just see me as a good marketer. They're going to send me to their thing thinking I'll then promote it." I decided to go anyway, thinking it was free and at least I might get some ideas for how I could make money. I needed to make money. I went to this seminar, Landmark Forum, without knowing anything about it. On day two of Landmark, they get you out of your comfort zone, and I realized that I had "repair my relationship with Dad" on a mental to-do list with no priority. I hadn't seen him in 13 years. He had never met my sons, who at the time were 11 and 12 years old.

So, I called him and said, "I just want to apologize." I had every reason not to have a relationship with my dad, but at the end of the day, would I feel good not trying to have a relationship? The answer was no. So I made that call for me, with no requirement that he accept my apology or recreate a connection with me.

This was 2009. We reconnected, and because I was broke, he flew me and my sons up to Indiana to see him. We still don't have the greatest relationship, but we have something, where we had nothing for 13 years. The boys and I flew back home, and less than a week later, I was introduced to the network marketing company in which I would go on to become the number one income earner.

I really believe that when you have past garbage, you think it's behind you, but it's also in front of you. It's blocking your access to create something new. Going to see my dad had nothing to do with money, but that led to an opening in my mind, allowing more things to come to me. I ended up making millions of dollars with that company.

Innovation Inside of Network Marketing

It was never an intention of mine or Jessica's to build a training company. Because of my pain with real estate, I wanted low risk, low overhead residual income, which is network marketing. My mission was to make it work. In July 2009, right after I came back from seeing my dad, I joined this network marketing company.

I had tried network marketing in the past and had some bad experiences with uplines. Because I've always been a marketer and a student of marketing, I decided I was going to use YouTube, Facebook, and Myspace to build my business. This was in 2006, and my upline said I couldn't do that, so I was the black sheep, the rebel. I didn't know why it had to be only home meetings and face to face. I did thousands of home meetings and thousands of Panera Bread and Starbucks meetings too. I wanted to use the internet to do things a little differently, and no one was teaching this back then. In 2009, I happened to join a company that wasn't so old school.

They didn't really understand what I was doing, but it was working. Back then, very few people in network marketing were using social media to effectively grow their business.

I remember going to a company event after I'd been with the company for a couple months. This guy came up to me and said, "You're the guy that recruits a lot of people on social media. I prefer duplication." He just couldn't comprehend that something technical could be duplicated. When they announced me as the number one income earner about three months later, I found him in the crowd and gave a little wave. Jessica, who was my girlfriend at the time, joined a couple months into that journey and went on to become the number one female earner.

We got married in 2011 and were doing things no one else was doing. I would get calls from people and other organizations saying, "I hear you guys like doing social media. How are you doing this? What are you guys doing? How do you run a group?" All kinds of different questions. My focus was only on building my network marketing business. I wasn't looking to sell coaching or training.

Then, in 2011, two companies came to me asking if I had any courses they could promote. I didn't know what they were talking about. I didn't have courses, but they suggested I do a course for them. They would sell it and pay me for it. So, I created a course for those two companies by teaching just like I trained those in my business. To this day, one of the companies sells that course from 2011 and I still get residuals.

While we were still actively building our business, other companies would ask us to teach on their stage. I became the number one income earner of a company, speaking on all these different company stages. Then, on one of these stages, I bumped into Eric Worre, and he invited me to speak on his stage. I did so for several years in a row, and things just blew up big.

In 2013, one of the company founder's wives had an aneurysm and almost died. He had been working himself to the bone traveling around with us doing meetings. They decided, based on a couple of factors, to merge into another company. We stayed with that company for three years, but the demand for our training was through the roof. At that point, we started taking on clients and launched our mastermind in 2013. We didn't think anyone would buy, but a whole bunch of people did.

We still had our team, which was doing great, and we had our training, but we didn't feel that we were giving a hundred percent to either. I like being all-in on one thing, and I found myself being torn. So, we sold our position in that company and focused on our coaching and training for the network marketing space.

What to Look for in a Network Marketing Company

I have such a love for the network marketing space because I see it as the lowest risk way for an ordinary person to start a business. The only people who don't see that are people who have never had other businesses. This model enables anyone to start a business. Literally, anyone can do network marketing.

While one of the greatest things is that it's low risk, low overhead, one of the worst things is that it's low risk, low overhead because some people come into this industry and don't take it very seriously. You can join most companies for a couple hundred to a thousand bucks. For some people, the potential loss of that money is just not enough pain for them to take it seriously.

People from outside of network marketing say only a small percentage of people make serious money. That's true, but there's a lot of benefits in network marketing in addition to income. I've made some amazing friends and used amazing products. I've enjoyed amazing development, inspiration, and motivation. I know people that have been in network marketing for 20 years and never really made much money but love it and would never leave it. Are there sleazes in this industry? Like any industry, of course. Sometimes people get in and, because they have no marketing training or psychology training, think they need to hype people and make promises that aren't real. That happens in many industries, but it doesn't have to be that way and isn't the core of the industry. The core of the industry is that the average, ordinary person can create a business and create residual income. Outside of network marketing, most people don't have a way to do that. You're going to learn the skills here that you would need in any other business: promotion, marketing, sales, closing, follow-up, plus personal development and maybe apply those skills to an amazing invention or idea down the road.

When looking for the right network marketing company, I'm not of the mindset that you've got to love the product or the service. Sometimes people get tangled up in the idea that you've got to be a product of the product, you've got to have your story. You do need to know stories of how it helped people, with their sleep, or weight loss, or energy, or aches and pains, or whatever, and if you do have a personal story, that is definitely a bonus. But I don't see it as a requirement.

For me, it's more about what the environment of the opportunity is. Are the leaders flexible in how you market and run your business? If they're giving you massive restrictions on social media or telling you don't dare learn from anyone outside the company, that's a big red flag. There are leaders that seek control more than production, and that's a warning to me. Is it a product that you believe helps? Does it solve problems? Does it help people attain desires, whether it's a service or a product? Do you feel good being a part of it? Do you feel good bringing people into the organization and then also knowing that you can build your team and create your own culture?

Consistency and Bringing Value

On July 15th of 2009, I decided that I was going to start doing a video a day, and I have not missed one day in over 11 years. There's a big difference between commitment and creativity. When you're committed, creativity is forced. If you wait for creativity before you're committed, it never happens.

People ask me how I came up with 11 years of topics? Simple, one day at a time. I have a very different energy when I commit to talking than when I am waiting for me to come up with something. I have to be putting value into the marketplace or I get weird, agitated, and anxious.

For Jessica and me, the biggest thing is presence. I have two sons that are over 21 now, and when they were younger, I would be at the dinner table still either mentally working or working on problems from my job or on a computer. I literally was never present, and I learned from that. It does help to have a daughter that's a total firecracker. She kind of makes me present, even when I might not want to be in that moment.

That doesn't mean that while I'm at my laptop I feel guilty working because I'm not being present. I'm being present in my work.

Be present. Be present when you're with your kid, be present when you're at the dinner table, be present when you're in your work. Be present.

Connect with Ray and Jessica Higdon on Facebook for Free Coaching Friday (https://www.facebook.com/ rayhigdonpage). Find their newest book Time, Money, Freedom: 10 Simple Rules to Redefine What's Possible and Radically Transform Your Life *at TMFbook.com. Learn more about RankMakers today by visiting BecomeARankMaker.com*

Tweetable: I'm grateful that whatever happened in the past got me to where I am today because I love my life now.

RAVIN S. PAPIAH
A Mentor Is the Bridge

Ravin S. Papiah is highly decorated in the industries of professional speaking and direct selling and is passionate about helping others reach their highest potential. He is a founder-partner, certified coach, speaker, trainer, and executive director of the John Maxwell Team, a Gitomer Licensed Trainer and a Distinguished Toastmaster (DTM).

Living Beyond My Dreams

This will be my fourth book with Kyle Wilson! Kyle has called me the Jim Rohn of my country, Mauritius. If, 20 years back, someone would have told me that I would be co-authoring four #1 bestselling books with the marketing genius behind the great American philosopher Jim Rohn's roaring success, I would have rolled with laughter.

How can someone who was born and raised in a third world country, who was condemned to a short life at birth, who was bullied at every level in school, and who was a super-ultra timid guy, become an Amazon #1 bestselling author, not one time, not two, but three times and running? Good question!

My life was a bag of problems starting when I was a child. If you read my first three co-authored books published by Kyle—*Life-Defining Moments From Bold Thought Leaders*; *Don't Quit, Stories of Persistence, Courage and Faith*; and *Success Habits of Super Achievers*— you will understand my challenges and how I solved them along the way and turned the problems into possibilities, the adversity into diversity of opportunities, and the challenges into sweet lozenges.

Early Teachers and Lessons

My teacher, Chantal, introduced me to reading, but I believe she was far from imagining that she was inculcating the notion of giving in me. Giving back became a mantra for me at a very young age. Being sick and bullied is not a gift, but what I got from my family and my teachers was more than a gift. In fact, it was a real blessing. I entered the magical world of reading and met superheroes doing super things to help people. My inner self got attracted and addicted to this. I could see how my teachers and my siblings were also my superheroes, protecting me from the bullies and providing me with a sense of belief that I was valuable too and that I could also help and support others as well.

It all started for me when I was 11 years old, and I just entered college. Some of my parents' friends called and asked if I could help their kids in primary school by giving them private tutoring. I was a scholarship winner at my primary school final exams despite my frailties. The answer was a quick YES. I wanted to help these kids, not because I was smart (I didn't believe that yet!), but because, like my teachers, especially Miss Chantal, and like my siblings, I now wanted to help others, other kids like me, who were timid, a bit late in their studies, and looking for that helping hand.

The results were amazing, and very soon, I started being flooded with tutoring requests for more kids from more parents. It went on for a couple of years. Those were some amazing years indeed. I helped the kids by sharing what I knew, and more importantly, how I studied. At that time, there was no electricity at home, and I had to study till late while burning the midnight oil in the real sense. I didn't understand at that time that I was adding value, but I was.

Recently, I had one of my very first students call me and thank me for turning him from a math zero to a math hero. He shared with me how he is now teaching and turning his son into a math supremo. He connected with me when he discovered that my daughter and his son are in the same class. What a great testimonial of value from someone who I was able to help some 40 years back. As is said — You just plant the seed. You never know when the tree will bear its best fruits.

Solving my continuous series of challenges created a new mindset within me. If there are always people present to help me, and if I have been helped along all throughout my life, then I should also be available to help others. My life has been filled with tedious challenges and adversities, but at the same time, all throughout my life I have been blessed with loads of positive achievements. Was my life a curse, a blessing, or BOTH?

My answer: I was given the challenges and adversities so that I could emerge, like the phoenix, to greater heights. I don't think I would have achieved what I have achieved so far without those challenging times and events. No way!

Turning Problems Into Value

But turning problems into value does not just happen. I believe there are many things, but there are the vital things necessary to solve problems and produce value for the world and leave a legacy.

These three things are:

(1) The awareness that problems, adversities, challenges, or struggles are NOT there to punish us, but to test our resolve

(2) The presence of people (teachers, mentors, coaches) to enlighten us of that awareness, and provide us wisdom and tools to fight the odds and continue our march towards our purpose

(3) The attitude of a student—to listen, learn, respect, apply, observe, and record results and to continue to build upon past results, good or bad.

I am very blessed that I have been given a mother who fought for my survival beyond everyone's beliefs, siblings who supported me all the way through, and a father who spoke little but imbued me with values including always keeping my hands open to give, for there is no bigger pleasure than giving. He told me, "The whole world awaits getting, but only the chosen few are givers. BE one of them Ravin." But beyond my close family, there have been exceptional beings who have marched alongside me through a particularly difficult life— my teachers and my mentors.

The tree can be filled with excellent fruits in great quantity, but if there is no one to pluck them and share them with others, the fruits just rot and become useless. So is value. If you have value in you, but you are unaware of it, and more importantly, if you have value and don't know how to share it with the world, then you are like that abandoned tree full of succulent fruits going to waste.

Les Brown tells us to not die with the music within us. He asks us to die empty, meaning having poured out our gifts to the world. We must share what we have inside of us with the world, for the world is waiting for our voice and our gifts. This is why mentors are important. They are the ones who discover, or I should say, uncover, our gifts, make us aware of them, and teach us how to share them with the world, in the process, creating our legacy. Our legacy is that which we leave for the benefits of others, just like we are benefitting from the legacies left by others, such as Jim Rohn. The mentor who took me by the soul, made me see my value and my gifts, and crafted the way I can share them with the world, creating my legacy in the process, is none other than the great marketing genius, Kyle Wilson. Kyle is my friend and my mentor!

The Trip Across the World

It was a May day in 2017 when I was knocking at the door of Kyle's house. I had loads of butterflies flapping in my belly, for I was going to be face to face with the MAN who had been mentoring me virtually for more than 19 years! After 36 hours of flight and transits from the little island of Mauritius, I arrived at Kyle's house for a meeting of his mentorship group. It was unreal. It was a dream and a magical reality. This day I met incredible people—Bob Helms, Ron White, Tom Ziglar, Robert Helms, Tim Cole, Kelli Calabrese, and so many more. It was a day that completely changed my life, but I would soon have a better day, a full day with Kyle one to one—a gift from the MAN for my dedication to being present, traveling the world to be the only foreigner in the house on that day.

That day, as Jim Rohn would say, turned my life around. While I was complaining and bemoaning my broken life, Kyle listened to me studiously, without interruption, taking copious notes and giving me that mentor's look that calms you down and gives you that space for a breather. Then, he started showing me how my broken life had pieces of genius that could help the lives of so many people around the world.

You see, I was only looking at the challenges that were falling on me. I didn't focus on the fact that I conquered those challenges and kept advancing through my path, which led me to meet Kyle 16,820 km away from my home. While I worked hard to be able to take that first trip to meet with my mentor, I was not realizing the feat. Yes, it was a feat, especially for someone who was saying his life was in tatters, to work hard and save money to do the kilometres to finally meet with his mentor! That was an achievement in itself.

Discovering My Value

Kyle showed me that my life and its turn-around was a piece of art that should be shared with the world. I would tell my story so the many others who STAY at the moaning and complaining stage can take inspiration and move to the next level of conquering their demons.

Kyle has showed me the way and identified the point where I was stuck. I was afraid to take action, I did not have the courage to ACT on my decisions, which was stalling me in my endeavours. I had come a long way. I was very near my breakthrough, but I was lacking the courage to take the actions necessary to liberate myself to fulfill my purpose. That was a revelation for me because I believed I was courageous. Yes, I was courageous but it was physical courage, while Kyle was talking about INNER courage—the courage of the heart, the courage of will, the courage to believe in your purpose and go for the actions needed without worrying about other people's opinions and comments. Inner courage—that's all I needed.

Three years later, I am writing my fourth chapter for my fourth book, I am hosting an international radio program with the International Business Growth Radio Network, I have launched a podcast and *The Ravin Papiah Show* which reached 155 episodes while I was writing this chapter, and there are many more great things unfolding soon.

You may be good. You may be very good. You may be a star, but you may not be aware of it. As I say, "if you are not aware, you are nowhere!" It takes a genuine mentor to uncover your potential and unleash it to the world. For me,

I will be leaving my legacy in books, radio shows, podcasts, and many other forms, thanks to my mentor, Kyle Wilson.

Who will you choose to mentor you to solve your problems, bring value to the world, and leave a legacy that will act as a benchmark for the benefit of the future generations?

Connect with Ravin S. Papiah, professional speaker and trainer, in The Life Defining Leadership group on Facebook, on LinkedIn, on his website www.plcleadership.com, or by email at plcjmleadership@gmail.com.

Tweetable: Solving my continuous series of challenges has created a new mindset within me—if there are always people present to help me, and if I have been helped along all throughout my life, then I should also be available to help others.

JEFF MCKEE

It's Never Too Late to Learn New Skills

Jeff McKee is a 30+ year, full-time sales and business development executive in the software industry who also specializes part-time on real estate investing. He is an active and passive syndication investor in 2500+ apartment units valued at $100M+. Jeff is passionate about introducing multifamily syndication investing to family, friends, and those wanting higher returns to achieve financial freedom.

Mindset Shift

At the age of 52, I found myself 30 years into a successful career working in high tech with a single source of income from my W-2 job. I heard about others investing in real estate and creating multiple streams of income while continuing to work their W-2 jobs, but I was a typical investor with a company 401K and holdings in stocks, bonds, and mutual funds. That year, I read Robert Kiyosaki's *Rich Dad Poor Dad*, and it shifted my mindset to thinking about real estate investing, which then spurred me into action.

Over the next three years, I read more books than I had in the prior 30 years. In 2017, I didn't know what a podcast was, and now I have listened to over 1,000 real estate and personal improvement podcasts. As I reflect, I'm most proud of the action I took to start to build and leave a legacy for my family by learning new real estate investing skills in contrast to my previous 30 years of "traditional" investing. I now believe it is never too late to learn new skills such as real estate investing.

Life Is Short

My dad died suddenly from a heart attack when he was only 55 in 1998. That was a difficult time for our family since he was such a family man. Fortunately, he was able to spend a lot of time with all seven of his grandkids before he died.

In 2020, I turned 55, and I realized how short life really is. I am a cancer survivor. I was diagnosed with cancer as part of a routine physical in 2009. I had the cancer removed, followed by treatment, and have had no recurrence of cancer during the past 11+ years. Now, I balance working a W-2 job, enjoying family time, sports, vacationing, and building our real estate legacy to last well beyond when I am gone.

Based upon my family history and my own health scares, I do not take tomorrow for granted. One of the legacies my dad instilled in us is camping, so my wife and I have camped a lot over the years with our kids and are passing this legacy down. My dad loved camping so much, we donated a playscape at Inks Lake State Park in Texas with a plaque dedicating it in his name.

Never Too Late to Start Investing in Real Estate

After college and starting my career in high tech, my high school sweetheart, and now wife of 32 years, and I quickly started a family. We were focused on family, raising three kids and working, with little long-term financial planning. We assumed our 401Ks and social security would be enough to save for a good retirement.

There's a saying: when is the best time to invest in real estate? 30 years ago! And the second-best time is today. It took 30 years of my adult life for me to discover real estate investing could accelerate our financial freedom. My missed opportunity was not investing in real estate during those 30 years to generate multiple streams of income. I suggest people invest time into expanding their personal education and skills now to see what is possible, then execute a plan that drives long-term success, including developing several sources of income beyond the traditional W-2 income.

After 30 years of working and paying high federal income taxes, I finally started reading real estate and self-help books along with listening to many podcasts to educate myself. At the time, our net worth was less than $1M, with only two streams of W-2 income between my wife and me.

For much of my adult life, I worked hard, saved mostly through my employer's 401K plan, and paid lots of taxes since I figured that was the American way. I had no idea you could change your facts, as Tom Wheelwright advocates, and pay way less in taxes.

What spurred this enlightenment? After hearing of others becoming financially free through real estate investing, I dedicated myself to becoming educated in these areas of investing I was not familiar with.

With my newfound wisdom, in 2018, my son, Brice, and I attended a local REIA (Real Estate Investment Association) meet up in Austin, Texas. Later, the three of us, my son and I plus my wife, attended the workshop, where we became excited about these single family investment opportunities and ultimately joined this group.

Homestead and Short-Term Rental Strategy

Based upon what we learned from the founders of the Austin REIA, my wife and I decided to be aggressive and implement a homestead exemption and short-term rental strategy. Since we were part of this single family investment group, I was on the email list of a few single family wholesalers that were locking down properties under contract then assigning to an end buyer and taking a fee during a double closing where they don't take title.

Within a few months, I received an email about a teardown house in South Austin on the same street as our condo where we were living. Long story short, after two and half years in real estate investing, we had paid $500K for a teardown house and put $700K into construction costs. The resulting ARV (after repair value) is $1.8M—thus creating $600K in equity (forced appreciation)!

We live in the main house, and we are on track to drive $50,000 per year in net revenue on the short-term rental, which my wife is managing. She quit her W-2 paralegal job in July of 2020 after we moved into the new property to focus 100% of her time on real estate.

Our goal is to live here for two or three years, then sell both houses, realize a $500K homestead exclusion non-taxable gain on the main house, and take a long-term capital gain on the investment house to then invest in multifamily apartment syndications with cost segregation/bonus depreciation to offset this taxable gain. For some W-2 earners, this homestead tax exemption strategy could create a good amount of capital, whether you sell your house or cash out refinance, to use to begin investing in multifamily syndications.

Fix and Flip

We purchased a house in East Austin with a business partner for $250K from a wholesaler, put $70K into rehab including $15K for foundation repair, and ultimately sold this for $420K, realizing a before-tax profit of $40K, $20K for our partner and $20K for our family LLC.

Our partner brought great value with her rehabbing skills, and we brought value by being able to secure funding with our W-2 incomes and personal funds. Identifying win-win partnerships is key to a lot of business but especially real estate when you are new.

We realized this type of fix and flip income is treated as a short-term gain and taxed at your current ordinary income tax rate. So, there is no depreciation or tax benefits from this type of investing, but it can generate a good amount of capital.

We quickly learned it is hard to scale and drive tax benefits with a fix and flip business.

Scaling With Multifamily Investing

After one year of executing our plan on single family homestead build strategy, fix and flip, wholesaling, and buy and hold, I learned we could scale faster with multifamily apartment syndications, so we quickly pivoted.

In year two of our real estate investing journey, I became educated through weekly apartment investing meetings and many podcasts that other investors had been scaling their multiple streams of income faster through multifamily investing in apartments.

What I like about multifamily apartment investing is the cash flow generated from taking over an existing apartment community and improving operations to increase the NOI (net operating income). With apartment investing, unlike single family homes, we can "force" appreciation through increasing rents once the exteriors and interiors have been renovated. Single family homes are valued on "comps" (comparable sales per square foot), whereas commercial property such as apartments are valued on NOI, which can be increased through improved revenues and decreased expenses. Like single family homes, the tenants in multifamily are paying down the principal on the loan, thus we are using other people's money to increase equity in the asset.

One of the most important aspects of multifamily investing is the ability to scale. We decided to partner with others to syndicate apartment investments to be part owners of 100+ unit apartment communities instead of trying to buy and hold fifty single family homes as investment properties.

Joining Multifamily Ecosystems

My wife, son, and I attended a weekend multifamily real estate seminar in Dallas then joined that apartment investing syndication group. The primary takeaway was learning the impact of dramatically increasing the value of an apartment community by increasing the NOI (net operating income) with small reductions in expenses and small increases in revenues. The general partners (sponsors) of these multifamily syndications, partnering with the property management team, have direct influence on executing the business plan for the property and improving the NOI. This contrasts with how single family homes are valued on comparable properties and the lack of influence investors have on stocks, bonds, and mutual funds.

Over the next six months, we invested as passive investors with this group in five deals across Dallas and San Antonio, thus becoming limited partner owners of 1,000+ apartment doors across five apartment communities.

Looking back, I could have spread out our capital investment analyzing more deals over a longer period of time. Our goals were to increase cash flow through passive investing, generating multiple streams of income, and to evaluate moving from LPs (limited partners) to be active GPs (general partners) on these multifamily apartment syndications. One more step I took in that direction was becoming a KP (key principal) on an investment. Without taking on personal liability, I signed on the Freddie Mac non-recourse loan using our net worth and liquidity to help the sponsor team qualify for the loan.

Another fascinating aspect of multifamily investing is, the larger the deal, the more non-recourse debt you can sign on without needing W-2 income. But, for the most part, small, single family deals require high W-2 income and recourse debt and signing on the loan personally. To invest in these five deals, we used after-tax funds from the sale of stocks, capital from our LLC, and my solo 401K (eQRP), which I rolled over from a prior employer IRA, which originated from my 401K with a former employer.

During our multifamily investing journey, we started evaluating other programs which were focused on helping families, including children, join in on the education and investing benefits. Due to the COVID-19 pandemic of 2020, our participation in events was delayed, but my wife and I were able to attend an event in August 2020 and joined our second multifamily apartment investing group. After returning to Austin the day after this event, my wife started listening to the recordings of their latest group calls.

Our First Deal as General Partners

On a recorded group call, one of the GPs was sharing his new deal and asking for volunteers to join the on-site due diligence of a deal under contract in Fort Smith, Arkansas. My wife and son drove that week and supported the due diligence, along with analyzing the competition in the area. We ultimately became co-general partners on that deal and helped raise capital, including investing as LPs ourselves. That deal closed in December 2020 and led to partnering with others in the group on deals in Lubbock, Texas, Jacksonville, North Carolina, and Montgomery, Alabama. My wife, the trooper, traveled to support the on-site due diligence on two of these next deals as well.

We have been fortunate to have some net worth to invest our own capital in these deals and are glad to share the opportunity by bringing new investors to these opportunities. We also bring value to the investment team by putting in time to support the on-site due diligence and providing some multifamily real estate experience. Other members of the investment team bring value in ways such as finding the deal, negotiating with the brokers and sellers, heading investor relations, marketing, signing on the loan, managing the asset, and in many other ways.

As mentioned previously, part of our capital has been generated from single family strategies such as our homestead forced appreciation strategy. This plan did involve some risk, but the rewards for us have been tremendous. We would rather have 10% of a 200-unit deal than 100% of a 20-unit deal. Today, we are part owners of 2500+ apartment units across six communities, of which we are GP's on 700+. Larger deals with experienced partners can grow your wealth faster than doing smaller deals on your own. Within three short years, through massive education and action, we have more than doubled our net worth through real estate investing, and we have built more than eight streams of passive income from real estate while lowering our federal taxes paid.

What I Learned Throughout This Journey

1. It's never too late in life to learn new skills such as real estate investing. For our family, having both partners on board has been a key success factor. Involving our children helps us ensure we build a legacy of investing that will continue for generations.

2. Having good W-2 income(s) can help you qualify for single family loans to generate capital for other real estate investments such as scaling with multifamily. For us, the homestead strategy has been a catapult to our investing, as we can add value to teams by providing capital. Our homestead strategy also included a cash flow investment property to offset the overall costs for the construction and add another source of income.

3. I've learned you can't use debt with your 401K/IRA, but you are able to leverage debt in a solo 401K to invest in multifamily apartment syndications which use 60% - 75% low-cost debt, thus driving up your returns.

4. Being around like-minded people and the power of partnerships have accelerated our real estate investing path.

5. If one strategy isn't working for you, then learn from that and quickly move on, applying those lessons learned to your next strategy.

It really is never too late to learn new skills and begin your journey towards financial freedom. Shifting our wealth-building strategy to multifamily apartment investing has been a key factor in our success. Adding value to partners and investors has enabled us to scale in this investing business model while working to leave a legacy for our family and network of partners and investors. Take massive action and enjoy the journey!

To download Jeff McKee's free eBook about multifamily investing, generating multiple streams of cash flow, and achieving financial freedom, please visit www.mckeecapitalgroup.com. To connect with Jeff directly, please email: jeff@mckeecapitalgroup.com

Tweetable: It's never too late in life to learn new skills such as real estate investing. You never know, that new skill may change your life and better the lives of those you love.

WANDA SANTOS-HAYNES
It's Cheaper Than Divorce

Wanda Santos-Haynes is a certified positive psychology educator who works with men, women, and couples to help them improve their relationships and harness their sexual energy. Her passion is to apply positive psychology and sex-positive education to support adults of all ages in sustaining their pleasure and happiness.

My Fairy Tale

Till death do us part.

I was so very much in love with him, I believed it would be forever. Isn't that what all the fairy tales promise?

I was sure I had finally found my life partner. I'd had several relationships previously, but none of them seemed to bring the lasting joy and satisfaction that I was seeking, and eventually, I would move on. But with Daniel (not his real name), it was different.

He was—and still is—a good man. I was a single mother in my mid-thirties, with young children, and Daniel happily accepted them as part of our family. We were both active, enjoyed the same things, had common goals. We married, pursued our careers, and were very happy. I thought we could overcome anything.

The Early Years

My upbringing in New York City gifted me with grit, resilience, and street smarts. I was raised by my mother and step-father, a man I grew to admire and respect. He was hard-working, cerebral, and always looking for ways to improve himself. His work ethic and thirst for knowledge greatly shaped the way I approach the world. However, my relationship with my biological father was always strained, and this influenced my early relationships, often drawing me toward unhealthy, emotionally-distant men.

I longed for those things that many women want: happiness, comfort, security, fulfillment, and to be loved. I thought I'd found those things in Daniel. For years, I thrived within our marriage.

A Familiar Story

Eventually, the day came when I realized that Daniel and I had drifted apart. The intimacy I craved was gone; my needs weren't being met, and my husband wasn't getting the best of me.

I resisted it for a while. I didn't want to become a statistic. But we had become two separate people, living separate lives, and I was self-aware enough to know that, for me, my happiness needed to come first. There was no infidelity, as there often is in these situations, but I decided I needed to move on. Daniel was disappointed, to say the least. While I grappled between his needs and my own, I knew I had to follow my heart's calling. This was my first major leap into the unknown.

Of course, I second-guessed myself—had I made the right decision? Was this another failure on my part to maintain a healthy, growing partnership? What would people think? After all, I'd had a number of previous failed relationships, though they had, thankfully, not involved the complications of marriage. When my mind would tell me I had failed, I would tell myself that the marriage had failed, that it takes two to tango. And, eventually, it sunk in.

The story of my divorce is far from unique. It's the story of thousands of couples around the world. Over the years, we become nothing more than roommates and discover we need more in our lives. Many people think that, because the issue is in their relationship, the pathway to happiness is to move on to a new one. Although it wasn't the case in my situation, too often, people move on without attending to the needs and feelings of those to whom they made a solemn commitment.

For years, I asked myself: *Did it need to turn out this way? Could there have been another way to rekindle the passion, interest, and intimacy of our marriage?* I didn't think the answer to that question was going to lead me to the path of becoming a sexpert, yet it's safe to expect the unexpected when you follow your heart.

Today, I am remarried and incredibly happy. This journey has taught me that when there are two willing partners, relationship challenges need not inevitably lead to divorce.

Discovering a Better Way

I'm a lifelong learner who's always been keen on self-improvement. Between my step-father's influence and that of my grandmother, who immigrated to the United States in the late '50s and poured herself into work so she could eventually bring her five daughters to her, I felt driven to improve myself and my circumstances. I read nearly every self-improvement book on the bestseller lists from the late '80s onward: the works of Dale Carnegie, Tony Robbins, and Jim Rohn... *The Secret, Chicken Soup for the Soul, The Celestine Prophecies, Women Who Love Too Much, Men Are from Mars*—you name it, I devoured it. I filled my schedule with personal development workshops and watched hours and hours of videos. I took up running, went back to school, and earned my degree in business administration.

Those habits, teachers, and resources carried me quite a ways, helping me succeed at work and eventually thrive as a single parent. I was feeling strong and productive, but I was still yearning for something more.

One day I received an email advertising something new to me: a tantra workshop. It promised new perspectives on human relationships and on sexuality in particular. Around this time, Sting was openly talking to the media about his relationship with his wife and the benefits of tantric practices. I was intrigued but a little nervous, since I really didn't know what to expect. Nevertheless, I signed up for a weekend seminar.

It was...not everything I'd hoped it would be. While that first one didn't hook me, I remained curious enough to sign up for a second, two weeks later. *That* workshop set me on a voyage of self-discovery.

My interest in sex-positive education took me to California once a month for several years to study sexuality, character structure, somatic practices, and personal energy, giving me valuable insights into my own character. I grew to understand myself in ways I never had before, coming into a deeper understanding of how and why I interacted with the world in the way I did—particularly with men. Through the theories I was studying, I began to experience how pleasure is tied to life satisfaction. Feeling sexy and sensual in my body, and knowing how to express that to others, gave me a more poised, self-assured outlook. I felt powerful—in some respects for the first time in my life.

Initially though, it was difficult for me to focus on bringing more pleasure to my body. I had to give myself permission to be human and to ignore the shame that society has often attached to self-exploration. With lots of patience and understanding, I learned that pleasure can bring happiness and contentment beyond a fleeting moment. Self-exploration is the path towards personal mastery; after all, what is personal mastery other than discovering and satisfying one's needs?

Courage

As I progressed, I kept telling my body: *I want to know you more. I want more pleasure in my life.* And the more I learned, the more I wanted to share what I was learning with others. Yet, I feared I would be judged and then rejected. Even though the survival of our species obviously depends on sex, as a society, we tend to gloss over it as a taboo, to be kept behind closed doors. If I talked about all of this, shared what I was learning, would people see me as some kind of sex-crazed degenerate? Would my friends abandon me? I struggled with it for a long while.

It took another leap of courage for me to begin to share my work. In all honesty, I did lose some people along the way, but many others flocked to me. More than a decade later, these areas of interest are becoming mainstream. I was just ahead of the curve. I'm glad I had the courage to pursue what, for me, was the right thing to do. My experience was profound, and the lessons I learned now form the core of my personal philosophy and the foundation of my work.

Here is what I now know to be true:

- Pleasure is our birthright.

- Sexual vitality is important to our well-being.

- Sexual performance is a skill that can be mastered.

- Sexual mastery is empowering, particularly for women.

- You can use sexual energy to heal yourself and your relationships and to achieve your personal goals.

- By understanding your needs and your sexual energy, you become a beacon for your personal destiny.

I loved learning to use this knowledge to become a more powerful woman. I began coordinating and teaching at tantric workshops and retreats. My newfound confidence and magnetism completely changed the dating game for me. Men went from talking about their golf game to awkwardly dropping their forks during dinner dates when I would start discussing my work—my passion. I explained that I taught sex-positive education and that I could teach men to provide heightened pleasure. They were mesmerized.

Then, in the midst of all of this, I realized, in order to most effectively teach others what I had learned and experienced, I needed more formal training. And, so, the next leg of my journey unfolded.

Advancing My Dream

With a dream of becoming a licensed clinical sex therapist, I embarked on a licensure program through the South Shore Sexual Health Center in Massachusetts, endorsed by the American Association of Sexual Educators, Counselors, and Therapists (AASECT). I wanted to work with men who were experiencing dysfunctions and with women who were experiencing difficulties during intercourse pre-, during, or particularly post-menopause.

I also wanted to work toward a graduate degree, so I began taking psychology courses at Harvard Extension School. One course in particular absolutely captured my fascination: positive psychology. Positive psychology is the scientific study of what drives happiness and enables us to lead a flourishing life. A relatively new discipline in the field of psychology, it is perhaps best known outside academia from *Flourish*, the bestselling book by Dr. Martin Seligman, a professor at the University of Pennsylvania. I was thrilled to combine positive psychology with sex-positive education!

Today, I fuse my passion and years of tantric studies with the application of positive psychology principles. In particular, I'm passionate about supporting our aging population in sustaining their pleasure and connection. Sixty is indeed the new 40. I truly believe that pleasure and happiness ought to be available to anyone, regardless of age. I've even coined the phrase "sassy centenarians."

While the manner in which we achieve our pleasure goals and pursue happiness changes over the years, happiness and pleasure are our birthrights. We all need sleep, food, and exercise...and healthy sexuality. When we rewire our brains to access deeper levels of pleasure in our bodies, we tap into a wealth of vitality, one of the tenets of a flourishing life.

At one point in my life, I didn't feel much pleasure in sexual intimacy. If I can learn how to embrace sexuality as a cornerstone of a happy, healthy life, anybody can. My goal is to make sure that people are sexually alive well into their elder years—after all, that's what I want for myself!

You Can Have It Too

I have four pieces of advice for those who want to experience a lifetime of pleasure, happiness, and fulfillment.

First, don't worry what people will think.

It's your life and your happiness. If you need to make changes that will bring you fulfillment and support your own flourishing, then make them. I'm not suggesting that you renege on commitments or vows that you have taken. Consider all your options before making far-reaching decisions. If you conclude that you need to take drastic action, and that is what is necessary to achieve your goals, then it's what you probably need to do. Just know that there are other paths to happiness, pleasure, and fulfillment. Give them a fair shot, but don't allow fear of someone else's opinions to prevent you from making the choices that are right for you.

Second, face your obstacles head on.

We all have challenges in our lives—some greater, some smaller. I've never been one to avoid conflict or tough decisions—ask my husband, he'll confirm that! Perhaps that's a by-product of having grown up on the streets of New York. Perhaps it was drilled into me by several years of military service. I don't know where it comes from, but I am grateful that I have the courage and determination to stand up to life's challenges and make the decisions that are best for me. And if I can do it, you can do it too!

Third, say "yes" to where your instincts guide you.

Be curious. See where your instincts take you, even if following them places you in an uncomfortable or unfamiliar setting. My first few tantra seminars were definitely uncomfortable, yet I was curious, and once the door was thrown open to this new and exciting place, I found it thrilling and rewarding. Tantra may not be your path, but everyone deserves something to be passionate about. Just follow your heart to see where it leads you. If the first door doesn't bring you joy and fulfillment, try another door. It's a journey about discovering your true self, and the path there is sometimes as important as the destination.

Lastly, pleasure is a goal, and you should not shy away from it.

Anyone can learn how to overcome their personal blocks to feel the full extent of pleasure. Pleasure is a positive, and sexual mastery is powerful. It's your birthright, so claim it. Embrace it. *Anyone* can become a master lover. Regardless of whether you are young or young at heart, pleasure and happiness are something to be attained, not just yearned for or reminisced about.

I sometimes wonder, given what I know now, whether Daniel and I could have found a path back to happiness and fulfillment. Of course, we can't turn back the clock. I'm not suggesting that I made a mistake in divorcing him. I expect many couples whose relationships have eroded—or even soured—who feel trapped with only one choice in front of them, could benefit from the lessons and insights I've gathered over the years. They deserve a chance to renew their love and to cherish one another once again.

After all, pleasure is cheaper than divorce.

Don't worry what people will think. It's your life and your happiness. Say "yes" to where your instincts guide you—be curious. And never forget that pleasure is a goal: embrace it! To learn more about working with Wanda Santos-Haynes email wanda@itscheaperthandivorce.com, visit her website positiverelationships.com or follow her on Instagram @cheaper_than_divorce.

Tweetable: Pleasure and happiness should be available to everyone, regardless of age or circumstance. How people achieve their pleasure goals and pursue happiness changes over the years, but both happiness and pleasure are our birthrights.

ROCKY MCKAY

A Lifetime of Learning Can Lead to a Lifetime of Success and a Lasting Legacy

Rocky McKay is the co-founder and CEO of Peak Care Assisted Living Homes. Since 2016, he has managed residential assisted living homes with the goal of leaving a legacy of setting new standards in senior care. He is an entrepreneur, mentor, real estate investor, consultant, and president of the Arizona Assisted Living Homes Association (2019-2021).

My Parents Gave Me a Dairy Cow

I grew up on a farm and ranch in a small town in southeastern Idaho. My parents taught my siblings and me how to be business owners at a young age. Instead of paying me, my parents gave me a dairy cow. From that one cow, I was able to get the profits from its milk and any calves it produced. The female calves it produced added to my weekly income from the milk profit. The male calves I would raise and sell for beef, and then I would take that profit and buy more cows. This kept recurring every year until I sold them to go to school. My parents encouraged me to go to school and get into a different field because ranching and farming were changing and making a living was getting harder and harder.

I went to school and learned about emergency power. Once I was out of school, I was offered a job and moved to Phoenix, Arizona. I worked in that field for 20 years. During this time, I learned about how to run a business, understanding profit and loss statements, balance sheets, and return on investments.

One of the best lessons was learning how to think critically to solve complex problems for our clients. We provided backup power to hospitals, so if the client was without power for an extended time, lives were on the line. We had to come up with creative and safe ways to get power back online in a quick manner. It was a great learning experience on how to look at the big picture and to explore every option. I learned quickly that it takes a team and I would never succeed by myself.

Do More

After going as far as I thought I could with the company, I kept having a nagging feeling I needed to do something more with my life. In 2015, I started to explore different things I could start doing while I was still working. My business partner was already investing in apartments, and she introduced me to *Rich Dad Poor*

Dad and the rest of the series. That led me to focus on real estate investing. I started to take seminars on how to invest in different classes of real estate.

Why VIP Was Worth It

I was still going to education events and networking with other individuals. During these events, senior living kept coming up in small private conversations. It was not a main topic, but everywhere I went, I could find someone that was talking about senior living. This really piqued my interest. Perhaps this was going to be a movement and it was just getting started. I thought to myself, *I need to learn more about senior living and find out how I can get into it.*

I started to research and came across an individual named Gene Guarino at The Real Estate Guys Secrets of Successful Syndication event during the first night's happy hour. He was going to talk about residential assisted living for seniors in a special breakout for the VIP group, which I was not part of. After sitting with him for almost two hours, I was even more excited about opportunities in senior living. The next morning, I went to the registration desk and asked if I could purchase a ticket to be part of the VIP group. They had a couple left, and I bought one for my partner and one for myself. That day ended up being a big turning point in my journey.

I went into the VIP lunch and sat down at a table. People started to come in and sit down everywhere. Then an individual, the author of multiple books I'd read, came in and sat down next to me. This individual was Kenny McElroy, a Rich Dad Advisor to Robert Kiyosaki. I was so excited to be able to talk to him about his journey and ask him questions. Kenny was so giving of his time to our table during lunch. We listened to Gene speak and tell us more about residential assisted living homes and the opportunity and need in the niche segment.

Kenny leaned over to me and said, "I just told Robert to come. He will be here in five minutes." Next thing I knew, Robert Kiyosaki was walking into our private luncheon, and he and Kenny just started to talk and educate everyone in the room. It was such a great experience that I never miss an opportunity to purchase VIP tickets anymore. You never know who you will meet and what you might learn.

Gene has an academy to teach residential assisted living. I got his information and started to research what it was. After researching residential assisted living, my partner and I signed up for his next three-day class, then started the process of creating our own residential assisted living home and business.

A Business Model to Serve Families

During our research of the market and competitors, we found out that we did not want to operate the same way they were operating. We could not get a fixed price on what it would cost to take care of my dad, who we were using as our example customer to gain information. When we asked for pricing, they each came back to us saying their price was dependent on the amount of care needed or desired, incontinence supplies, and a few other up charges.

We asked ourselves, How can a family budget? If the family could only spend four thousand dollars a month for three years, how much would these up charges take away from the three years? Would their family member have to move after they spent the money? We knew we had to come up with an answer to the budget question.

We also found the homes to be mostly older style and not wheelchair or walker-friendly. This was our driving factor. We had to set new standards on what we would want if our parents were living there.

We started looking at homes. During this time, we started interviewing contractors and explaining what we wanted to do. We found one that was great. He was even going on the tours with us and explaining what we would need to do or telling us if the house would not be able to meet our requirements. We all agreed upon one home that would meet our requirements with a major renovation.

With the home under contract, we started to put together a budget and drawings of what the house would look like. We made sure the home was ADA compliant with zero transition showers, wheelchair friendly bathrooms, and wide hallways. We were excited about how the home would look.

Make It Happen

We worked with a local bank that specialized in SBA loans and submitted everything they required. We were asking for a loan for the purchase of the home and tenant improvements (the remodel cost). It took four months working with the bank and SBA to get approved. One of the obstacles we came across was our lack of experience in this industry. When we went through the Residential Assisted Living Academy, we purchased their inner circle package so we would have access to them and so we could have them advise us through our journey. We asked them if they would be on our board of advisors, and they agreed to it.

With them on board, we updated our business plan to include them as our board of advisors and the bank agreed to it. With this off our list, the loan closed. The total time was just over four months.

Innovation and All-Inclusive Pricing

We were able to break ground in March of 2017, and the construction took six months to complete and another month to get licensed from the state. During this time, we came up with a solution to the question of how families can budget. We decided to do all-inclusive pricing that did not change with the level of care, including the incontinence supplies, and the majority of the other up charges. We had already planned our staffing, which made it so we did not have to charge more for the level of care, so we increased our prices a little to cover the cost of the additional charges.

We set our prices on the room size. The bigger the room, the more it would cost. We started working with placement agents to get the home filled and explaining how we are doing it differently both with the home and how we charge.

We Could Handle the Toughest Cases

Everyone was loving what we were offering, but we were still struggling to get the home filled. We did not yet have the experience that the placement agents and families wanted. We had hired a state-licensed manager and certified caregivers, and they were doing the work, but that was still not enough. We had to prove ourselves. We accomplished this by accepting residents who required the highest level of care.

We now have a reputation that we can handle almost any resident and provide the best care. We went into this to set new standards, and we have. We make sure our staff understands our mission statement: Care for our residents, as if they are our own family members, in our own homes.

This started out as us investing in senior living, but it has turned into so much more. We are being entrusted to take care of our most precious individuals who deserve to have their final days be some of their best days and to be respected. In each of our homes, we have a saying posted that a fellow friend and assisted living owner gave to me.

THE PEAK CARE TEAM WAY

WE TAKE INITIATIVE

We do what we say we are going to do.

We treat others how we want to be treated.

We are accountable, we own it, and we do our job.

We hunt for problems so we can deliver solutions.

We follow up and follow through. We do not complain.

We know that performance can be learned and behavior is a choice.

WE ARE RELENTLESS.

Relentlessly positive. Relentlessly ready. Relentlessly quick.

Everything, every interaction, every person matters.

Our work is our passion.

WE HAVE EMPATHY,

not egos. We are loyal and we are kind. We are patient.

We believe caring is giving, not taking.

We listen to respond, not just to reply. We are incredibly self-aware.

We love to give back because

we are part of something bigger than ourselves.

WE RESPECT

the residents, the families, the process, the brand, our team,

and the energetic spirit. We are honest and we are authentic.

We smile, we have fun, we reach our goals, and we provide

EXCELLENCE in senior living!

We have worked hard to live up to what is expected of us, and we have had to make changes along the way. I would not change anything about this journey. I have learned along the way and have even more passion for providing the best care possible to our loved ones.

My advice is to find something you are passionate about, surround yourself with people that encourage you, get mentors, and do not be afraid to change course when you need to. I have been extremely fortunate to have great people around me and people that I can call upon in my hard times. They have been through their own challenges, and they give me guidance and positive support while also keeping me in check.

I hope my story can help others on their journey to fulfill a purpose and serve as a reminder to always give back.

Rocky McKay would love to give back with the great fortune that he has had. If you are looking to learn how to invest in different avenues of senior living or if you need a consultant to help you start or manage your own assisted living, Rocky McKay would be privileged in helping you. Contact Rocky by email at rockymckay@peakcareliving.com and on Facebook as Rocky McKay.

Tweetable: Find something you are passionate about, surround yourself with people that encourage you, get mentors, and do not be afraid to change course when you need to.

KAREN NEWTON

One Door Has to Close Before Another Can Open

Karen Newton is founder of a global education company helping clients generate wealth through business, property, digital investments, and precious metals. She's the author of 21 books sold in 13 countries. Her philosophy is you can have anything you want in life. It starts by taking one small step.

My life was perfect, or at least I thought it was at the time. I lived in the perfect home in a perfect village. I had the perfect job and the perfect husband. Little did I realize, it would all change so quickly and drastically.

October in New Zealand is springtime. My husband and I had spent the winter months learning to ski, but now it was time to put the skis away and transition into my next passion, tennis. It was the 5th of October as I drove home from my banking job. I had started working with Eastern & Central Savings Bank within a couple of weeks of arriving in New Zealand. There were several promotions during my time there, and as a result, I was now a senior supervisor with the Stortford Lodge branch.

At the end of the day, I locked the door to the branch and started my drive home. I turned left out of the bank carpark onto the main road, then I was turning right onto the long straight road that would take me out into the country village of Havelock North where I lived when a white flash blinded me.

Three days later, I awoke in the hospital. My body was wracked with pain. My eyes not focusing properly, slowly I became aware of a police officer sitting at the foot of my bed. He started asking questions about what I remembered. All I could remember was the white flash. He filled in the blanks.

A white car had come speeding through a stop sign and we collided. The impact spun my car, which hit the white vehicle a second time. My car flipped, landing on the other side of the road where it was hit by another vehicle. Today, I still have no memory of the accident. I just remember the white flash and waking up in hospital.

Although my battered and broken body didn't think so at the time, I was very lucky that day. My usual car was in the garage being serviced and a friend had lent me his car—a little yellow mini that he used for motor racing. I had been strapped into a racing seat with a four-way harness and a roll cage protecting me. Although my life had been saved, the injuries were substantial and would have a major impact on the rest of my life.

There are two things I remember vividly during my hospital stay. First was the pain. It wasn't constant but rather would start as a tingle and build to a crescendo that put my body into spasms and then stop only to start again a few minutes later. Second, was the bright yellow bruising, a color I had never seen before, which took weeks to turn green before fading. That particularly stuck with me. As before I had only seen red and purple bruising, I didn't realize that deep internal bruising was yellow.

After three months in hospital, I was sent home in a wheelchair. The surgeons said I may be able to walk with walking sticks, but it was unlikely due to the problems with my right arm, which had very limited movement and couldn't grasp anything, let alone hold and support a walking stick. I would need to take drugs permanently for the neck pain, which was caused through the damage to what the surgeons referred to as the nerve junction box.

It did not go down well with the specialist when I refused to be on drugs permanently. He decided he would send the details to my GP, who would know what to prescribe when the pain became too much to handle—I never took them. I had a neck brace to support my head as my spinal damage meant I couldn't hold my head up on its own accord. My eyesight and speech, both affected through the nerve damage, would not improve according to the doctors. The government paid me a one-off disability payment, saying there was nothing more they could do for me. The payment was the end of their responsibility to help me recover. My perfect life had come to an end.

"There's nothing to be done," my GP said. "You'll have to accept this is your life now. You have to move on and start planning a future in a wheelchair."

It was now several weeks since I had left hospital, and I got the same response every week. This time I wasn't accepting it. I insisted there must be something that could be done to help me get my body working. My doctor's reply: "This is the telephone number for a psychiatrist. He'll help you deal with being in a wheelchair."

I sat in the psychiatrist's room answering his questions. He asked, "Why did you agree to come here?"

"Because I want you to go back to my GP and tell him I can walk with the right support," I retorted.

I continued answering his questions when finally, he asked if I would come back again the following week. I agreed.

The following week, I was extremely nervous, worrying. *What if this was it. I might be in this chair for life*, when the psychiatrist started talking about his brother-in-law:

"He's a doctor who specializes in sporting injuries. Would you be happy to see him?"

"Yes," I replied. "I'm happy to try anything."

"I thought you might. He's in the next room waiting to see you."

The next day I was back in hospital for surgery. My journey to learn to walk again was just starting.

A team of people was assembled with the sole focus that I would walk again. The doctor was head of the team, together with a physiotherapist, a Feldenkrais practitioner, and my husband. There were several more surgeries and physiotherapy to help rebuild the muscles because after months in a wheelchair, there was horrific muscle wastage. Feldenkrais helped to create new neural pathways between my brain and limbs. The surgeon told my husband that I needed specific treatment three or four times a day, and he taught my husband how to do those treatments.

My day started as soon as I woke up, and for five minutes every hour, there were exercises and treatments continuously until I went to sleep at night. This became my daily routine. Just five minutes every hour.

Was this plain sailing? No. I had good days where I made progress and bad days where everything seemed to grind to a halt and even go backward. I was often frustrated because what I had done the day before now couldn't be done. *Patience* was the word repeated over and over. "You just have to be patient. Let the body adjust. It's working hard and needs a rest," the surgeon would say.

There were times when being patient didn't work and a new strategy was needed. Eventually, though, I got to the stage where I looked for the setbacks because I knew a change of strategy would often see me take a huge leap forward in progress.

Imagine a young child learning to walk for the first time. The parent walks backward holding their arms out, ready to catch the child when they fall and help them back up again. Only, I wasn't a child, I was an adult, and the person walking backwards ready to catch me was my husband. It had taken around four months to get my legs to the stage where I could get my feet flat on the ground so my legs would support me and I could try to walk. There were tears running down mine and my husband's faces when I managed to put two steps together before falling. Those two steps felt like I had walked a mile, but they were two steps, which generated so much hope, belief, pride, and joy.

Those emotions were soon replaced with frustration when my legs refused to work for a couple of days after those first two steps. Try as I might, my legs would not work. A change of strategy didn't help, and a couple of weeks later, I was back in for more surgery, after which the progress can only be described as a miracle. The wheelchair became a thing of the past, quickly replaced with crutches, then one walking stick, and 19 months after the car crash, I was walking unaided.

There was just one problem. I couldn't get up or down steps.

Walking on the flat was one thing, but when slopes were involved, or even worse, steps, my legs just collapsed under the strain of trying to support body weight while bent. A new plan was put together which involved spending five minutes every hour stepping on and off an A4 sheet of paper. Gradually, that became a piece of cardboard, a wooden plank, and a Reebok Step, until almost 12 months later, I could walk up or down average size steps unaided. Today, high steps are still a problem. Luckily, there are few of those.

My banking job became a casualty of the changes taking place, and the door closed on my perfect job. Banking is a job which requires a person to handle different stress levels throughout the day. I was unable to adjust to those levels of stress anymore. I seemed to be operating at maximum stress levels in my recovery. There was just no room for more, so I had to resign. The focus had to be one hundred percent on me and my recovery, or there wouldn't have been a recovery.

I have been blessed to have incredible parents who taught me I could do or be anything I wanted to be. My mother always told me not to let anyone tell me I couldn't do something. My father always said there is no such word as can't, only that you don't want to do something or you don't know how to do it. If you don't want to do it, get off your backside and go do it. If you don't know how to do something, then find someone who does and learn from them. These were incredible lessons that helped me keep motivated to walk. When I was told I wouldn't walk, I persisted until I found the right people to work with to achieve my goal of walking.

My husband is also an incredible person who has the same ethos as my parents. When he accompanied me to see doctors, it was always "Why are we doing this?" and "What is the expected result?" He would even question, "Why do it this way?" if he thought something else might work. He was as determined as me that I would walk again. Between us, there was never any doubt allowed to creep in. There was only the focus to master one process in my recovery and then move on to the next.

The accident shut many doors in what I thought was my perfect life. As those doors closed, other doors opened—doors I would never have previously considered. I became self-employed, building several businesses. Through one of those businesses, I made history by becoming the first woman to own a fire protection company in New Zealand, and later the first woman to chair the Fire Protection Industry Contractors Association. I learned how to become an investor and later developed an investing strategy that allowed me to build sufficient wealth within four years so I was able to retire at the age of 43.

I then started writing books about investing, which led to a man stopping me in the street to ask if I was the author of the book he was holding and if I would coach him. That, in turn, led me to build my current global business. I teach clients how to create wealth and build a dream lifestyle using the lessons I gained through learning to walk: patience, persistence, and taking lots of little steps every day to build my dream future.

Next time a door slams shut, move your focus to where the next door will be opening and the incredible journey the new door has to offer. It might just lead you to what you are meant to be doing. It could be your legacy.

Your journey to achieving whatever you desire in life starts by taking one small step.

Connect with Karen Newton and take your first step to financial freedom and living your dream lifestyle at www.facebook.com/karennewtoninternational or https://karennewton.co.uk

Tweetable: Your journey to achieving whatever you desire in life starts by taking one small step.

PANCHAM GUPTA AND RAJAN GUPTA

Solving the Investment Problem for High-Paid Tech Professionals

Pancham Gupta and Rajan Gupta are first-generation Indian immigrants who worked in the financial technology industry for 14 years and now are full-time multi-family syndicators. Through their company, Mesos Capital LLC, they provide investment opportunities to high-paid professionals outside of Wall Street.

So-Called Success

"I'm making plenty of money in NYC, but where is it all going? How come I am running around all day like a chicken with its head cut off with not much to show?"

That is what I used to think during April tax time every year. In 2011, I was working at a financial technology (FinTech) company in NYC with a handsome salary. I was flying business class, staying in nice hotels, managing exciting projects, and leading an incredible team of people. Life was good. Everyone thought that I, or anyone in my position, had made it.

However, when tax time came each April, I would start reflecting on the past year and evaluating how I did. I would realize how hard I had been working to make that high salary, all the sacrifices I was making to achieve the so-called success.

Trading Time for Dollars

I grew up in India in a middle class, small business family. As a kid, my parents made sure that I went to a good school and had access to a good education. I was very good with math and science, so I chose to become an engineer. After graduating with my bachelor's in computer engineering, I came to Carnegie Mellon in Pittsburgh to pursue my master's in 2003. I had the entrepreneurial genes of my dad. At the time, I thought I would get some work experience in the US and then move back to India to start a business of my own. However, right after graduating from CMU, I started working for a big financial technology company in New York City as a computer programmer. I started making a six-figure salary, and every year that salary grew.

But as successful as I was, every day felt like a grind. As soon as I woke up, I had a list of items for myself. I got ready for the office, got the kids ready for school, commuted, worked 8-10 hours, commuted back home, and by the time I was done with my dinner, I hardly had time or energy to do anything. This did not include the time I spent running around taking the kids to classes, working out, or spending time with friends or my wife.

Knowing this was unsustainable, I started educating myself on how I could make money work for me so I could spend more time on the things I care about. As part of the education process, I started reading books, and I came across *Cashflow Quadrant* by Robert Kiyosaki.

That book really opened my eyes to the fact that the 90% of people on the left side of the quadrant control only 10% of the wealth and they trade hours for dollars. However, the other 10% of the people on the right side of the quadrant control 90% of the wealth and have their money work hard for them. The book discusses how employees and self-employed people on the left side of the quadrant pay the highest taxes, and business owners and investors on the right side of the quadrant pay the least taxes. That was when I decided to move to the right side of the quadrant, start investing, and have my money work for me.

Learning to actively invest in asset classes available to accredited investors felt like an overwhelmingly big mountain to climb. Since we are limited in our exposure and not taught investing in school, most of us know the stock market as the only investing opportunity. If you want to create another stream of income by actively or passively investing outside of Wall Street, you really have to spend a lot of time and energy to learn how.

After all this rigorous hard work, and after acquiring investments and the risk that comes with them, my tax situation still looked bad. Like most high-paid professionals, I had a huge tax bill. It was my biggest expense. As Robert Kiyosaki says, "It's not what you make, it's what you keep." If you look at your income and all taxes—income tax, social security tax, medicare tax, sales tax, property tax, mortgage tax—you have paid about 50% of your income in taxes. Given that I was already feeling so overwhelmed with my work and family life, I consistently felt that I was falling behind and that there was no one to guide me in my investing strategy. I had learned and grown a lot, but I was still in the grind.

Rajan and Pancham

A few years later, my good friend and colleague Rajan and I were having coffee and talking about this exact problem. We had both been diversifying our investments outside of Wall Street for a number of years. Rajan was heavily focused on the local real estate market in New Jersey, whereas I expanded into five different states.

As our discussion progressed, we shared the same sentiment. We really felt the need to find a solution to this problem that all high-paid professionals like us face. All the high-paid professionals we knew made a good salary but did not have the knowledge, time, or motivation to learn about different asset classes.

Rajan has a background in computer science and a long, successful career in FinTech, spanning multiple asset classes and products. He has been very successful in solving this problem for himself and his family. Rajan discovered that he could effectively reduce his tax burden by investing in real estate with tax-efficient, positive cash flow streams.

Rajan spent a lot of time learning about different asset classes within real estate. Over the years, he invested in a wide variety of real estate, from small condos to mixed-use commercial buildings. His investments were generating 20% or greater return on his investment and creating multiple passive income streams for him. At this point, he had a deep understanding of a wide variety of investment options in and outside of Wall Street.

Rajan and I discussed how investing really could solve our tax problem. Since then, we've been proving it to others like us. We decided we should team up to solve the investment problem for high-paid professionals.

Friends in Tech

Most of our friends work in the tech industry, and the tech sector has been booming for the last two decades. Many have their incomes tied to the stock of their employer via a large amount of stock options they receive as compensation. Now, this part is very scary. It is great to have a lot of company stock when your company is doing well, but this can be fatal when a company goes down.

I personally saw this play out at a previous employer. When I interned at Lehman Brothers in 2004, a lot of my colleagues who had worked there for decades had the majority of their 401K tied to Lehman Brothers stock, and on top of that, they had a lot of stock options. When Lehman Brothers went down during the 2008 financial crisis, not only had my colleagues lost their high paying jobs in the middle of a deep recession but also they had most of their life savings wiped in a matter of weeks!

Rajan and I see many of our friends potentially facing a similar outcome. Whatever diversification they have outside of their company's stock is in the also vulnerable stock market, and most of these investments are tax-inefficient.

Inception of Mesos Capital

Rajan and I started brainstorming ideas for how we could teach our friends and family about diversification outside of Wall Street and, for those interested, how we could help them achieve this with purely passive and tax-efficient vehicles. With this vision, Mesos Capital was born.

At Mesos Capital, we help high-paid professionals diversify outside of Wall Street investments. Rajan and I have a mission to optimize investing by making it easy for people to invest passively in tax-efficient investments. Being tech geeks, we named it after Apache Mesos software, which optimizes the use of computer resources across the cloud. We thrive to replicate the same success with the allocation of capital.

Since the creation of Mesos Capital in 2017, we have been able to help many of our friends and family diversify their investments into tax-efficient, cash flowing, multi-family real estate. We have worked diligently over the last three years to build relationships in multiple high-growth markets, set processes, and build teams to find the right investment opportunities and manage them efficiently. These opportunities are completely passive for our investors and provide benefits like income, tax-benefits, depreciation, equity, and the leverage of owning real estate.

We have successfully deployed over $20M of investor capital and have over $60M in assets under management. We have gone full-cycle on two syndications with an average 27% internal rate of return (IRR) and recently completed a large refinance. Additionally, as we have diversified our own portfolios into real estate, we have diversified our risk, lowered our tax burdens, and increased our freedom to spend our time how we choose.

Mentors

We would not have been able to do this without the help of our mentors. In the last four years, we have spent a lot of money to spend valuable time with and learn from the experts in the industry.

Being engineers, we have this tendency to figure out things ourselves. However, we soon realized that it's not about whether you can do it or not, it is about how quickly and efficiently you can do it! It is all about compressing the time-frames.

Challenges

It's not been all rosy. We have had many challenges that we had to overcome, and we are still working on many on a regular basis. As we embarked on this journey, we had to build a track record. We had never worked with investors or managed money. It was difficult to be confident in our ability to find interested investors and build a strong investor base. It was a classic chicken and egg problem: we didn't know whether to chase the money or the deal first. We knew that we could buy a $10M building and manage it effectively. However, having an investment with no investors or vice versa would not have been an ideal start. It took us almost two years to oil the machinery and become confident to find opportunities and investors when needed.

Moving from being employees to entrepreneurs was not easy, especially in this business because we are responsible for managing large investments for others. We have to constantly think and tune our approach as we both set processes to efficiently scale and stay prudent at the same time. The fruit of success is sweet, but it comes after a lot of hard work and patience. There are new challenges and lots to learn in every project. It is never a straight line to the exit.

Many residential multi-family projects have taken a serious hit with the COVID-19 pandemic lockdowns and the resulting job losses. That presented us with its own unique challenges.

Every challenge is an opportunity to learn, build trust in your abilities, and build a stronger bond with everyone you work with. These challenges have made us better investors, syndicators, and partners. We have grown into our roles, and we continue to do so as we do more and more deals. Our bigger vision is to improve lives through real estate and create an environment of success and freedom at Mesos Capital. Our mission is to focus on creating win-win opportunities for high-paid busy professionals so that they can design the life they want, for our employees to have a mission-oriented place to work in, and for our residents who can call our communities their home.

To contact Pancham Gupta and Rajan Gupta about their story, please email: pancham.gupta@ mesoscapital.com, rajan.gupta@mesoscapital.com.

You can subscribe to Mesos Capital newsletter by going to www.mesoscapital.com/ subscribe and learn more by listening to The Gold Collar Investor podcast (www.TheGoldCollarInvestor.com) wherever you listen to podcasts.

 Tweetable: As engineers, we have a tendency to figure things out for ourselves. However, we realized it's not about whether you can do it or not. When it comes to living your ideal life, it is about how quickly you can do it!

BRANDY VEGA

They Said I Couldn't

How I Landed a TV Reporting Job at 20 and Built a World Class Media Studio

Brandy Vega, owner of Vega Media Studios and the non-profit Good Deed Revolution, is a media and video production expert with over 25 years of experience. She's an award-winning news anchor, reporter, and Army Veteran broadcast journalist and public affairs specialist. She loves helping businesses grow through marketing, video production, virtual events, live-streaming, podcasts, TV, film, coaching, and more!

Desperate Measures

I was desperate. I was hungry. I had to find a way to get money! One of my earliest memories is going door to door at about five or six years old, asking if I could help with housework, yard work, or even scooping poop. We were poor. My single mom worked two and sometimes three minimum wage jobs to pay rent and cover some necessities. My dad wasn't around much. There were days when all my sister and I had to eat was a spoonful of peanut butter or a school lunch. I remember eating ice cubes as a treat, and if we were really lucky, we'd add Kool-Aid and make our own popsicles. We didn't know how poor we really were.

Being poor forces you to do things you may have never considered. It forces you to be creative. I started my own retail business shortly after kindergarten, a pet rock shop. I sold custom painted rocks on the corner of a busy street for $.50-$1.00. I even glued googly eyes on them. When I saw a return on my investment, my eyes were opened, and I've been hustling ever since.

I babysat, walked dogs, made dongle keychains, and anything else to make a buck. It became like a game to see what I could do and how much I could earn and save. This came in handy because around 12 years old, I became acutely aware of my teeth. I had a big gap between my two front teeth, and I was ashamed to smile or talk to a lot of people. We were poor, so I lied about my age to get a job as a maid at a motel so I could save money and buy my own braces. I worked all summer cleaning nasty motel rooms and saved up enough for a down payment on my teeth! That was the best money I ever spent. That's when I found my smile, which would soon give me the confidence to pursue my dream.

Finding My Passion

A few years prior, when I was around 10 years old, I was watching the news and thought, *That looks like a fun job. They get to tell stories, look pretty, and be on TV! What's better than that?!* That's when I decided, no matter what, I wanted to be a TV news reporter. I started watching the news regularly and dreaming about working in broadcasting. I didn't know what my career path would look like, but I was determined. I started writing for the school newspaper in junior high and high school, eventually taking broadcast classes in which I got to shoot, edit, and produce. In my senior year, I was anchoring the morning announcements.

Making TV History at Just 20!

Throughout high school, I worked as a waitress because I loved making money every day. While my buddies made minimum wage, I averaged about $20 an hour and learned how to talk to people! The nicer I was, the more I made. My senior year, I got an unexpected phone call from the Marine Corp asking what I wanted to do with my life, and without hesitation, I told them I was going to be a TV news reporter. As a spontaneous, open-minded girl, I jumped at the opportunity when they said, "We pay you, train you, and you'll be reporting in about a year." I ended up joining the Army Reserve as a broadcast journalist and public affairs specialist at only 17 years old! I graduated six months early and left for bootcamp, which was a million dollar experience I wouldn't give you two cents to do again. Even so, while I was in the Army, I got to interview President George W. Bush, Colin Powell, Donald Rumsfeld, Condoleezza Rice, and many others. I also dodged death when terrorists tried to shoot down my helicopter September 12th, 2001 while I was deployed to the Balkans.

When I got back from bootcamp and my advanced individual training in 1996, I immediately wanted to get a job at a TV station in Salt Lake City, a pretty large TV market. Everyone told me I was crazy and would never get hired.

I chose not to listen. After all, I wouldn't have a chance if I didn't at least try. To my surprise, I was hired by a FOX Affiliate. I was just 18 years old.

I was hired as a studio operator. I ran camera, ran teleprompter, ripped scripts, rolled tapes, and then volunteered to edit stories, run audio, and start technical directing. It was an amazing opportunity, and the more my supervisors saw my initiative, the more opportunity I was given.

A year later, I wanted to move to Phoenix, an even bigger market. Again, everyone told me there was no way I would get hired in a market that big. I was even told by my coworkers, "Don't waste your time." But, again, that's not how my brain is wired.

I always thought, *Why not me? What do I have to lose? All they can say is no, and if you don't ask, the answer is always no.* One of my favorite quotes is, "You miss 100% of the shots you don't take." So, of course, I applied anyway. I sent my resume to all five TV stations in Phoenix, and I was offered a job at three stations. I took a job at the number one station in the market!

I loved it. I was hired as a satellite coordinator and electronic news gathering chief at just 19 years old. I worked 2-11pm, and then I volunteered my time for the overnight shift to work on reporting and field producing. After about a year of that, I landed my dream job as a reporter for a FOX affiliate in South Dakota at just 20 years old. I was the youngest reporter they'd ever hired!

The people who are afraid to try are the same ones who tell you not to try. They are often the ones who settle for mediocrity because they fear trying! They are the same ones who tell you to think small and don't like to see you succeed. All my dreams came true because I didn't listen to the naysayers who told me I would never get hired and to not even try.

Imposter Syndrome, Realizing I Had Made It

Despite my success at 20 years old, I was still poor. I was living on a $17,000 a year salary, shopping at the thrift store, and eating ramen noodles. Those who think TV pays well are wrong, unless you're the main anchor in a top 10 market!

My whole life, I pushed myself, I tried and thought big. I achieved so much, but it wasn't enough. I think one thing that aided in my success was being humble. I always maintained a side hustle and didn't mind doing whatever it took to get the job done. Just because I was an anchor didn't mean I minded helping with other positions, carrying equipment, or taking out the trash.

It wasn't until I was 40 years old that I finally felt like I had made it. All of those years, I tried and pushed forward but never felt like I had quite arrived. I felt inferior and like a failure in many ways. Like many others, I suffered from imposter syndrome.

Finally, in 2018, Hyrum Smith, one of my heroes, a friend, a world-renowned speaker, and a founder of Franklin Covey, told me I was one of the most incredible humans he'd met in the last decade.

That was one of the most unbelievably wonderful compliments I ever received. I sat in my office in the beautiful video production studio I had just built and cried tears of joy. I had finally made it, and I made it while being single with three kids. I had a 16 and an 11 year old and a one year old baby I adopted from foster care who'd been born addicted to meth. And the kicker, on that day

I was also about five months pregnant with a baby girl! I was a surrogate for a family in need.

In 2015, I had launched a non-profit called Good Deed Revolution, and I had spent the past few years doing my best to help those in need. I knew what poverty looked like. I knew what it was like to be cold, hungry, lonely, and scared. I knew that God had blessed me in so many ways. He blessed me with drive and determination. He blessed me with health. And my mantra is, "Because I have been given much, I too must give."

By the end of 2018, I had made more money that year running my own company than I had made in the previous 20 years combined. I had nothing left to prove. I had put everything on the line. I put my heart and soul into building a business many said would fail. In fact, a so-called friend told me what an idiot I was to build a studio and that he hated to see me waste my time and money on something that would never work. I couldn't believe my friend thought I was stupid for following my dream, the dream I had at ten years old to tell stories, which had evolved into building Vega Media Studios. Those words haunted me, and I knew that I had to prove him wrong.

Around the same time Hyrum Smith gave me that compliment, my friend came to my studio, apologized, and congratulated me on the studio's success.

Sharing Success

With the studio's success, I've had the opportunity to help many other business owners realize their goals, crush sales, build their brand, and make a difference. I've been able to coach them on how to deal with the media, speak on camera, plus launch successful marketing and advertising campaigns. I wasn't born with a silver spoon. I had to find a shovel and start digging!

Often, I didn't even have a box to think outside of. I had to build a box, shovel all of the bad advice and burdens I'd been given into that lousy box, and then bury it. Once you bury the stuff that holds you back, you see a clean patch of land, giving you an opportunity to cultivate it.

If you look at things the same way everyone looks at them, or the same way you've always looked at them, things will never change. You've got to have eyes to see what needs to change, ears to hear the truths and silence the doubts, hands to do the dirty work, a heart to carry you through the ups and downs, and feet to move you in the right direction. You can't ask God to guide your footsteps if you aren't willing to move your feet. You'll find once you start doing this, not only will your business skyrocket, but also others will flock to you to see how you did it.

After working with me for just one year, a client of mine increased their social media presence and saw their sales nearly double with a 40 percent increase in revenue! I was able to look at their business through my eyes, analyzing it with a different perspective than big companies who only focus on numbers, programs, and analytics. What I saw allowed them to spend significantly less on marketing and advertising. By taking a guerrilla-style approach, we far surpassed their goals. I love what I do and how I am able to help other folks succeed through media, marketing, and advertising. I'm living the dream in every way!

Life Is What's Given, Opportunity Is What's Taken

I've always been the underdog. I've always had to work hard and believe in myself even when others doubted me. Looking back on my life and experiences, I understand that many people may have bought my pet rocks or let me clean up after their canines because they felt sorry for me, but they also saw that I was willing to do whatever it took. I was never too cool or proud. I knew I was no better than anyone else. I also learned a few other valuable lessons about treating people right, about encouraging them, believing in them, serving them, and telling them to try.

If we shoot for the moon, we'll land among the stars. We will always miss 100% of the shots we don't take. We will regret the things we didn't do, often more than the things we did do. My fight to the top keeps me humble and successful. It's the little things. It's the struggle. After all, life is what's given. We don't get to choose our birthright, sex, skin tone, geographic location, parents, or other circumstances. But we do get to choose what we do with what we are given. Life is what's given, opportunity is what we take. Take yours!

Brandy Vega owns www.vegamediastudios.com as well as www.gooddeedrevolution.org. She is a media and video production expert, coach, and speaker offering a range of services to companies worldwide. Contact her for a free consultation at 801-637-5416 or email her at Brandylvega@gmail.com

Tweetable: Life is what's given, opportunity is what's taken. You've got to have eyes to see truth, ears to hear the good and silence the bad, hands to work, a heart to believe, and feet to move you. Don't ask God to guide your footsteps if you aren't willing to move your feet.

DR. LEE NEWTON

Music, Optometry, and Real Estate Development: The Trifecta of My Life Passions

Dr. Lee Newton is an optometrist and real estate developer. His experiences have allowed him to help others build, develop, and invest profitably in commercial real estate.

A Road Less Traveled

I have always loved to learn because a product of learning is growth.

An insatiable desire for acquiring and applying new information and skills has prevented me from accepting that we were meant to do one and only one thing in life. I have intentionally ignored the tired mantra "go to school, get an education, get a job, make a comfortable living, save money, retire, and live frugally." I never thought that advice applied to me.

Though I enjoyed playing the saxophone, I chose eye care as a profession due to my interest in science and health care and because most career opportunities for saxophonists involved teaching—and I only wanted to perform. I had many great experiences collaborating with talented musicians, and I still love to play. Some of my fondest memories include meeting and associating with tremendously accomplished and Grammy award-winning musicians such as Bruce Hornsby and Branford Marsalis and performing at the Hard Rock Café in Las Vegas and Times Square.

A few years into my career, I became interested in real estate. This was a logical consequence of owning my office building, home, and other commercial and investment real estate. By owning real estate, I developed a working knowledge of construction and building science—the physiology of how buildings work. Building science was fitting given my background. I remember the event that stimulated my interest: after having a new roof installed, I had noticed an intermittent drip of water. Not wanting to draw inaccurate conclusions (the roofer was well-respected in the community and a friend), I asked him to help me determine the source of the drip. "Do you see that metal flashing up above?" he asked as we looked above the ceiling. "The warm, moist air from the office is hitting it, and moisture is condensing and dripping down." Building science told us that an imperfect air barrier was the culprit, not an imperfect roof.

I occasionally receive strange looks when my interests and activities are not totally aligned with societal expectations. In one instance, the words from my friend's social media message hit me like a slap in the face:

> "Your Facebook profile shows optometry at the bottom of your list.... Those who don't know you well will think you are unfocused on your real profession."

I couldn't help but think:

> *First of all, my patients generally aren't Facebook friends with me. And I don't believe I have any choice in determining the order of attributes on that platform. Finally, who is to say that I can't do more than one thing well?*

> *Is it the same voice inside of us that tells us that someone with more than one focus is, therefore, unfocused?*

"Jack of all trades, master of none" refers to a person superficially competent in many areas rather than proficient in one. Many grew up in an era where learning, polishing, and practicing one skill was the norm.

But times are changing. Les Brown, a prominent motivational speaker, has stated, "You have to develop at least three core competencies." In other words, we don't have complete control over our segment of the economy. Some industries that seemed infallible as recently as a decade ago are becoming obsolete. Having multiple skills and abilities allows one to pivot when necessary.

When I moved my eye care practice into a new facility and later expanded that facility to accommodate new tenants, I was the project's general contractor. These experiences taught me powerful lessons. Later, as general contractor, I put up an 8,600 square foot office building with two other investors. Blessed with talented and trustworthy subcontractors, I didn't have to babysit the job. I could work in my practice and check on the job status at the beginning and end of each day.

Experience Leads to More Opportunities

After finishing this build, I was approached by Ashley and Rob—owners of a medical practice—looking to expand their treatment facility. The building I had recently completed had 3,000 square feet available for lease. However, the vacant suite was barely larger than their present facility, and at their current rate of growth, I feared we could complete a build-out and find it obsolete within six months.

I was chairman of our local DDA (Downtown Development Authority, a quasi-governmental entity that collects tax revenue and uses it to entice economic development). Our DDA had stimulated economic growth by purchasing vacant commercial land and giving the land away in exchange for constructing a building on it. Everyone wins: the building owner receives the land free, and the local municipalities see their property tax revenue increase forever. It really was a beautiful mechanism for progress and development in the community.

As chairman, I had a fiduciary responsibility to act in the DDA's best interest. The DDA only had one vacant lot remaining, and I attempted to interest Ashley and Rob in this property. New construction was more attractive than rehabbing an old, tired building with outdated mechanicals and insulation levels from energy codes of decades past. They were enthusiastic about the opportunity and decided to construct their new facility on the DDA's last remaining parcel.

It was an exciting time for them because they could envision their hard work and practice growth leading to a brand new facility of their own design. The layout would be optimal for patient flow, and the finishes would be entirely their choice. Further, they could design the facility for future expansion.

They chose a reputable design-build firm and obtained architectural renderings. Satisfied with the footprint and aesthetic, they ordered a complete set of construction documents. Unfortunately, when the project was bid, they realized that the cost exceeded their budget by more than $1 million. Attempts at downsizing and value engineering did not help reach their target cost. To say they were devastated when they realized their contractor could not perform within their budget was an understatement! They had spent money on construction documents for an office that would never be built.

Architects are an invaluable resource and an indispensable part of a design-build team. I've learned through experience that architects are never anxious to start with their second-best design. They strive to impress you with the virtually unlimited possibilities of the design process. That's their job. And some, unfortunately, want to design a testament to their own ability. I believe the problem was the contractor failing to clearly articulate the budget. But the owners had asked for a functional new building for their business, nothing more.

Knowing that they weren't likely to reach an agreeable budgetary number with their contractor, Ashley and Rob asked me to construct their new office. The request was very flattering. I knew I had to keep things moving for the DDA, and I also wanted to help them as much as possible—especially since I had recently constructed a building at a cost that was well within their budget. But they were asking the DDA chairman to get paid to build their facility when the DDA was providing the land, and I could not imagine a larger conflict of interest.

I relayed all the facts to the DDA. Since I had not actively sought this work, the DDA and its attorney felt that my involvement was in the best interest of the community and we were granted permission to move forward.

The savings were immediate. As opposed to starting over with construction drawings, we were able to hire my engineer to simply modify the structural prints of my previous build to suit their needs for the new construction.

Value engineering is about saving money without compromising function. I have found that almost every area of the construction process can be value engineered: the layout of the build on the property, the footprint of the building, the foundation, the framing, the superstructure, the rooflines, windows, doors, the wall and roof assemblies, the interior layout, all the mechanicals (plumbing, electrical, heating/cooling) as well as where they are placed, the modularity of interior wall construction, the ceiling height and layout, and the finishes.

The initial construction documents proposed a building design with a footprint shaped like a cross, with eight outside corners and four inside corners. By changing the design to a rectangle and altering the rooflines to add visual interest, we experienced savings in materials and labor during every step of the construction process. As an added bonus, the final design had a much smaller heating and cooling load, meaning lower utility bills for the life of the structure.

We engaged many of the same tradespeople who had helped with my earlier building. Additionally, I was able to leverage the time and talents of two of my real estate partners, Matt and Doug, to oversee this build, as I had my own health care practice to run. Other than some minor challenges with soil quality, we finished the project on time, during a pandemic, and saved about $1 million compared to the first bid.

Reflections

Why are societal expectations considered "norms"? Why isn't it considered normal to follow where our passions lead? Why do we place limits on ourselves? Should I worry about what others think if they know that their eye doctor put up that new office building?

I have learned not to dwell on the cognitive dissonance of thoughts such as these. I continue to enjoy my primary occupation after 20 years of practice growth. I truly enjoy interacting with and treating some of the most sincere people who need medical eye care or vision care. With the help of my wife, I started a charity providing eye health care and vision correction to those with needs but without means. By financial metrics, my practice is thriving. But dollars are only marks on the scorecard of one's passion, drive, and skill; they shouldn't be a source of motivation. If I were not successful in my primary occupation, I would not have developed the connections that provided opportunities such as this.

I realized that I was able to help Ashley and Rob solve their construction problem not because of my own innate abilities, but because others had previously brought value to me. Mitzi, who serves on the hospital board with me (and was their landlord), referred them to me because she trusted me to act in their best interest. Ed, my friend and commercial banker, helped me secure financing early in my career to move my practice to a better location so I could reach my full potential. Fred, my late friend and architect, taught me much about building design and construction management. Even more importantly, he taught me that one of the most important things in life is to help others.

By leveraging lessons learned from building science, value engineering, and many real estate development projects, I am able to help other health care providers save money on designing and building their new facilities. I am frequently asked to lecture on building science topics such as indoor air quality. And I enjoy donating time and resources toward developing affordable housing for the homeless population.

Never underestimate your ability to redefine the limits of your comfort zone and accomplish something remarkable. By looking for opportunities to help others, you can solve problems, experience incredible personal growth, and change lives.

Dr. Lee Newton maintains a successful optometry practice while building, developing, and syndicating real estate. He is an expert in building science, value engineering, indoor air quality, and affordable housing. Learn about opportunities for connecting and consulting by emailing Lee@DrLeeNewton.com.

Tweetable: Learning, polishing, and practicing one skill was the norm, but times are changing. Industries that seemed infallible are becoming obsolete. Developing multiple skills and abilities provides the versatility to pivot when necessary.

ROBERT HELMS

Becoming the Next Best Version of You

Robert Helms is a professional real estate investor and host of nationally syndicated radio show and one of the most downloaded podcasts in real estate The Real Estate Guys™ Radio Show, *now in its 25th year of broadcast and heard in more than 190 countries. Robert's investment and development companies have past and current projects valued at $800+ million in nine states and six countries. As a real estate agent, Robert ranked in the top 1% of sales in the world's largest real estate organization.*

Getting Around Good Ideas

There's nothing more important than your development as a person. The first time I sat in a room with Jim Rohn changed my life. A great way to develop yourself is to immerse yourself in good ideas. You get around good ideas and they take hold.

When you're getting around people that have earned the right to have an opinion, even if you don't agree, you'll have the chance to grow. It can be the most powerful thing to listen to someone else's path and how they've figured things out for themselves. I think, in personal development, when it comes to finding out who you are, you recognize pretty quickly that you don't have it all figured out, which is why you have to get around other people and their great ideas.

Then, try those ideas for yourself. Sometimes an idea leads to massive positive results in your life. And sometimes, something that works for somebody else doesn't work for you. Okay. Then, try something else.

Types of Investors Listening to Our Show

We're blessed with the most amazing listeners! Many of the people who listen to The Real Estate Guys have busy lives. They do something they love and are learning to invest on the side. They're not full-time investors—they want an income property portfolio that doesn't run their whole life.

Then we have the folks that are professionals—real estate attorneys, brokers, and property and fund managers. They tune in to keep the pulse on what's going on and what opinion makers are talking about.

Finally, a big part of our audience is next level investors. These folks got serious about real estate and eventually deployed all of their resources. An investor's ability to apply for loans is not infinite. The natural evolution beyond investing in your own account is to put deals together through real estate syndication, where you're utilizing the efforts of lots of people to do bigger deals. Some people put up the money, some people put in relationships, some people put in the research and the expertise, and you put together a plan that allows everybody to achieve more.

Syndication answers a need in the marketplace for the busy professional to invest passively, get exposure to multiple types of real estate and multiple markets, but not have to do all the work while still retaining many of the tax benefits. Passive investors in syndication also get exposure to deals they couldn't otherwise do.

Learning from Our Failures

If you go through something terrible and it makes you a better person for doing it, then mission accomplished. Too many people don't want to pay attention to their mistakes. They think mistakes are bad when mistakes are actually the way we learn. If I invest money with someone, I want to make sure they've been through the wringer. I want to hear the horror stories and what they did to get through. I want someone who's seen battle and lived to tell.

Things that happen to you aren't necessarily good or bad. It's the lesson you learn that matters. Because when you are faced with decisions, regardless of the outcome, you become stronger. It's not that people that are dedicated to personal development have perfect, happy, wonderful lives. It's that we try to get the lesson when something goes wrong and become a little better as a result.

Lots of real estate investors were burned in 2008. Some never invested in real estate again. Others went through that ugliness, but did not wallow in it and used it to propel themselves forward. When something goes wrong, whatever it is, see if you can pause, set the emotion aside, and get the lesson because that's the thing you've paid for.

Whatever happens to you isn't you. When something goes bad, that doesn't make you bad. It's just something you stepped in. If I step in something yucky, I just need to wash it off, be disgusted for a minute, and plan to be more careful in the future. But I don't take it on as an identity.

It's true on the positive side too. When you have success, it's really easy to believe your own press. You can rest on your laurels and say, "Well, I'm done now. I don't need to keep pushing. I'm good." Instead, I recommend the opposite. Every time you have success, allow it to drive you to be better and to do more. That's how you develop. You don't need to make sure you make every decision correctly and do everything right. Rather, recognize that we're all a bundle of good and bad, and we want to take in all of it, learn from it, and make the future better than the past. You are a work-in-progress.

If you know what you want to accomplish, you know all kinds of things are going to happen on the way there. But that's what drives you. Personal development is so important because you must get in touch with who you are and know the goals you have in life. Whether yours are monetary goals, relationship goals, health goals, spiritual goals, or any other goal, you have the ability to drive towards something that's bigger than you.

Learning from My Father – Bob Helms, The Godfather of Real Estate

I always tell people that my dad taught me everything I know about real estate but not quite everything he knew. Bob was amazing. He got the real estate bug early on, and his passion created abundance for our family. When my mom got sick with cancer, one of the greatest assets we had was a portfolio of real estate. We could spend time with her and not have to worry about making ends meet.

Bob had a genuine love of people. I remember going with him to listing appointments. I had a mentor who taught me to get in and get out: get the listing, get the key, and go because that's dollar productive behavior. And then my dad and I would go out to talk to a couple about listing their fourplex, and he would go for four hours just talking, asking questions, and noticing things on the walls in their home. It wasn't a sales technique. He just loved people. In those four hours, people were falling in love with dad, and that was the most dollar productive behavior we had because, then, they weren't just people selling their house, they were clients. And many of them, of course, went on to become friends.

When he got to the point when he didn't need to sell real estate anymore, he got just as excited watching the lights come on for other people. When he was 80 years old, he set a goal to write a book. To be 80 and have a new goal is pretty awesome. And then to do the work. He worked so hard on that book. When he passed away, I was so grateful he finished and published *Be in the Top 1%: A Real Estate Agent's Guide to Getting Rich in the Investment Property Niche*. He wanted that so much, not because he wanted to be a bestselling author, but because he wanted to share his ideas with a group of people he cared about. His strong belief was, if you're going to be a real estate agent, you better learn to be your own best client and invest in the very product that you sell.

Dad left an amazing legacy, and it started when he was a young man. You don't leave a legacy at the end of your life. You create a legacy as you go. He lived such a good life. He made such a difference to people and made everyone he met feel special. That is how you help make the world better.

Bringing Value

The great thing about bringing value is it happens at every level. It doesn't have to be a massive thing. When someone gives you one little idea and you take action on it, that's huge value. Still, some people provide tons of value—your mentors and role models, people that speak into your life regularly, in your spiritual life, in your personal development life, and in your business. A lot of times we're influenced by people that bring value by just sharing education.

I believe everyone that enters our lives leaves us a little bit better or a little bit worse. Intentionally approach each relationship asking yourself how you can improve it. How can I have a positive impact? If I inspire somebody to do, have, or be more because they can relate to me and my story, that's the value.

Solving Problems

Many people want to avoid problems. They hate problems. I take the exact opposite approach. I had a mentor early on who was one of the top 10 real estate agents in all of Century 21. He used to say, "When you come back to the office after lunch, you better hope that in your inbox is a huge pile of problems because you get paid to solve problems."

As business people, we can't exist without problems. If someone doesn't have a problem in their life, then there's not a whole lot they need our help with. Jim Rohn would say, "Don't wish it were easier. Wish you were better." You don't want to wish that you have no problems. You want to be the person that can conquer bigger and bigger problems.

Early on in our business, we gave everybody the same title. We didn't have director or vice-president. Everybody was a Solutionist™—a person that looks for solutions, which is a little different than a person that solves problems.

I'm big into solving problems. It's like a puzzle. I get joy out of it. A problem is a challenge. That's all it is. Challenges are not a bad thing. They're a good thing if you approach them the right way. Be the person that can solve the biggest problems. Be the person that can find the best solutions.

That's really the essence of investing. The problem most people have is they want more money. They need to put their money to work. Real estate becomes a solution for that. In real estate, there's better money to be made the bigger the problem is.

We want the things that aren't necessarily easy. Take the example of the classic fixer upper. If the house needs paint and carpet, almost anybody can figure that out, so it's not worth as much to solve that problem. If the property has major foundation issues, a zoning problem, or it's functionally obsolete, you get paid more to solve those kinds of problems.

If you figure out how to bring value to the marketplace, you get a reputation for being a fixer. When that happens, watch out because you're going to be in demand. People will start coming to you with their problems, and you'll have a never-ending stream of business.

Leaving a Legacy

We live our lives on a pretty superficial level most of the time. We don't give ourselves the opportunity to really go deep. One of the silver linings of COVID-19 for many has been the opportunity to spend more introspective time. Legacy starts at figuring out who you want to be when you grow up and then designing a life that you want to live. You figure out who you are at your core and all the things that you'd love to have, see, do, and become, and then chart a path to get there.

I think written goals are a driving system to propel you towards the things in your life that you've decided are important to you. Some of those things are monetary, but a lot of them aren't. Why not have a life that when you're done, you go, "Man, that was awesome." And it wasn't accidentally awesome. You set out to make it awesome.

And yet, where are we trained to do this? School doesn't teach us that. Your parents probably didn't teach you that. To me, the whole idea of leaving a legacy is deciding in advance who you will be when you're done. And then how do you become the next best version of you?

People talk about being the best version of you. My actual belief is that there's not really a best version of any person. My belief is that we're all constantly improving and getting better. We refine ourselves based on the good and bad things that happen. They all chip away to create the masterpiece that becomes us. At the beginning of this year, at our annual Goals Retreat, I challenged everyone to begin working on the next best version of them. What's next for you? What's the next iteration of what your life's going to be? Every year is different. You continue to evolve, and you make changes and decisions based on where you've been and then based on what you want. That's why goal setting is so powerful. For me, goal setting is more than writing it down and reviewing it every morning. You've got to figure out who you are, where you're going in your life, what matters to you, and what you stand for.

That's how you leave a legacy. One person at a time, one change at a time, one idea at a time. It's a big concept to think about. How can you make a lasting impact after you're gone? So, start now. While you're still here.

Robert Helms is co-author of Equity Happens. *Robert's annual* Create Your Future *goals retreat provides a blueprint for achievement in life. Listen to The Real Estate Guys™ Radio Show at www.RealEstateGuysRadio.com. To learn about The Real Estate Guys™ programs, email SuccessHabits@realestateguysradio.com.*

Tweetable: You don't leave a legacy at the end of your life. You create a legacy as you go. One person at a time, one change at a time, one idea at a time.

MARK LIVINGSTON

From Conflict and Failure to Corporate Executive and Real Estate Syndicator

Mark Livingston is a corporate executive and CPA who has built successful teams in various industries and currently leads finance teams in three states and three countries. Mark uses 35+ years of experience to create profitable investment strategies with real estate and natural resource projects.

Crisis

On July 20, 2011, I sat in my living room, thinking about my life. How did I get here? I had just finalized my divorce from my wife of 25 years and moved to my own house to live by myself for the first time ever; my children would only be there part-time. I was 48 years old.

My teenage children would soon be in college. My ex-wife and I had done a terrible job of saving for retirement. I wasn't thinking of retiring yet, but it would be nice to do that in 15-20 years, and my savings were definitely not on the right path for that to happen, let alone pay for college.

Additionally, I was getting pretty bored with my job. I was successful in my career by most standards. I loved the company I worked for and the people I worked with. But it felt like I had no more challenges. I wanted to be more valuable to my company and to do something new.

These were not the challenges I expected to be dealing with at age 48. I should have been on the right path to retire in my 60s, have money saved to pay for my kids' college, be at the top of my game in the corporate world, and enjoying what I did every day. But that wasn't so.

I felt like a failure in so many ways. There were so many things I was lacking. What I did have was a lot of people who relied upon me. And that was something that I could wrap my head around. I would build a new strategy for my life that I could be happy with.

My Background

I earned a degree at The University of Texas at Austin in 1985 specializing in accounting. I followed a very common path for accountants spending the first 15 years working my way up through a few companies, first auditing client companies and then auditing internally for my employers. I learned to help other managers develop processes to reduce the risks in their business. In this capacity, I felt like a partner to those in operations and finance to help our company be successful.

In 2001, I got the opportunity to lead my own department at a new company. A few short years later, I got the opportunity to join a much larger company's internal audit department. This was an interesting time in the US for corporate financial responsibility. There were accounting scandals at Enron, WorldCom, Tyco International, and others. As a result, Congress passed the Sarbanes-Oxley Act, adding significantly more regulations regarding how public companies accounted for their business and how they were audited.

This larger company I was joining had also made several material accounting errors that could have been misleading to investors and had recently changed their CEO and CFO. I took the job because I thought the company was at rock bottom and could only go up. I couldn't think of a better place to learn from all the wrongdoing and errors of others and bring value to a struggling company.

I spent two years helping this company get back on the right path. By the time I left, they had re-stated two years of financials and developed new processes and controls to prevent this from happening again. I don't think I could have been in a better place to learn during that period.

From 2004-2011, I followed more opportunities to lead and provide value to companies. By 2011, I had been through a lot and had accomplished a lot. But I started to find myself at a CRISIS. I had this feeling that if I stayed in internal audit for the rest of my career, it would just be like *Groundhog Day*. I would keep moving from company to company and doing the same thing for the next company that I did for the last company.

What I really wanted was to be even more valuable. My goal has always been to keep moving forward, do new things, learn new things, and provide more value to my company.

In November of 2011, I met two people that would have a huge influence in changing my life in positive ways and helping me solve my problems.

Finding Love Again

November 16, 2011, I met the person I would fall in love with and marry. We had been messaging each other online through Match.com for a couple of weeks and found many things in common from our pasts. She had a child very close to the age of mine. We previously had lived in the same neighborhood, only a couple streets apart. Our children attended the same pre-school, but a year apart. As a teenager, I lived near New Braunfels, Texas and spent a lot of time there with my friends. Her family had a house there and spent a lot of summers there as she grew up. I drove by that house numerous times while in high school. Yet we never met. Maybe it was serendipitous, but late 2011 must have been the "right" time.

On the evening of September 7, 2013, I asked Liz to marry me by proposing on the balcony of The Foundation Room in Las Vegas, which has a great view of the Strip. This had become one of our favorite spots in Las Vegas. We got married the next year and honeymooned on the Big Island of Hawaii.

Now, I have a partner again. She supports everything I want to do and is the rock of my family life and emotional well-being.

The Opportunity to Change

Also, in November 2011, I met someone who helped me make a huge change in the path of my career that has enabled me to accomplish my goals. In 2011, I got a new boss, and he quickly identified the CRISIS I was having in my job. He also realized that I had been valuable and would be a loss if I left. Within six months, he identified a position in the accounting department that would give me the opportunity to move my career in a new direction.

Moving from internal audit to accounting came with some challenges. In my 25+ years as a professional, I had never done any true accounting. In internal auditing, not only did I assess the accounting processes, but I also focused on the operational areas of the business. I had moved to the top in internal audit, but as part of accounting, I was back in the middle again.

Now, I was responsible for the SEC reporting of a public company and advising the company on applying accounting rules. There are a lot of gray areas and judgment calls in applying the accounting rules. But the job also required some strict attention to detail.

I struggled quite a bit. But my new manager was very supportive and gave me helpful feedback. After a few quarters, I settled in. I made improvements, including installing software that helped automate drafting and filing required documents with the SEC, and developed an advisory relationship with the rest of the accounting team. I stayed in this position for three years.

Opportunity to Be a Leader

In August 2015, I was offered the opportunity to be the Chief Accounting Officer and controller at another public company. This was why I moved out of internal audit. Now, I had the opportunity to be an executive officer at a public company and be valuable in a whole new way and at a higher level. As expected, there were a lot of new challenges. But I had been through similar challenges throughout my career. I had the confidence to believe in myself and meet these challenges head-on and create new value for the company.

After three years, the company was acquired. It was a new learning experience. I was working with the acquiring company to get the most value for our shareholders, knowing throughout the process that if we were successful, our positions as executives would be eliminated, along with most of the headquarters.

As 2019 began, I took a position with a new company, again as the Chief Accounting Officer. This is where I still work today. And again, there have been new challenges, including having accounting teams in several locations around the US as well as the UK and Germany. In 2019, I spent a lot of time traveling and getting to know the teams very well. Early in 2020, I felt very good about the culture that was developing. I was looking forward to continuing to make improvements in delivering better accounting information and being more efficient, including consolidating more processes and building more capabilities across the company.

In the Spring of 2020, COVID-19 changed everything. We could no longer travel or even work at our offices. We were forced to adapt very quickly. I knew we had to continue to communicate regularly, and everyone needed to know what everyone else was working on so that nothing would fall through the cracks. In the first month of working remotely, we had many daily group status calls to check in with each other.

I was very pleased with how well we worked together in this remote manner. I think the thing that got us through 2020 was that we had spent 2019 building a culture. We knew each other well, and this made communicating through the phone and video much easier.

Diversifying to Real Estate

In 2015, I had decided I would get serious about starting to invest in real estate and started executing my plan to develop multiple streams of income. I started by creating Match Real Estate Partners LLC. My company name had significant meaning to me. Match related to Match.com, where I met Liz. I also knew that I wanted to partner with other people who were experts in real estate investing. Matching appropriate skills with each other would bring the most value to a project and its stakeholders. The "partners" part reinforced that I fully expected to "partner" with other people.

I really love the multiple ways to create value with real estate. People always need physical spaces, whether it's a place to live or operate a business. Communities are improved when real estate is improved, making the community more desirable to live and work in. Finally, investors get profits from cash flow, appreciation, and tax benefits. These are win-win outcomes that help so many different stakeholders.

Currently, there are tailwinds creating strong demand for certain sectors of real estate, and most experienced real estate investors estimate that the opportunities to take advantage of those tailwinds will continue for years to come. I have already completed dozens of transactions and plan to continue adding to and diversifying my portfolio.

Because I have become educated about real estate, developed relationships, and started investing in real estate, I now feel much more certain that I will have strong cash flows to support my family for the rest of our lives.

Learning, Growing, Solving Problems, and Bringing Value

In the corporate world, I have learned to lead functions including accounting, cash management, strategic planning, reviewing legal agreements, and navigating through significant transactions. Now, with real estate, I had to learn sales and marketing as well. Without a strategic focus on sales and marketing, virtually no business can survive. I have studied the principles and tactics of marketing constantly and tried and failed on many initiatives. But I have learned that the faster I fail, the faster my business will grow. I firmly believe that trying and failing is the best and fastest way to learn.

When I started investing in real estate, I viewed it as similar to investing in stocks and mutual funds. However, I was more interested in putting my investing efforts into real estate. As I have refined how I invest in real estate, my education and background working on the financial side of corporations have led me to focus on the financial strategies of investing in real estate and all the financial ways to benefit from real estate investments. This includes creating multiple streams of income and using tax incentives to reduce the burden of income tax.

What I have learned over my career is applicable to any business venture, whether in the corporate world or real estate. We always have investors, customers, employees, and communities that we operate within. We have to understand what is valuable to all four of those stakeholders as well as the risks and problems to solve. When we understand the value, the risks, and the problems to be addressed, we can design and build the appropriate teams, processes, and systems to solve those problems and deliver value.

I strive to be approachable, listen, and respond effectively to achieve "win-win" results for all parties. I value open and honest communication with my investors, customers, and employees. I have learned to take responsibility for everything I can influence by continually anticipating problems and risks and developing ways to improve and innovate so that we can continue to be valuable for our customers, employees, and investors.

Leaving a Legacy

In my corporate position, I want to leave a legacy in the people I work with. I want people to know who their true customers are, develop open and effective relationships, communicate openly and honestly, and continuously make improvements to effectively serve their customers.

My goal in my real estate business is to educate people that through investing in real estate we can improve housing for people, create facilities for businesses, and improve communities. While doing this, the investor can also benefit from multiple streams of income and legally reduce their tax burden. This is not generally how most people are taught to invest, but I find it more gratifying and profitable.

Finally, I have a huge goal to create a charitable foundation where I can direct profits from my investments to improve the lives of less fortunate people.

I think any problem can be solved if you bring the right people together to work as a team with respect, honesty, and open communication. And by all means, *just do the right thing.*

Email Mark Livingston at Mark@MarkLivingston.me. Ask him how he handles being a corporate executive and running a real estate business.

Visit MarkLivingston.me for events Mark Livingston attends, podcast interviews, or to schedule a call with him. Visit MatchRealEstatePartners.com to see where Mark invests.

Tweetable: Be open with honest communication. Understand your customers, employees, and investors. Always Do the Right Thing!

VANESSA CANEVARO
I Am NOT Ordinary!

Vanessa Canevaro is a mindset coach, the founder of The Dream Big Life, and a John Maxwell coach, speaker, and trainer based in Canada. She is the author of three books, I Want a Dragon, Zero the Superhero, *and* Of Lions and Lambs, *and co-author of a bestselling book titled* Still Beautiful.

The Damage of Chocolate Pudding

I never really understood how powerful my words were until I actually started to listen to my husband.

For years, he would talk about the power of thoughts and how thoughts become things. What I heard: "Wa wa wa wa wa!" What he was actually saying: "Vanessa, pull your head out of your butt and pay attention to what you're saying about yourself!"

I get it now!

I remember, as a kid, sneaking a large bowl of chocolate pudding from the refrigerator and stealing away to the mechanical room in our basement to hide in the corner between the furnace and the wall so I could eat it.

I recall my delight as I ate spoonful after spoonful of the cool, rich goodness. I found pure bliss in the dusty darkness of my furnace hideaway. But soon, the euphoria of the moment started to fade to be replaced with damning guilt and the realization of how bad I had been for gorging myself. I was a bad girl—a fat, dumb girl with a dirty food-stealing secret.

I buried that empty bowl at the bottom of my toybox and hoped my mom wouldn't figure out it was me who had taken it.

The fact that I remember that day so vividly is proof of how an insignificant event can have an impact on self-worth.

Bullied as a Kid

As a kid growing up, I was shy, respectful, and unsure, qualities that I would cling to my whole life. My need for comfort, reassurance, and protection I fulfilled with food, and those moments when I would gorge on something I knew I shouldn't eat were moments of pure pleasure. But, after that feeling of elation subsided, a dark presence hung over me and the tears of self-loathing would overflow, tears that would leave scars on my memories.

I was an insecure kid who was bullied at school. The bus ride each morning was time to strategically plan how I would try to avoid those bullies and their stabbing words of ugliness that tore at my gut. The taste and feel of food delighted me, and I used that false happiness as a temporary shield to block the sting of their painful words.

At the time, I had no idea why I was hiding food or why I felt so badly about doing it. As a kid, you don't think about why you do anything. You just do it and face the good or bad consequences later. My mom never mentioned the chocolate pudding, but I hated myself for eating it.

Hard Lessons to Learn

I was a single mom when I met my husband. Tony is the exact opposite of me. Where I was insecure, he was self-assured. Where I'd focus on the negative, he'd shine the positive. Where I'd falter, he'd lift me. We're like the dynamic duo of push and pull. He taught me that it's okay to want something more.

To say we were financially set would be a lie. When we were first married, we owned a gas-service station. Two 22-year-old kids owning a business we knew nothing about and using money borrowed from our parents to do it, what could possibly go wrong? Three years later, because the environmental rules surrounding in-ground fuel tanks had changed, the company we leased the business from decided not to update the tanks. You can't have a gas station without gas. We filed for bankruptcy. We struggled so badly that when my parents would visit, I would fill margarine containers with water and put them in the refrigerator so my mom would think we had food.

That same year, my father passed away after a long battle with his health. The day he died, a representative from the power company was at our door with a notice to turn off our power because of unpaid bills. It was a very bad day.

We managed to keep the lights on and then relocated to another province with a company Tony was working for. That relocation changed my perspective on the possibilities open to us. We bought a brand-new home and were happily comfortable, but there were limits to what we could earn, and we both wanted something more. We ventured into business again, this time with a partner.

The construction rental business went well for a few years. Then, in 2008, the recession hit. At the same time, an under-construction commercial building we owned and were planning to flip came to completion, but we couldn't sell it because of the economic downturn. Our business partner pulled out of our business; the business closed. Because the business closed, we went into arrears on the payments for our commercial building; we lost the building. Because we didn't have money to pay for our home's mortgage, we lost our home.

I felt defeated and like a failure. We were building a future and a stable home for our family and somehow permitted it all to crumble by making decisions that were dependent on conditions not within our control. We weren't willing to let that happen again.

The Birth of a Dream

Becoming an author had been a life-long dream of mine, and after my father died, I started submitting my children's stories to publishing companies. Back then, manuscripts had to be printed and physically mailed for a publisher to receive them. I did get a few handwritten responses back and was thrilled to read the editor's suggestions. I can't tell you how many submissions I sent before finally receiving a response from a publisher wanting to sign me to a six-book deal. I was overjoyed. Five months later, that publishing company went bankrupt.

Out of frustration and with a whole lot of coaxing from my husband, I started my own publishing company. I was indie when indie publishing wasn't cool. I published two books on my own. I was living my dream but felt guilty, because to me, it meant that I wasn't good enough to be an actual published author. I felt I had cheated the process. I thought everyone would know I was an imposter posing as an author.

There's a reason publishing companies only commit to publishing a few books each year. It's a huge investment without a guarantee of return. Each year, thousands of fantastic stories remain untold because of cost.

I understood how powerful it was taking on my own project by hiring an editor, hiring an illustrator, and seeing it through to print. I knew I had done something most authors at that time would never have considered trying, taking on a financial risk because of a dream. My quirky little books were engaging and sold well. I was profitable.

I Went Through the Change

It was a weird series of wins and losses, and my fragile confidence cracked. Because of the financial crashes surrounding the businesses, I began to question every decision we made, replaying circumstances leading up to and after each event. I became afraid of making the same mistakes over and over again and wanted to avoid running towards my dreams. Fear can play tricks on rational judgment and logical thinking, whether it's fearing failure or success.

My need to dream bigger and control our destiny propelled me forward. I dove into personal development like it was a life preserver I was desperately clinging to. John Maxwell, Jim Rohn, Ed Foreman, Les Brown, and Zig Ziglar became my best friends, and they moved me to the next level—loving myself.

I would never have guessed that my love for personal development, my curiosity about how the mind works, and my finally understanding who I was would lead me into building a successful home-based business with a team in six countries, a six-figure income, and the opportunity to speak on stages all over Canada.

I discovered I wasn't the only one having secret, sabotaging self-talk. I embraced the struggles I had as a kid and the financial hardships we had faced as a family. I love sharing the lessons I have learned with people wanting more from their life and business. No one needs to feel alone without the right voice cheering them on. We're all here to help each other along. We're all in this life together.

around the country

At the beginning of each year, I create my big audacious goals list. It's a list of things I've always wanted to accomplish. Every day I do something that will bring me closer to achieving one of those goals, and eventually, it pays off. I have been in a commercial, been a voice actor, become a bestselling author, started a podcast, and moved into our dream home.

Every morning at 5:00, I get to hang out with my "best friends" by reading at least one chapter of personal development gold. Then I spend an hour writing so I can share what I've learned and then plan out my goals for the day.

Each night before I close my eyes, I review everything I am grateful for that happened that day, and I fall asleep with a full and happy heart because I know I am winning.

I Am a Rock Star

Okay, I'm not really a rock star, but I can sing-ish and do own a few killer outfits. Where I do rock is in my ability to understand other people's limitations and thought processes surrounding failures, because I have had wonderful successes and a few massive un-successes along my journey. Over the years, I have come to understand that you can change your direction at any time. Life has no map, only a bunch of squiggly paths leading to an epic ending.

As Jim Rohn said, "If you're not willing to risk the unusual, you will have to settle for the ordinary."

I am NOT ordinary!

To connect with Vanessa Canevaro about her books, podcast, blog, and coaching, visit www.thedreambiglife.com and www.vanessacanevaro.com.
Email vanessa@vanessacanevaro.com
Facebook: https://www.facebook.com/vanessa. canevaro https://www.facebook.com/thedreambiglife,
Instagram: @vanessacanevaro

Tweetable: Over the years, I have come to understand that you can change your direction at any time. Life has no map, only a bunch of squiggly paths leading to an epic ending.

PAUL ARAGON

From Prison to Profit

Running a Multimillion Dollar Award-Winning Company

Paul Aragon overcame the odds and now runs a multimillion-dollar, award-winning company he started from nothing. Paul started his construction career once he earned his GED, religious education degrees, and a degree in machine technology while incarcerated. Paul is a man of integrity, striving for excellence and to make a difference in the lives of everyone he meets.

Negative Role Models

Growing up in a broken home and around alcohol early in my life and looking for love, acceptance, and affirmation, I turned to the wrong people, which led me to a life that spun out of control.

My friends and I had discovered beer and marijuana and stole some from their dad. I was the youngest in my family and had three older sisters who had older boyfriends that soon allowed me to drink and smoke marijuana with and around them. I was only 11-12 years old. They were involved with gangs and sold drugs, so I thought I was cool because I got to hang out with them.

I soon became one of the drug dealers at our school after being taught in middle school how to do all those things. Then, the rest of my schoolmates would buy marijuana from me, and that soon moved to other things and I dropped out of school because I was chasing money.

I finally was caught smoking marijuana and drinking underage and got arrested for it. I had to do diversion classes and lost my driver's license. Then I was caught another time driving in possession of marijuana and drinking as a minor.

Rap Sheet

By the time I was sixteen, it had gone from marijuana to cocaine, ecstasy, you name it, we could get it for you. I would be in bars, and they allowed me to drink underage because people would stay at the bar and drink. The owners knew what we were doing but did not mind 'cause they were making money by us selling our products to people at the bar. I soon got addicted to drinking, partying, fast money, and girls. I thought I was untouchable, carrying guns. People were scared of me and the people I hung around.

I would soon find out that those were all wrong choices and not to follow the crowd. I was making a lot of money, anywhere from 50-80K a month profit, but it soon caught up to me. Friends were getting jealous. And my girlfriend's family was buying from me. I was 21 years old and she was 16. I was arrested for possession of a controlled substance and other charges. We were under investigation by North Metro Task Force.

I went to jail and had a bond reduction hearing. The judge lowered my bond, and I was out in three days, then back doing the same thing. I still did not learn my lesson.

God and My Son Changed My Life

During all this, my mom had turned her life to God after a head-on car collision, and she tried to reach me. She would always try to talk to me about Jesus, but I would treat her badly. But she continued to love me. She would always say, "I am praying for you, and I love you."

I was back at it, at the bars and partying and facing time. I just didn't care. Then my sister's husband and his brothers were arrested. Actually, they were set up and robbed, so the sheriff's office said they must be doing something. There was a deeper investigation. I kept going on my own until my friends finally told on me. They called the police. I was drinking and driving and was caught with large amounts of money and cocaine in my possession.

I was back in jail, and now my charges were aggravated because I was not sentenced on the first case with drugs, racketeering, organized crime, and kidnapping. Plus, people were telling, and it was looking bad. I was facing 25 to life in prison.

That is when I realized my girlfriend had given birth to our son. I was not going to be an alcoholic, womanizing, drug dealer. I didn't want that life. I didn't want to be like my dad in and out of jail and work release programs. I looked around at where I was, and I told myself this is not for me. I didn't want that for my life and said there has got to be more than this!

So, I started to work out and got healthy after my withdrawal from alcohol. It was cold sweats at night and shaking when I would wake up from not having any alcohol. I was so used to it in my body.

I finally got through it and started to get my GED and attend prayer meetings, church services, and Bible studies, and I gave my life to Jesus Christ. I prayed: *Lord, if you exist, help me to change. Bring my family back together, let me see my son, and help me get married to my girlfriend, make things right, leave a legacy, and change my family tree forever!*

Sure enough, my girlfriend and my son came to see me. After my visit, I went back to my cell and was screaming, "God answered my prayers. God is real!"

People in the cellblock were mocking me, but I didn't care. Ever since then, I have committed my life to Christ.

I was attending a prayer group in our pod/cell block, and the guy leading it was getting out. He told me he saw the passion inside me and that I was to take over and lead the prayer meetings. I said, "I cannot. I am new and need to learn." I finally decided to lead it because others in the group said God was teaching me so much, and I was memorizing scripture and growing in my faith very quickly. I started sharing Bible studies and leading prayer and had a desire to become a pastor.

Another Setback

My charges were lessened, some were dropped, and the amount of time I received changed. It seemed like there was a change of heart in the prosecuting attorney and the judge. Things started to turn around for me, and I was denied probation, but community corrections (which is a halfway house) accepted me, so that is where I was sentenced.

I proposed to the mother of my son as soon as I was released. At that time, my girlfriend, soon to be wife, got the modified order from the judge for us to see each other, but the halfway house counselor would not accept it. But that didn't stop us. We continued to see each other and later realized we should have waited. I was caught. The girl that worked at the halfway house front desk saw my fiancé pick me up when I was walking down the road and had the sheriffs follow my fiancé after dropping me off to find out it was her.

And then, one day, they called a lockdown, and they called me down, and the sheriffs were there to take me to jail. We were not supposed to be seeing each other. My sentence was no longer a halfway house sentence that was six years but four would have been suspended if I had completed two years in the program successfully. I would have been done, but now I had to appear in front of the judge.

He told me last time that if he was to see me in his courtroom again, I was going to get the full six years DOC—and that is what I got sentenced to. I had got my fiancé pregnant again, now with our daughter, and I had to serve time. The good thing is I did get time credited for the time I was in jail and at the halfway house, and then we got more good time in prison than in county jail, so I only ended up serving under three years. During that time, I earned a janitorial certificate, an associate's in machine technology, and four religious education degrees, and I read a lot and got really fit.

It Was a National Scam

I was released and was paroled homeless. Once again, the odds were stacked against me. I found a church that my fiancé started to attend, and a pastor started to mentor me. I got flagger and asbestos certified and found a job doing asbestos removal. I did as many programs as I could that could help me stay out and find a good job that could potentially turn into a career.

I had to work at a metal fabrication plant because the asbestos company had to lay us off. Then I met a guy in church, but he was playing the part. He had a bunch of the church brothers working for him, but he was taking extremely long to pay us. Well, I did learn some things from him, including some roofing skills. I had done tear off before and screen repair, odd jobs, and some small paint jobs. But, I also learned how not to treat people and to never be dishonest with customers or employees.

This guy had me knocking on doors and setting appointments. Then I did really well, and we were supposed to be a sales team, but he wasn't paying me and taking draws towards the jobs. The office called me and told me they knew I was involved in the sale of these jobs because my signature was on a section of the contracts. I could not prove the jobs I did not get paid for because he was teaching me. So, I learned another lesson: get things in writing, fill out proper paperwork, ask questions, and know how you are getting paid. Then the company owner did the same thing, and we found out the company was part of a national scam that came from Florida then moved through Ohio, Kentucky, and Georgia to Colorado and Wyoming. He filed bankruptcy once again, shut down, and didn't pay many of us.

Starting a Million Dollar Company from Nothing

There were three other sales guys that had been burned by that company that started their own company. So, they reached out to me about working for them. But I was broke and had been burned for almost $50k. They helped me with gas and gave me leads, and there I was again, starting over.

I walked with a 13-foot, fold up ladder when I started out. I bought my first car, for both the business and my family, through the church's donation program, then eventually got better vehicles over time. Then the three gentlemen had a falling out and fought over money. The one gentleman who was left with hardly anything offered me co-ownership of the company, but I soon found out why the other two had left him.

I had already registered a business name for them to pay me as a subcontractor, so after the short-lived partnership, I decided to make a logo, get a website, claim online listings, and start out my business with the money that I had saved from working for the company and in that partnership. I paid my personal bills for a month and started my company with $5k and a dream to one day run a multimillion dollar company that would change people's perspective on contractors, all while I had no business degree and knew very little about business. I knew I had to start this on my own to be challenged, to grow, to learn, and to make the impact that I have always wanted to make. That is where I am today.

Nine years ago, I was successfully discharged from the Department of Corrections. I completed parole and became debt-free in 2018, paying off more than $106K in debt that my family and I accumulated trying to get a good credit score to buy a house. Once we paid that off, we bought our first home.

Now, I coach others to manage their money, live debt-free, and teach their families how to do things right, leaving behind a legacy that impacts lives and continues to echo even after they die. I have learned to persevere when things look dim and goals or dreams seem unreachable. Starting with very little kept me pushing for more, for myself, for my family, and for others like me in our community.

I would stay up at night working on my website, finding photos, trying to proofread on my own, claiming my business listings on free sites, reaching out to previous customers for referrals, handing out flyers, sponsoring schools and volunteering, networking with whomever I could, wearing all the hats and doing things by myself from sales, to production, service and collections, and marketing. There were times I felt like giving up but knew that to change the course of my family tree, I could not give in to the frustration and pain. I would tell my wife, "I hope this is worth it," but knew it would be one day.

When I was just starting out, driving cars that ladders wouldn't even fit on, using fold up ladders and shoving them in the trunk, doing what I could, I had goals to be featured in publications, to be mentioned by the Better Business Bureau, to win the Torch Award for ethics, to win best of business awards, and to make an impact in the community. That is all starting to happen for us now. It has taken time, but this is just the beginning. It has been four years since I started off on my own, and I would not change this path for anything. It has its ups and downs, but to be where I am from where I came from, I know the Lord has more in store for us.

I have learned to just keep pushing and good things are worth waiting for. I know the effect I have and will have on my family tree I may never fully see the fruit of. I look at my kids and other people who grew up like I did, or who just need encouragement, and I know it is all worth it. Even if I can touch one life with my story and encourage others to do the same, I have done my job!

To book roofing and exterior services, reach out to Paul Aragon and the Jireh 7 team by phone 720-429-9274 or email paularagon@jireh7enterprises.com. Website: www.jireh7enterprises.com.

Inspired by this story? Invite Paul to speak at a church event or to a group that can be impacted by this story by email at paularagon5@live.com

Tweetable: There is no such thing as an overnight success. There is blood, sweat, tears, and sleepless nights. If you want success, you must be willing to make the sacrifice. God never wastes pain and trials. He always will utilize them to bring freedom and healing in the lives of others.

KERRY FAIX
Grow and Scale Through Adversity

Kerry Faix is an entrepreneur, real estate investor, plus COO and founder of Stone Bay Holdings. With extensive experience in building companies from the ground up, she owns and operates a $150 million real estate portfolio. She is passionate about helping others achieve their dreams and build their businesses.

Successful Businesses Can Scale

Adversity is something every entrepreneur faces on a regular basis. The ones who succeed are those who learn how to harness that adversity and use it to grow and scale up their business. They look at obstacles as opportunities to learn rather than problems that are holding them back.

Throughout my career, I've worked for and owned multiple businesses, finding ways to grow and streamline each of them. Along the way, I've developed the ability to look at both the big picture and the incremental steps needed to get there. Being able to create and then execute that blueprint is the starting point for every successful entrepreneur.

My mission is to help other entrepreneurs avoid the pains and struggles I've experienced.

Overcoming Roadblocks Early On

I currently own and operate a $150 million real estate portfolio, but I started out as a data entry clerk without a college degree. I was working full-time while attending college part-time. I hit a glass ceiling at the company pretty quickly. There was a trifecta that kept me from breaking the glass: age, education, and gender. I desired more than what was being offered. Desire fueled me to overcome my fear and insecurity that I wasn't good enough. This obstacle was a blessing that led me to an equivalent management position at PNC Bank with a much larger staff and greater opportunities for growth.

Too many times, we hit roadblocks in life and freeze, but God used this to leverage me into a much better job at a much better company where I was valued and respected for my skills regardless of my gender or education level. We have to always be searching for another way in when a door is shut and believe that we have the power to make changes in our lives. If you find yourself stuck, believing you can't change your situation or feeling sorry for yourself, push through that quickly. The power is within you. Doing something is better than doing nothing and living life with regret and unfulfilled dreams.

While continuing to move up at PNC, my husband Will and I started a construction business and expanded our family, doing both in tandem until we had our third child. We then made the decision for me to leave my financially stable job, which we depended on for steady income and health benefits. At the time, it didn't make financial sense. That job supported our growing family, and it was a huge leap of faith to leave. We burned the boat and went all-in with our business.

I felt strongly that it was what God wanted me to do, even though it didn't make sense. Sometimes we know in our gut and our heart that a decision may not make sense to the outside world, but it is the right decision. It may be hard to follow through, especially when outside voices may be loudly discouraging you, but don't discount what you know in your heart to be true. Heed the advice of people you trust, but always follow the voice inside you. We had a growing family on a single, self-employed income. It was through these challenges that I grew and learned the most.

By pushing through the struggle, I continued to develop a strategic sense of problem-solving, and our business was able to flourish. We started taking on bigger jobs, becoming more profitable, and increasing our staff. Burning the boat gave us no other option but to push forward at full speed, and while it was challenging, it was also invigorating and exciting.

The Crash of 2008

I started flipping houses in 2006 with my husband, and I was thriving. I was starting to make progress and finding my groove. The first few deals went great, and it looked like my financial dreams were finally within reach. After so many years of struggling financially as a young family, it felt amazing to finally have money in the bank and to be doing fulfilling work for ourselves. Finding what you are passionate about is so critical. Living in your purpose and doing what fuels you is exciting and feels so much better than becoming stagnant in an unfulfilling career.

Like most entrepreneurs, I was all in, usually infusing all of our money into every deal in our flipping business. I had a gut feeling to put a little money aside in reserves, which I later realized was God preparing us for what was coming next. Always listen to the voice inside you! So, I put aside some money for a famine, not knowing it was right around the corner. This was challenging because, as entrepreneurs, again, we want to be all in and tend not to think about potential famines that could happen.

The crash of 2008 ravaged our construction business. All of our high-end work completely dried up, and that almost completely put our family under. If it weren't for that money we'd set aside, we would have lost our family home that we were raising four young children in.

While grappling with the fallout of the crash and the beginning of our next flip, my husband cut his thumb on a job site. There was a period of time we thought he might lose the thumb entirely. As a carpenter and the sole income source of our family at the time, the loss of his thumb would have been even more financially devastating for us. He was unable to work for several months during recovery, which made us burn through our savings even faster. We were going deep into a financial pit. God wanted to take us all the way to the bottom so that something stronger and better could emerge.

This was a dark and uncertain time. I knew and believed that it would somehow work out, and we never gave up. It was a milestone that defined where I am today. We need the struggle to grow as business owners. We need to face adversity. We need to learn how to problem solve and figure out how to make something beautiful out of a mess. I strongly encourage you to learn how to love the obstacles and appreciate them for how they help you. When you get knocked down, you don't have to stay there! You get back up stronger than you were before.

A typical entrepreneur is extremely passionate about their business and often lives by an all or nothing mentality. We lived that way for a long time, but the events of 2008 taught me that you can never have all your eggs in the same basket. It's hard to plan for the what if. Most entrepreneurs are more concerned with going to work and keeping things moving. But as we've seen with the COVID-19 crisis, there is always going to be something coming down the pike, and it will usually come unexpectedly. It's important to adjust your mindset from "what if" to planning for "when," because when you stay ready, you don't have to get ready. You may feel overwhelmed with the daily operations, but making time for strategic thinking is what is going to prepare you for when crisis strikes.

The Always Critical Pivot

Complete trust and faith in God saw us through the crash. I moved out of self-employment for the first time in over 12 years and took a job in operations at Partners for Payment Relief (PPR). This was the avenue I needed to take at the time, and through doing that, I met my current business partner Steve Lloyd, who was part of the pivot that brought me to where I am now.

It's difficult as an entrepreneur to go from running your own business to being a W-2 employee for someone else. I chose to see this obstacle as an opportunity instead of letting pride keep me from taking action. I found myself excited to be working alongside these four entrepreneurs helping them grow this new business.

Steve was also developing off-campus student housing at Temple University in Philadelphia, which had taken off. I left PPR to partner with him and form a new property management company to streamline the operations and growing business. We found a good niche in raising private money and developing real estate for student housing, a market that was actually thriving in the post '08 fallout.

Steve and I then took what we'd learned and founded Stone Bay Holdings. Stone Bay is an investment fund focused on a variety of undervalued real estate opportunities. We started the business from nothing, the two of us plus some part-time staff working out of Steve's basement. I built out the structure, systems, and processes of the business and staffed up to a fully operating, multimillion-dollar real estate fund.

One of our most notable deals was a 558-unit apartment building, Clifton Glen, that we purchased in Georgia for $27.5 million and sold a little over a year later for $41 million. This deal radically changed my business and my entire mentality. We need to constantly be thinking and dreaming bigger. If your goals don't overwhelm you, you're not dreaming big enough!

Our first hockey stick moment hit just a couple years after the inception of Stone Bay Holdings, prior to Clifton Glen. If you visualize a graph, a hockey stick moment is when you are growing steadily, and then all of a sudden, you go off the charts. I was constantly chasing to keep up with the growth. I've always thrived under pressure, and I think it's important as entrepreneurs to come to that place of loving and appreciating adversity. I realize that is really what has made me. I was regularly in the fire, and I had to figure it out. Not everyone has that passion, but I loved the experience. It really empowers you and excites you to be pushing through adversity and solving the problems in front of you. I've always been a firefighter, which helped me push through without getting bogged down. There was no time for exhaustion because every day brought new opportunities and challenges. I've learned the hard way that setting time aside to strategically plan better prepares you for unexpected growth and eventual crises.

I developed the mentality of taking one bite out of the elephant every day. You can't always solve a problem, fix a business, or dig out of a crisis in one quick fix. You chip away at it slowly and consistently, in manageable pieces. This keeps you from feeling overwhelmed and helps you see the steps to completion. I'd regularly find myself firefighting in my business, and I've learned to focus my energies and take it one step at a time.

If you find yourself struggling to get your mindset right in the midst of a crisis, change your state by putting on music, lighting a scented candle, or going for a walk. Write a short mission statement of your goal on a Post-it Note, put it around your home or office, and read it frequently. Self-motivation can only get you so far, so be sure that you have an accountability partner that you can trust and confide in. Having someone in your corner to help encourage you when the road is rough is invaluable. As much as I have learned to love adversity, I've always had a great support team encouraging me and cheering me along through the challenges I've faced. Keep people in your circle that see the best in you, cheer on your success, and pick you up when you fall.

The Basis for Scaling Your Business

One thing I've found to be crucial across every industry and business that I have managed is the importance of continually streamlining systems and processes. Without this solid foundation, it is incredibly difficult to grow and scale your business. You need that framework to sustain business at that level and really move up. It's become a passion of mine to help struggling entrepreneurs in this phase of their business, where they have an idea, dreams, and goals, but lack the knowledge or foresight to take the steps needed to achieve them. I meet entrepreneurs where they are stuck, in a business that is struggling to grow or in a solopreneurship where they own a job instead of a business generating income without them. I've always loved problem-solving, and I have the ability to see the blueprint that not everyone else can see.

My kids are now entering the world as entrepreneurs themselves. They have big dreams and know that anything is possible. They watched the hard times I went through and where it led me. I've laid a strong foundation for them to break through obstacles, and they are empowered with confidence and have my support and encouragement along the way. Letting them learn through adversity is at times a challenge, but to see them become self-sufficient entrepreneurs brings more joy than I can express. I've broken the mold and changed my family tree, leaving a legacy that goes beyond an inheritance.

I'm currently at a reset in my life as a new empty-nester. Many see this as a sad time—their identity changing, missing their kids, etc. Not me. This is an exciting opportunity to explore new ideas and ventures. I plan to begin angel investing and continuing to mentor business owners in breaking out of their ruts to develop mature, thriving companies. I've achieved the goal of most entrepreneurs when they decide to go into business for themselves—financial freedom. The hard work, long hours, disappointments, struggling to make ends meet, and no savings created a massive financial pressure that was the why that kept me pressing forward. The worry and fear that kept me up at night have disappeared. I'm now free to live life on my own terms. I own vacation rentals in Siesta Key, Florida that I frequently visit and bring family and friends to. I've also been able to take my family on some amazing family trips out of the country, creating family memories that I've always dreamed of having. When you achieve one dream, you just reach higher! And I love getting to see what I can dream up next.

The best thing you can do for yourself as a business owner is don't feel like you have to do everything or do it all perfectly. This is the easiest trap to get caught in. Often there is beauty in just making progress. Sometimes good is good enough, and when you realize that, you release yourself from an enormous amount of stress. Outsource the things you're not good at or don't enjoy, and ask for help when needed. Find what you're passionate about. Find what fuels you. Know that if you're not where you want to be, intentional progress every day will get you there in the right timing. There is a lesson in everything. Always get back up quickly when you fall and pivot when necessary. Keep cultivating relationships, yourself, and your business. The pieces will start to come together when you visualize and focus on where you are going as well as the joy and happiness that achieving your goal will bring.

Kerry Faix has over 20 years' experience in building businesses and real estate. For advice building and scaling your business, contact Kerry by visiting her website at www.KerryFaix.com or kerry@kerryfaix.com. Follow her on Instagram and Twitter at @KerryFaix.

Tweetable: We have to always believe we have the power to make changes in our lives. If you're stuck, believing you can't change your situation, push through quickly. The power is within you. Doing something is better than doing nothing. Intentional progress every day will get you there.

BRANDY WILSON EDWARDS

How I Turned Burnout Into a Blessing

An Attorney's Journey to Meaningful Happiness and Motivational Speaking

Attorney, passionate speaker, thought leader, and founder of The Self-Love Challenge™ Brandy Wilson Edwards empowers the legal community, business professionals, and students by speaking on happiness, confidence, and stress management. Brandy is also an authority on teaching self-love as a lifestyle.

Spiritual Awakening

I was unhappy driving to work one day, which was not unusual. But what happened as I drove to work that day felt like divine intervention. I was hanging onto every word of an audiobook and intuitively felt that both the book, *Light Is the New Black*, and author, Rebecca Campbell, were going to change my life.

I felt burned out and imbalanced in my legal career and desired more fulfillment in my life. At the peak of my unhappiness, I often felt stressed and anxious and I regularly had headaches and stomachaches. I turned to alcohol for stress relief and fun, which provided a temporary illusion of happiness, but it left me unfulfilled and pushed me further away from who I was and where I was meant to be.

When I took time for myself by practicing yoga, I noticed a gradual shift in my thoughts about myself and my life. While I sought out yoga to physically change my body, I unintentionally discovered how to love my body, and that allowed me to transform my life. For years, my body was my passion project, and interestingly, that passion project led me to others.

In my search for more happiness, I took a solo trip to New York to attend a retreat hosted by the author who changed my life. I desired change and was seeking clarity in my life, and I knew I had to be there, even though I was out of vacation days at work. I needed a break from my day-to-day life before I had a breakdown, so I took a chance on what my soul was calling me to do. I did a lot of soul searching, journaling, and meditating during my transformational week in New York. The retreat was a pivotal moment in my self-discovery journey, and when I arrived back in Texas, I had a new outlook on life. I had more direction, and I created new goals which led me to create and host my first workshop to positively impact the lives of others.

A few months after the retreat, I set a goal to train for my first fitness competition. I wanted to challenge myself to become the strongest version of myself, physically and mentally. My training goal required a secondary goal to stop drinking alcohol for six months, which I knew would be quite the challenge! I quickly adapted to my new lifestyle, and it turned into an epic self-discovery journey. I noticed I was receiving clarity as well as creative downloads. When I stopped drinking, I had more energy, I slept better, and my skin was reverse aging. After training religiously for six months with phenomenal results, I decided to push my competition back and then ultimately decided not to compete. Although my training goal changed, I became so much happier without alcohol that I kept counting the days without it.

A year later, I attended the same retreat in New York and left a more empowered version of myself. I had a breakthrough and gained more clarity and courage. I had a burning desire to discover and passionately pursue both my potential and purpose. On the last day of the retreat, with a grateful heart, I promised myself that I would use my voice, share my stories, and follow my happiness. This transformation happened while I was experiencing extreme burnout in my career. Interestingly, during this time, I almost skipped into work glowing with happiness because I felt so rejuvenated with more purpose, life, and light. While little changed at work, I was evolving daily.

Within months of my newfound clarity, I followed through on the promises I made to myself. I booked my first keynote, which led to many more speaking engagements in person and virtually. I also gained coaching clients, did radio and podcast interviews, and wrote for blogs and had articles published in magazines. I collaborated with other entrepreneurs and also became certified to teach yoga and mindfulness. I started hosting more events, including a transformational women's retreat, so others could experience the power of investing in themselves and the clarity that comes from it.

My most memorable moment to date was when I spoke to my professional peers for the first time. As I waited to be introduced, I experienced imposter syndrome. To quiet my inner critic, I reminded myself that I was asked to speak by the president of the organization because she knew I had value to provide the prestigious audience. I kindly reminded myself that I had lived what I was speaking about, and I wanted to empower and challenge the attorneys in the audience to become zealous advocates for themselves, not just for their clients. To my surprise, a Justice on The Supreme Court of Texas was in the audience and approached me afterwards to thank me for my presentation. I challenged myself to be strong and courageous that day. The experience boosted my confidence and increased my happiness, and it was confirmation that I had unique gifts and was on the right path.

Prioritize a Passion Project

As a multi-passionate person with many interests, skills, goals, and dreams, my soul was craving creativity and excitement that could not be found working behind a desk. Once I discovered and prioritized my current passion project, speaking to the legal community as well as business professionals and students, I felt a magical shift.

Change is good. Consider changing something in your life that allows you to prioritize a passion project. While happiness might feel elusive at times, a passion project will give you something to do that excites you and feeds your soul. Your primary goal is to make time for something that makes you happy, even if you are busy and stressed. What do you lose track of time doing? What have you always wanted to try? What hobby has taken a back seat to your demanding job or chaotic life? What would you do for free? Your responses will guide you towards possible passion projects in your pursuit of more happiness.

Your passions, just like your goals, can change over time and will be revealed to you as you take action towards them. Release any ideas that your passion project should yield a specific outcome. While you have many obligations, prioritizing a passion project is imperative to your overall well-being and does wonders for your mental health!

Five Steps to Meaningful Happiness

A powerful concept that I often share when speaking to audiences is this: To pursue meaningful happiness in your life, you must take courageous action towards change. While there are many things you can do to follow your happiness, when you commit to five specific actions, you will transform your life.

I changed my life in many ways, all while working at my firm. I realized the happiness I was searching for was waiting on me to prioritize the five C's—change, clarity, courage, confidence, and celebrate.

Step 1: Desire Change

Acknowledge that you want more in your life and be kind to yourself during the process. Adopt a mindset that it is never too late to start, or start over. While being able to embrace change is certainly a skill, I think of embracing change as something you must do when change is out of your control. Alternatively, desiring change is a decision you make. When you desire change and choose to take courageous action towards change, you take control of your life.

When you feel like you are going through the motions, know that you have a choice to stay stuck or to take action. Make a choice to stop settling and demand fulfillment in your life. As you explore the changes you need to make, it is normal to feel unsure where to start. You can begin with working on your mindset by believing there is more to life and that what you desire is possible. Perhaps it is only your mindset that needs to change, but most likely, it is both your mindset and activities that you engage in, or refrain from, that need to change for you to become happier.

When you feel unhappy, notice how you cope with your feelings. It might take time to notice your thought patterns as well as your empowering and disempowering habits and routines. During this process, try judging yourself less and loving yourself more. Give yourself grace and compassion. Ask yourself if your actions propel your forward or push you back. For change in any area of your life to be effective, stay patient, persistent, and consistent.

Step 2: Seek Clarity

As you seek clarity, have an open mind. When you have an open mind and are flexible with your goal timelines and outcomes, each action you take towards your goal will reveal more to you. Give yourself permission to try things so you can see for yourself whether you like it, love it or could live without it. Start asking yourself this question: *Why?*

Why do I desire change? Why do I feel unhappy? Why am I allowing fear to hold me back? Why do I self-sabotage my success? Why am I not showing up as the most confident version of myself? The more you ask yourself why, the more clarity you will receive on what is holding you back and what you need to do about it.

While goals are important, know that all of your goals are not necessarily meant to be accomplished. Some goals serve the sole purpose of being stepping stones to experiences, people, places, and things that you might not have otherwise discovered. Never underestimate the power of your goals, both those that you achieve and those that you fall short of achieving. Unaccomplished goals still have the power to positively impact your life, as every life experience is a lesson or a blessing.

The more action you take, the more clarity you will receive. As you search for answers, know that inspiration, willpower, motivation, and discipline will come and go. There will be days you feel overwhelmed and want to give up. However, when you have clarity on what you are changing and why you are changing it, you will be more connected to your vision of happiness.

Step 3: Practice Courage

Allow fear to be your compass so that fear may fuel you rather than hold you back. Fear will guide you to where you need to be courageous in your life.

Instead of fearing failure, gift yourself an opportunity to fail. Failure is simply feedback. This step is where many people settle and allow fear to get the best of them. You can desire change and seek clarity every single day, but if you do not take courageous action in your life, you will be unhappy.

In thinking about where you can practice courage in your life, consider these questions: What would you do if you could not fail? What would you ask someone if the answer would be yes? If people would not judge or criticize you, what would you do and who would you be? What would you try if you believed in yourself more?

You must believe that you have not experienced the best days of your life yet. Make a decision right now to be strong and courageous in the pursuit of your happiness. Your best life depends on it. If you need a powerful statement to tell yourself every time you have fear around taking courageous action, adopt my life mantra: "I AM STRONG AND COURAGEOUS!" It has served me well.

Step 4: Build Confidence

To have once-in-a-lifetime experiences, you must believe in yourself and power through self-doubt! When you have butterflies in your stomach and have a choice to stay comfortable or to challenge yourself, ask yourself, "What would the most confident version of myself do right now?"

Comparison and self-criticism subtract from your confidence and can deter you from exploring what is possible. Rise above self-doubt by highlighting your strengths instead of your weaknesses. Build yourself up and become your own cheerleader with positive praises instead of negative statements. Confidence is a choice, and because it requires a mindset shift, it is something you can curate over time. Make a decision to show up for yourself, even when you doubt yourself. Each time you power through self-doubt and take courageous action despite fear, you boost your confidence.

The easiest way to increase your confidence is to invest in yourself. Learn. Read books and take courses. Attend events, in person and virtually, for both business and pleasure. Surround yourself with like-minded, ambitious individuals for inspiration, and see what is possible. Hire a coach or find a mentor. Invest in your health by moving your body more, hydrating, and eating nourishing foods. Meditate and allow your mind and body to slow down. Experience the power of pausing.

If you can choose to doubt yourself, you can also choose to believe in yourself.

Step 5: Celebrate Yourself

Stop waiting until you accomplish something to feel successful when you can celebrate yourself every step of the way. Success is subjective, and you can create your own definition for it. Push yourself, but also give yourself grace and compassion as you navigate change and prioritize your happiness.

Think about your accomplishments from this past year, or from your life in general, and write them down as your thoughts come to you. Include accomplishments that are both big and small. Think broadly and focus on different categories beyond your education and career. Challenge yourself to fill up an entire page. If you are struggling with your list, perhaps you have unintentionally overlooked certain accomplishments and moments in your life and you are not giving yourself enough credit. Sometimes what you find easy to do is challenging to other people. Count these. List anything and everything you can think of to celebrate yourself for.

After you create your list, acknowledge all of the things you have done, experienced, overcome, achieved, or learned in your life. When you choose to celebrate yourself as you take action, remember to prioritize self-care. It is not selfish, it is necessary.

Take Courageous Action and Crack Open Your Unhappiness

Change: What is one change you need to make right now to enhance your quality of life? (*Use this as a guide to create mini-goals.*)

Clarity: Why do you need to make that change? (*Think about how the change will positively impact your life.*)

Courage: How can you practice courage around this change? (*Notice what you fear. It will guide you towards actions to take.*)

Confidence: How can you build confidence in yourself around this change? (*Notice where you doubt yourself. It will guide you towards actions to take.*)

Celebrate: How will you celebrate yourself for taking action towards change? (*Celebrate each step you take!*)

Challenges Give You Choices

Choose to be grateful for your unhappiness because it is guiding you to what needs to change. Trust that your unhappiness is happening for you, not to you, and know that you have the power to bridge the gap between where you are and where you want to be.

Happiness is a choice. Change can be uncomfortable but you have the choice to choose courage over comfort. As you take steps to transform your life, it is critical that you love yourself while you work on yourself, without conditions. That means you love yourself during the work, rather than after it. Make a choice to be a zealous advocate for yourself, not just for your clients and those that are near and dear to your heart. Make yourself and your happiness a priority, not an option.

When you become intentional and prioritize your happiness, it has a ripple effect in all areas of your life, personally and professionally, and the possibilities are limitless. Happiness in one area gives you a return on investment in other areas. Your stuckness and unhappiness are stepping stones. Those feelings are leading you to discover more—a place where you can thrive, not just survive.

To book attorney, speaker, and certified mindfulness and yoga instructor Brandy Wilson Edwards for speaking engagements, or to schedule a confidence and clarity strategy session, email TheSelfLoveChallenge@gmail.com.
www.SelfLoveChallenge.com
Instagram: @TheSelfLoveChallenge
Clubhouse: @BrandyEdwards

Tweetable: Be a zealous advocate for yourself and make your happiness a priority, not an option. Take courageous action and adopt a mindset that it is never too late to start or to start over. Love yourself while you work on yourself. Trust your unhappiness is happening for you, not to you.

RACHELE BROOKE SMITH
Becoming the HERO of Your Own Story

Rachele Brooke Smith is an actress, host, coach, and motivational speaker seen frequently on Hollywood screens, modeling for major brands, and motivating fans around the world. After starring in the sequel to the film that changed her life, Rachele is on a mission to help people overcome obstacles and create the life they really want.

Dreams Come True

Everyday, I feel so grateful that I get to live my childhood dream. Through a crazy road of many challenging twists and turns, I get to wake up and continually create and fight for a life that I really love living. I went from being an all too stressed out, not very happy, and not very healthy young girl in Phoenix, Arizona to being the lead actress in several hit films and TV shows. My first lead in a film, *Center Stage: Turn It Up*, was my childhood dream come true! This road has come with many struggles, tears, and seemingly impossible to overcome challenges, and it is far from over, but I have learned so many amazing life lessons along the way which have helped me always get back up, create a happy and healthy lifestyle for myself, and remain unbreakable.

Competitive Gymnast

Before discovering my love and obsession with storytelling, acting, and performing, I was a very competitive gymnast (and a very stressed out little girl). Being a young competitive gymnast was incredibly demanding, but it wasn't necessarily the demand I received from others that made me live in an awful, and pretty constant state, of worry, fear, and anxiety. It was the stress and pressure I put on myself. I was anything but my best friend and biggest supporter. I felt this extreme pressure to be the best at whatever I was doing, so much so that the concept of just hanging out with my friends was pretty foreign to me.

This overwhelming stress ended up taking a severe toll on my physical health and is something I still deal with today. It was so bad that I stayed home sick half the school year and would throw up on a weekly basis, not because of an eating disorder but because of how nervous I felt all the time. Mind you, this was from about 8-12 years old. Crazy, right? While most other young girls were playing with baby dolls, I was just hoping I wouldn't be getting hurt or yelled at in practice that night.

I feel I learned the power of my thoughts in a negative way. I used this power so I didn't have to deal with life. I knew if I were sick (and not just faking sick, but really sick), I could stay home with my mom (and my best friend) in my safe, warm bed. And what kid doesn't want to feel safe? On that same note, what kid wishes they were sick all of the time so they don't have to go to gymnastic practice?

After breaking my hand during a competition and having surgery, I began to realize how truly unhappy I was. Even though it was ridiculously hard to quit, seeming almost impossible at the time, I eventually found the strength to do so.

Gymnastics was all I knew. It was my life, my friends' lives, and my mom's life. For the first time, I felt incredibly lost. I went from being extremely dedicated to something for a long time to feeling like I had nothing. I went from having goals, dreams, purpose, passion, and a schedule to nothing, and on top of all that, I felt like I had lost my best friend, my mom, myself, and my close friends (my team). I spent countless days crying alone in my room feeling so alone, so scared, so helpless. I don't think I will ever forget how sad and lost I was back then.

The Transformative Power of Film

Around that same time, I went with my family to see the movie *Center Stage* by Nicholas Hytner. This film was so powerful for me, especially because the only reason I really even liked gymnastics was the dance and performance element. Throughout the film, I had crazy goosebumps and chills and was filled with a ridiculous amount of inspiration. I never wanted to get up from my seat. I wanted to stay in that magical moment forever, and for quite a while, I just sat there in the dark theater feeling so overwhelmed with new drive and passion for life. I started visualizing myself up on that screen playing characters like I just saw. I actually still do this practice after every impactful movie I see. I probably would have stayed there all night but I knew my family was looking for me. I walked out of that theater a changed girl. I knew right then and there that was what I wanted with my life. I wanted to act, tell stories of overcoming struggle and challenge, make people laugh, dance, perform, inspire, and change lives just like the actors in that movie did for me. That film and that moment changed my life, and I will never forget it.

I had always loved movies, but this was a whole new level of obsession. Could movies really be that powerful? I went from feeling so sad, lost, and alone to feeling more alive and full of joy and wonderment than ever before. I wanted to act, dance, and perform more than anything, and I wanted to do it for the rest of my life. After that moment, there really was no looking back. I just knew that performing and storytelling was what I was born to do.

Right after seeing *Center Stage*, I lived and breathed dance and acting. For the first time in a very long time, I felt so free, so happy, and so driven. Yes, I was still a perfectionist to a fault, and yes, I still put a ton of artificial pressure on myself to be the best at everything, but I wasn't living in fear anymore. I was living for my absolute love of music, movement, creativity, and storytelling.

I believed I was really good, however it took a very, very long time before anyone really gave me a shot. I wanted to be good so bad it hurt and got very little sleep all through high school in pursuit of that goal. I even got the "Rat" award at my studio because I would stay and practice well after my daily 5-10pm classes were over.

The plan was to go to my dream college that had one of the best performing arts programs then go to LA to follow my dream of being a lead actress.

Challenges May Lead to Opportunities

Fun fact: That plan failed big time and I didn't get into my dream college (even though everyone thought I would be a shoo-in)!

After a few weeks of coping with my complete devastation, I did not feel right or happy about going to Arizona State University even though I was accepted with a scholarship and all my friends were going there. I saw an opportunity to audition for a super intense performing arts scholarship program in LA.

I flew last minute to LA with my mom, auditioned alongside hundreds of kids from all over the world, got in (oh my gosh!), and then found out I had two weeks to move to LA and be all set up and ready to go. Nervous excited energy flooded my body. This was epic. This was amazing. This was freaking scary, especially since I just got out of high school, I didn't know LA at all, and I didn't know anyone there or have a clue where or who I would live with.

That program was one of the most difficult and best experiences of my life. Looking back on it, I really don't know how I did it. There were no excuses, no vacation days, and no sick days. You had to be there six days a week all day long, and if you had to miss, you had to make it up somehow. 9am to 7pm was jam packed with the best (and emotionally and physically challenging) classes Hollywood, maybe even the world, had to offer.

As challenging as it was, I just loved it so much. In fact, there are many days I wish I could go back to that time when all I had to worry about was showing up for class. During this program, you were not allowed to audition, have an agent, or work at all in the entertainment industry because it would take you out of training.

Serendipity

As soon as I finished the program, I got signed to an amazing dance agency (yay!) but got turned down from acting agents because I didn't have an acting reel. How could I have? I had been in a performing arts program where you couldn't work or do anything else since I moved to LA. To say the least, I was discouraged and confused about what to do next.

A couple weeks later, I saw a sign advertising auditions for the lead girl in *Center Stage: Turn It Up*, the sequel to the very film that changed me as a little girl. I don't think I had ever seen a sign posting about auditions, let alone an audition for my literal childhood dream. My heart dropped. I couldn't believe it.

My initial reaction was there was no way this could be happening. Is this some sort of joke? Am I being punked? Where's Ashton? It seemed so surreal, almost not even possible. *Center Stage* was my movie. It was the whole reason I started acting and dancing. How was it even possible that they would be casting the sequel at the exact moment I could finally audition for it and that I just happened to be in the right place at the right time to become aware of the opportunity? Most auditions you never even hear about, hence why you have to have an agent to know about them.

I almost didn't even go. I went home trying to justify all the reasons I shouldn't go: I would make a fool of myself, All those acting agents had turned me down, I wasn't ready, I really hadn't done an acting audition before. I almost convinced myself, but then, this overwhelming feeling came over me and a voice said, "You have to go," and I swear, it pushed me out the door.

I ended up having to go in and audition six different times and experienced a rollercoaster ride of emotions that comes with your childhood dream seeming so close yet so far. There were lots of tears, prayers, and sleepless nights. Then finally, after about a month, I got the call that Sony Pictures wanted to book me to play the lead character in their new film and the sequel to *Center Stage*. I would be playing Kate Parker, and I would be filming in Vancouver for a couple months, and I would be leaving in a couple days.

AHHHHHH HAAAAAA YAHHHHHHHHHH!! Yes, that was me screaming in my car! It was a childhood dream come true. I was about to play the lead in the sequel to the movie that changed my life as a little girl. I was going to get to be "that girl" that inspired me so much. This crazy, beautiful, overwhelming, and to me, miraculous experience has shaped my entire brand and company.

A Deeper Look

That defining moment in my career was not something that happened without years of preparation and dedication to learning my craft. Even as a young teenager, I was always on the go. I would wake up at 6am every day and struggle to balance an exceedingly full school day with additional before school study as well as competitive dance and acting classes immediately after school.

At that time, I was also captain of the dance line, in student government all four years, and often, I would not even turn in until after 1am. Every morning, I would wake up and do it all over again. This didn't leave much time for hanging out, but at the time, I really did not know any different. This was what I considered normal. That fast-paced lifestyle created a constant high stress level, and by the age of 16, I had already developed an ulcer.

These stomach problems continued into my early adulthood and were my ultimate motivation to search for a more stress-free lifestyle. Amidst amazing things that happen in life, sometimes life has a way of blindsiding you and many times the things you think will never happen, well, they do. In the moment, those personal setbacks might seem like the worst thing that could ever take place, but what do you do when those unexpected things happen in your life?

You choose to be unbreakable. Being unbreakable is about knowing who you are, living from an authentic place, and going after your goals and dreams every single day. It is knowing that when life gets hard, you will allow yourself to bend but never break. Nothing is going to break or stop me from living my purpose, and nothing should break you from yours either! If you are open to turning all of those feelings of frustration, sadness, and anger into fuel for your fire, you will always be able to figure things out and be better and stronger because of it. That is what being unbreakable is all about.

Having big goals and dreams is a wonderful part of life, but making them come true is even more extraordinary. What is it that allows us to actually get to live our goals and dreams? I am convinced that our overall happiness, productivity, and ability to achieve any goal all comes down to the story we are telling ourselves—who we truly believe we are deep down. I believe we all have the power to choose a story that will allow us to achieve the life we want to live, a life where we wake up every day full of love and intense passion.

These lessons have helped me not only to achieve success, but also be able to live a happy and healthy life. After many ups and downs, I have learned what it feels like to live by these principles, and what it feels like when I am not, and I do not ever want to go there again. I now come from this strong and grounded place and view the world with a new perspective that is humbled, authentic, and empowering.

In your life, you are the actor, writer, director, and producer of your own movie. You are already writing the story of your character. Your strength is the realization that you have the ability to change whatever story you used to believe about yourself into whatever your heart desires. You are living your life every day, so why not write and act in an incredible movie and play the hero of that empowering story?

I believe greatness is a choice, and we choose to be unbreakable.

After years of applying everything I've been learning, I can look back and proudly say, I played the lead role in the sequel to the film that changed my life as a little girl, and since then, I have played countless dream roles in major films and TV. I overcame some major challenges to create the most loving, supportive, empowering relationship with myself. I am also engaged to the most amazing man who is even better than my absolute dream guy, Emilio Palafox, and we are on a mission to co-create a world where healthy relationships are the new norm. This did not all come easy, and I'm nowhere near perfect, but I've learned a lot and I LOVE coaching people and sharing all that I know.

When in doubt, and you don't know what to do, do the BRAVE THING.

Rachele Brooke Smith plays hero characters in films and on TV and will help YOU create "hero habits" to become the HERO of your own life's movie. Rachele and her partner, Emilio Palafox, co-created "Relationship Renegades" and co-host the @Relationship.Renegades radio & Youtube show. Follow @Rbrookesmith on IG. Subscribe at www.rachelebsmith.com

Tweetable: Let go of outcomes you can't control, and just keep doing the brave thing. Every time you take action you win.

CHARLES VINCENT KALUWASHA

Leaving Zambia

My Journey to Becoming a Million+ Dollar Multifamily Investor

Charles Vincent Kaluwasha holds a Master of Clinical Nursing and has worked in Zambia, New Zealand and Australia. Charles is a visionary entrepreneur, author, and multifamily investor at CJ Investiment, providing real estate education to high-paid professionals who lack investment experience in apartment buildings.

Childhood in Zambia

I am the third born of seven from a village south of Zambezi district in the northwestern province of Zambia. Growing up rural was not pleasant for me. I envied children who grew up in town. Occasionally, mom would take me to the city to visit some relatives. I admired the children in those homes.

My father was a peasant farmer. Later, he became a well-respected cook for the district commissioner. He was a firm believer in hard work and self-reliance. He taught us efficient ways to become independent, socially and financially. His teachings inspired me to remain focused on education as a tool to secure my future.

In my final year of school, my father was hospitalized. The doctors diagnosed an unexplained illness, and there was nothing they could do but encourage us to take him home and try traditional medicine. That was painful!

My Father's Passing and Legacy

We risked taking him home in a trailer pulled by oxen. I asked for two days off of school, and the headmaster urged me to report back for the final examination.

At home, I assisted my father with the activities of daily living. Before I left for my final exam, he kissed me and whispered, "My son, go in peace and know that your ways will be blessed."

I'm indebted to his unconditional love, care, and commitment to educating us. His legendary gifts inspired me to do more for myself and my family. He was all I strive to be in this life, so I hold onto his legacy and pass it on to my children.

My father's death inspired me to pursue medicine. I wanted the responsibility of helping people in hospitals. I wanted to become a doctor, and to do that, I needed a Division 1 certificate on my final exam. But I was grieving my father, so I got Division 2. That decided I would become a nurse, but it would not be an easy path.

Working in the Mines

Everyone who left school needed to serve in the Zambia National Service. Due to fortunate and unusual circumstances, I did not go. I started working in the mines as a general worker. The job involved loading heavy semi-crushed copper ore into a wheelbarrow then tipping it onto the crusher to be conveyed up to the smelter. Sometimes I carried heavy timber and pipes to the drilling areas. It was challenging, but I remained resilient.

Interestingly, an internal advertisement came up. The company was offering a course to train first aiders to man first aid stations underground. Since I wanted to pursue my career in helping people through medicine, I applied. After the interviews, the matron recommended that I train as a registered nurse instead.

My wife Joyce and I were thrilled and thanked our Heavenly Father for the great opportunity.

In July 1986, I commenced training as a registered nurse with four other boys in a class of 35 girls. I was the oldest student in the class. I planned to study harder and be top in class.

In 1989, I graduated with the prestigious award of the best student in humanitarian and good behavior. I joined the Kalulushi mine hospital in Kalulushi and worked in all departments, including emergency, children, obstetrics and gynecology, and I was promoted to head the medical ward. I gained a reputation as a nurse who provided holistic care to patients, and I could get along with anybody and work with everyone, even with aggressive patients.

I enjoyed my job and kept working and eventually bought our first house. I wanted more opportunities for my family and my children. I wanted to build a legacy.

Opportunities Overseas

In 1996, I applied to undertake a degree in nursing at the University of Zambia. I wanted to continue growing into more responsibility and a higher salary.

My application was accepted, and I applied for company sponsorship to cover tuition. The company accepted, but two weeks before starting the course, I received a letter stating all sponsorships were suspended until further notice. I never gave up.

I started applying to programs overseas and received a favourable response from New Zealand. This was the opportunity I had been waiting for.

I had to find the money to not only buy an air ticket but also to live on while I was in New Zealand and solve how the family would survive without a steady income. I came up with three solutions.

I started a drug store in our town. A friend and I obtained a license to sell essential drugs and first aid items. After work, I would go straight to the shop to take over. I would conduct free blood pressure checks and refer to doctors. That type of service made an impact on the community. In record time, the drugstore was known by everyone in the community and surrounding farms.

I bought a small farm to grow tomatoes, onions, and other vegetables to sell at our market. I earned some profit, but the money was not enough for the journey to New Zealand.

I ventured in keeping chickens in the backyard to sell too. To beat the competition, I added four tomatoes, two onions per each chicken bought, and that made a difference to the customers. I was above the competition, and the business was prosperous.

Additionally, my brother, David Musema Kaluwasha, gave me ZMK500 (Zambian Currency), boosting my savings closer to the funds I needed to immigrate.

I was afraid to go to a new country for the first time. The details of my travel, especially my fear and uncertainty, were engraved into my mind. I was fearful of the potential dangers of passing through Johannesburg in South Africa and the foreignness of Hong Kong, but I was determined to do this for the benefit of the whole family.

It was tough to say goodbye, especially to my wife. I only focused on my mission. I would go to New Zealand and work very hard to support my family and to bring them to live with me.

Building a Life in New Zealand

I arrived in New Zealand with only US $5000. After three months of hard work in school, I was deemed competent to work in New Zealand hospitals. Although I had graduated, I had to wait for my nursing license, and that left me without much income. I could not apply for a position until I had my license, but my finances were dwindling, so I started looking for jobs with nursing agencies.

I negotiated and told the agencies of my predicament: I was from overseas and did not have enough money to either go back or buy food and accommodation. Thankfully, they understood and employed me as a casual nurse.

I opened my first bank account. Now, I could send money back to Zambia. The sense of ownership and responsibility became real. I had to work hard to boost my bank account faster, knowing that my casual contract could be cancelled at any time.

Thankfully, I continued working as a casual until I received my license in January 2004. I began a full-time position at Hutt Valley Hospital, Wellington in the emergency department, and I didn't stop learning. I began a masters' program to increase my skill, education, and pay.

It was challenging to take courses while working full-time, and I made full use of all resources available to me, including the university's free editing services for students who spoke English as a second language. I needed to remain motivated at all times.

When I left Zambia, the family vacated our house and rented it to a tenant to start getting ongoing income. The family was scattered. Each child was kept by our brothers and family friends in different towns. I sent money fortnightly to my wife, who was staying with her sister. She would then distribute the money fairly.

I started the process of applying for immigration for the family to come and join me in New Zealand. First, I applied for a permanent visa. I qualified as a skilled immigrant. It was an expensive process. I paid for medical exams, visas, and air tickets for the five of them. I lived on a tight budget, moved out of the nurses' hostel, and found a three-bedroom apartment.

On December 29, 2005, the family joined me in New Zealand. We thanked our Heavenly Father for the family reunion. It is not always possible, as many immigrants remain separated from their families, only seeing them for short visits once a year.

From Single Income to Multiple Incomes

I was the only breadwinner, and the cost of living in New Zealand became unbearable. Before coming to New Zealand, I thought money was easy to get. I was wrong. All I needed was to work hard to exchange time for a dollar. We needed to adjust to the Western world mentality.

However, I was open to learning and associated myself with positive and successful people. I was introduced to Melaleuca, a company involved in wellness products. After my due diligence, I joined and started sharing the products with friends and families. That helped me to have supplemental income to pay for increasing bills. My wife found a job with a cleaning company. The extra income started trickling, and our financial life started getting better, stress levels came down, and we found the opportunity to enjoy life.

Two years later, we decided to buy our first home in New Zealand. African families who had been in New Zealand before us were amazed by how we got the money to buy a house so fast. We showed them that banks were available, and we were working smart by having additional income from Melaleuca.

I created a money-making website, providing advice to newbies about leveraging the power of the internet to make money working part-time from home as entrepreneurs. Ten signed up and started making money by learning how to sell online. That encouraged me to scale my business to a higher level.

Meanwhile, I continued to pursue a masters' degree. Each year I improved, gaining more experience working in the emergency department. I progressed to level three as a senior nurse, and I mentored others to advance their professional careers by applying to the master's degree program.

By the time I completed my master's degree in 2012, there were six nurses I worked with who had enrolled. It only takes one person to show others the ropes and inspire.

Australia and Multifamily Investing

Eventually, we wanted to move closer to Zambia, and we decided on Perth, Australia. We moved in 2014 and kept our real estate in New Zealand. In 2017, we moved into our new property as new homeowners in Australia.

My idea of investing in real estate traces back to Zambia when I rented out our house and received rental income every month.

My desire to build a real estate business was strong. I invested in a three-day workshop, a real estate rescue program, which aimed to help homeowners facing bank repossession. I was intrigued by the training and system.

In 2018, my wife and I decided to sell the property in New Zealand, paid off the remaining balance on the mortgage, and transferred the balance to our bank in Australia.

I continued training with DG Institute and started building our team of experts: lawyers, accountants, mortgage brokers, and solicitors, and built relationships with three lending institutions in Australia.

While searching for investment properties to buy in Perth, a family friend phoned us about EK Capital, which was looking for people to invest in multifamily units.

We did our due diligence on the deal they were proposing, then signed the contract and put down deposits on three units, two apartments in Melbourne and one townhouse in Brisbane. Our units are under Motion Property with loyal tenants giving us income monthly.

Lesson

I wanted to change my situation. Although I started making good money as a clinical nurse, I did not become a millionaire until I bought rental properties. That is when we achieved stability, and my net worth took off. I didn't want to keep doing the same thing over and over but instead work smarter by leveraging systems, resources, and the internet. I learned how to live on a tight budget to fulfill my responsibilities and save for future projects. But I needed some further support to get through the learning and action phase as quickly and efficiently as possible. Being open to new ideas opened doors to opportunities and shaped our lifestyle to be what it is today. As I have grown, I am delighted to have the chance to inspire others to improve their situation too.

If you want to change your situation, get a clear path for action and set yourself up for success, then Charles Vincent Kaluwasha's simple but effective strategies can make all the difference. Send an email to info@cjinvestiment.com and request JV partnership application or visit https://cjinvestiment.com

Tweetable: There is a saying that states knowledge is power, but I would add that knowledge is the dollar in one's bank! Mindset matters most when it comes to all forms of success, so keep feeding your mind with the good stuff.

EBERHARD SAMLOWSKI

Former Board Certified Surgeon Leaving a Generational Legacy

Eberhard Samlowski passionately teaches people how to create financial freedom by using a little known concept called infinite banking. He was a board certified surgeon with a 30 year history of investing in real estate and the market and has used the infinite banking concept for over 12 years to help himself and others achieve financial freedom.

Money Is the Answer

What if everything you and I have been taught about money, wealth, retirement, and leaving a legacy is a blatant LIE? I'll bet it would make you mad as hell, as it did me.

The wisest and richest man who ever lived, Solomon, wrote, "A good man leaves an inheritance for his children's children." He also wrote, "Whoever loves money never has enough; whoever loves wealth is never satisfied with his income," and "Wisdom is a shelter as money is a shelter." But, here is something that you most likely have never been taught, "A feast is made for laughter and wine makes life merry, but MONEY is the answer for everything."

A wealthy friend of mine once said, "If you can write a check to take care of an issue…you don't have a problem." Very wise and profound words.

I grew up in a middle-class neighborhood, the son of German immigrants. My father was a physician. My parents left Germany with the clothes on their backs. Instead of buying a big, fancy house, they spent their money traveling the world. Starting at an early age, they took us four boys all over the world on incredible adventures, some which you could not repeat today. These travels had a profound effect on my worldview. I saw everything from extreme poverty to extreme wealth. My parents also scrimped and saved to pay cash for college for us four and then medical school for three of us four. For the rest of their lives, they lived extremely frugally, some would say cheap. They bought their clothes at thrift stores and the Goodwill. But, when they died, they left a substantial inheritance for each of us. Their only expectation was that we "pass it forward" by doing the same for our kids and grandkids.

Growing up, I saw that all of our wealthiest friends owned real estate. The wealthiest friend didn't have enough money to pay for school and had a mentor pay his way through pharmacy school. Later, he began buying real estate and became a hugely successful developer of shopping malls. Through him, I learned individuals could own skyscrapers. Before he died, he left Ohio State College of Medicine the largest donation it had ever received at the time.

I ended up being a physician and surgeon. I spent 34 years of my life being educated, from homeschooling before kindergarten through surgical residency. I trained at Baylor, at the time known as the most brutal surgical residency in the country. Ironically, my first rotation at Baylor was with a world famous heart surgeon. But what got my attention was that he owned thousands of acres in the greater Houston area. He also owned oil and gas wells, a cement factory, and other enterprises. He told me, "Oil and gas is a boom and bust economy. It is far better to own the land and the minerals than the drilling company." In the subsequent years, I have seen two boom and bust cycles myself.

Living for the Future

I was single when I got out of residency. Other than splurging on a fire red Nissan 300 ZX Twin Turbo, all my money went into investments and real estate. I bought everything from raw land, to a 300-acre ranch, to commercial real estate.

I bought most on what I called "suicide notes," mortgages of 10 years or less, some as little as four years. Money was extremely tight. There was no room for hiccups. That was the case when I got married in 2004. All my money was tied up in investments. So, all we could afford was to buy a double-wide and place it on 82 acres that I owned, overlooking our town lake. If there was an error in my plans, it was that I always planned 20-30 years into the future, not living for the present.

During those years, we increased our tithe each and every year. At our peak, we were gifting over 50% of my pre-tax income. During that same time, the beginning of HMOs, my per procedure reimbursement was cut 75%. You can't make up those losses by working harder or longer.

Things remained extremely tight financially. Another problem in my plan was that most of my investments were not cash flowing, although they were growing on paper. You can't eat paper. If I have one other major fault, it is that I am overly optimistic and altruistic and have a strong need and desire to help and serve others. My entire life has been about service, often neglecting my own needs and desires. This can lead to problems, and boy, did it.

The Fault of Altruism

I wasn't your typical surgeon. Yes, I was a skilled surgeon, but I had a captive audience in the operating room of scrub nurses, scrub techs, anesthesiologists, and nurse anesthetists, so I would teach personal development and entrepreneurship. I played hours and hours of tapes of Jim Rohn, Denis

Waitley, Zig Ziglar, Brian Tracy, and so many others. One day, a nurse handed me a book, *Becoming Your Own Banker* by R. Nelson Nash and asked what I thought about the whole concept. I rapidly read it and quickly dismissed the idea. I scoffed, "It involves whole life insurance, and everyone knows that is the worst place to put your money."

For years, it had been grilled into me: "Buy term and invest the rest. Never, ever, buy whole life." What a profound lie. I asked the nurse if she wanted her book back, but she said she had no use for it, so I put it on my bookshelf.

I could see the stock market crash of 2008 coming, but I didn't know exactly when. Everyone I worked with had their money tied up in the market in IRAs and 401Ks. For years, I had been told about OPM (other people's money) and leveraging it. Being involved in real estate, I came up with an altruistic plan. What a fool I was.

I thought that I could protect those I worked with by borrowing their retirement money and investing it in a real estate project that I was involved in. This was a big mistake. Worse, I overpromised their return on investment and personally guaranteed that no one would ever lose a dime. I bought several vacation rental properties in Biloxi, Mississippi. I borrowed around $2.5 million. The crash did occur, and they would have lost 40-50% of their retirement savings. Real estate took a hit as well, but in that area, only 20% or so.

One thing I hadn't planned on was my hips going bad from overuse—standing on hard concrete operating room floors for 10-14 hours a day, plus years of skydiving, extreme snow skiing, running, and biking. In 2009, I had to have my first hip replacement. While on the table, my left ulnar nerve, which is responsible for sensation in the fourth and fifth fingers and some motor function, was injured. I was told it would most likely recover in three to four months. It never has. Lack of sensation and motor function in the hand is not a good thing for a surgeon.

My surgery career was OVER.

I Had Missed the Concept

During my recovery, I was a voracious reader. I happened to see R. Nelson Nash's book on my bookshelf and decided to reread it. The second time, it was like being hit over the head with a two by four. I thought to myself, "You fool! You missed the entire concept." From the picture on the book, I knew Nelson had to be up in years, if even still alive. Was he still teaching? I quickly got online, and a God thing happened. Nelson would be lecturing half an hour from where I lived in two weeks. I immediately signed up.

I was totally blown away by what he was teaching and called my wife from the meeting to tell her she needed to be there. Fortuitously, one month later, he was speaking in Waco. She joined me and was also blown away. We immediately started implementing his concepts in a big way.

The Most Powerful Tool

In 2010, three terrible things happened to us in rapid succession:

1) In January, without warning, my disability company cut off my disability checks, claiming that I could go back to work. My other hip was failing and would require surgery and the feeling in my hand had never recovered.

2) On April 20th, the Deepwater Horizon oil spill occurred in the Gulf of Mexico. Overnight, the properties became worthless and to date have not fully recovered.

3) By late June, natural gas prices plummeted from about $13 per MMBTU to around $3 per MMBTU. The gas companies stopped producing. Our gas royalty checks of $15,000-25,000 per month came to a screeching halt.

I owed about $2.5 million to investors with no means of paying it back.

Fortunately, that was not the end of the story. Nelson and I became friends. For the next 12 years, I read and reread Nelson's book at least two dozen times. Each time, I picked up another kernel of wisdom. During those years, I was able to hear Nelson speak at least twenty five times. I also was able to pick his brains in private. Because of our friendship, he was able to get my son an audition with the dean of the Samford music department playing organ as a sophomore in high school. He impressed the dean so much that he is now studying performance organ there on scholarship. I was fortunate enough to have lunch with Nelson shortly before his untimely death.

How infinite banking works and how it saved me financially is for a future book. It is the most powerful concept and tool that I have come across. In the late 1960s, The Who released the song, "I'm Free." The lyrics are, "If I told you what it takes to reach the highest highs, you'd laugh and say nothing is that simple..." That is the way it is with infinite banking.

Infinite Banking

The concept involves dividend-paying whole life insurance, banking, and taking out personal loans. For a moment, keep an open mind and forget what Dave Ramsey, Gary North, Suzy Orman, and others say about life insurance. We are not talking about your typical whole life insurance policy that is structured for the highest death benefit for the least amount of money. Nelson came up with the idea of structuring a policy with the largest immediate cash value with the least death benefit. It sounds counterintuitive, but by doing so, your death benefit will later be much greater than it would in a traditional policy. You do this by adding just enough short-term, term insurance. That term insurance drops off in five to seven years, before it becomes a financial drag on the policy. What many experts don't tell you is that less than one percent of term insurance ever pays and most people drop their policies in their sixties and seventies when it becomes prohibitively expensive. This shortchanges their family's financial needs.

I took this to heart and bought huge policies on myself, my wife, and my children. I was able to put over $200,000 into these policies, but I wasn't obligated to do so. Why would I do so? Because of the next step—the "banking process." Nelson told me over and over that infinite banking was not a product but a process and a total paradigm shift in thinking. It requires imagination, reason, logic, and prophesy.

Have you ever noticed that banks have the largest and nicest buildings? For every dollar deposited, the bank can lend out nine dollars. That is called fractional reserve banking. Additionally, as loan repayments are made, they immediately lend that money again, often up to seven times during the course of a loan. That is known as the velocity of money. So why wouldn't you want to get into the banking business? It just so happens, dividend-paying whole life insurance is the perfect vehicle for doing so. The only difference is life insurance companies by law cannot inflate money.

You can bank using a checking or savings account. You can borrow against a money market account or CD. You can borrow against held mutual funds. You can even bank using a buried tin can or with money hidden under a mattress. Or you can use dividend-paying whole life insurance. The problem with checking accounts, savings accounts, mutual funds, and CDs is that you will pay tax on any yearly gains, and shareholders of the institution will get any profits made from those accounts. The problem with the tin can and mattress method is no compounding and no dividends. The beauty of a dividend-paying whole life insurance policy is that all income grows exponentially, tax-free, and because you are considered an owner, you get paid interest and dividends even if you have outstanding loans.

The ideal storage for your wealth would have the following characteristics:

1. Liquid
2. Tax-deductible deposits
3. Withdrawals which can be tax-free
4. Ability to accept large deposits
5. Competitive to other financial products

6. Free from market loss
7. Accessible before age 59½ without penalty
8. Loans paid at the discretion and terms determined by the borrower
9. Judgement-proof in most states
10. No penalty for early withdrawal
11. Dividends and or interest can be used to pay the interest on any loan
12. In the event of death, there is a death benefit that exceeds any cash deposited
13. Basically no documentation needed for a loan request other than a simple loan request
14. Money can be used for any purpose with no rules on self dealing or what may be purchased

IRAs and 401Ks violate all of the above except number 3 and number 10.

CDs and money market accounts violate all except numbers 3, 8, 10, 11, 12, and 13.

For life insurance, all the above are true, except deposits (premiums) are not tax-deductible.

The System that Created My Family Legacy

Nelson's next big revelation was that everything that we purchase in life involves finance. We either borrow money, paying money to someone else, or we pay cash, giving up any future interest that money could have earned. The average person in this country spends 34.5% of every dollar earned on finance charges (mortgages, car loans, credit cards, or loss of interest when they pay cash). At the same time, they save less than 5%. That means year after year, they fall further behind financially. By the time the average person retires, 95% have to rely on government assistance. If you could capture any part of that 34.5%, you would be creating wealth for yourself and your family. That is exactly what I did. Over time, I took over my outstanding debt and paid myself interest instead of creditors.

Nelson further taught, if you ever borrow from a policy, you need to pay it back at the same or greater interest rate an institution would charge or interest rate you could make on an investment. A portion of that interest would pay the interest the insurance company charges. The remainder would buy additional "paid up" insurance, greatly increasing the velocity of your policy growth.

This was what I did. Over a ten year period, I used the policies to finance our lifestyle as well as pay down debt. We liquidated most of our properties, including our homestead, and dissolved many of our joint venture agreements. All of the investors have been made whole.

I still own several million dollars of property. When they sell, a portion of the proceeds will go to paying off policy loans and the remainder I will use in 1031-exchanges to buy income-producing properties. In this way, there will be over $2 million available (tax-free) for my retirement, that is still growing at four to six percent, tax-free. And I will leave an inheritance of over $8 million. Part of that money will go into an insurance trust set up for banking for future generations. The remainder will go to pay off policy loans on my children's policies which I will gift them (tax-free) when they can demonstrate to me that they understand the infinite banking concept.

As my parents did for me and my siblings, over the last 12 years, I have created this legacy for my family. There were obstacles, and if it weren't for this amazing wealth storage system, I may not have been this successful. I am compelled to share what I have learned with others who yearn to create their own financial freedom and generational legacy.

To get into contact with Eberhard Samlowski about how to implement the "Infinite Banking" concept, send an email to ebsamlowski@hotmail.com. His only requirement is that you have read Nelson Nash's book Becoming Your Own Banker.

Tweetable: Infinite banking is the most powerful financial tool that I have come across bar none. It saved me from financial ruin while, at the same time, setting me up for financial freedom and leaving a legacy for my children and future generations.

DENIS WAITLEY
Wisdom From an Iconic Thought Leader

Denis Waitley is a world-renowned speaker. He has written 16 bestselling classics including Seeds of Greatness, The Winner's Edge, Empires of the Mind, *and* Safari to the Soul. *His audio album* The Psychology of Winning *is the all-time bestselling program on self-mastery. Denis is the former chairman of psychology for the US Olympic Committee's Sports Medicine Council and in the Sales & Marketing Executives Association's International Speakers' Hall of Fame.*

Dysfunctional Upbringing

My parents divorced when I was in my teens. They were always arguing about money or my father's drinking, smoking, and socializing. I was always putting my pillow over my head in my bedroom to block out their constant bickering, and my little brother would hide. He was seven years younger than me and my sister was three years older.

My father joined the Merchant Marines at the onset of World War II and left when I was nine. He came into my room and said goodbye instead of goodnight. He returned briefly after the war, however soon left again, and I only saw him once a year thereafter.

Six years later, he came back from World War II as a Lieutenant and said to me, "If I were you, I'd head for the Naval Academy. If you can, get a congressional appointment and take the competitive exams." As a Merchant Marine, he couldn't give me an appointment himself.

During the Korean War, I was a senior in high school. As a kid in the 1940s, I grew up playing with army helmets, army men, and rubber guns. Then, as a senior and student body president at La Jolla High School, I believed I was going to go to Stanford on a Naval ROTC scholarship. I would only have to serve a couple of years. But when the Korean War came, my father encouraged me to go to the Naval Academy to become an officer the right way. It wasn't me, but at that time it was the right thing to do for the country.

When I was in the Navy in Washington, I got a chance to tie the Navy into the Blue Angels at the Ice Capades. I got a chance to do Sea Power, sell the Navy, and see how to promote. I became a Navy department head of media relations. Then I got the opportunity to work with Ampex, who had invented the video recorder in the early 1950s, and traveled the world selling the first instant replay videotape recorder. There was a little showbiz in that. People were wowed that the device could replay short bursts of video instantaneously without the need to develop the film first.

Early, Iconic Mentors

I then got the chance to work with Dr. Jonas Salk at The Salk Institute for Biological Studies in San Diego. He changed my life. He said to me, "Be careful. You're very bright and very optimistic, kind of like Jiminy Cricket. But don't tell people they can walk on water. They need pontoons." He said, "You're not a scientist. You're a promoter of self-awareness, but you're not magic." Dr. Jonas Salk introduced me to Abraham Maslow who was the head of the American Psychological Association. He introduced me to Carl Rogers at Center for Studies of the Person. And he introduced me to Viktor Frankl, author of *Man's Search for Meaning*. This connection with Jonas Salk in the 1960s helped me develop into who I would become.

Then the Apollo Program came along. My classmate, astronaut Bill Anders orbited the moon with Apollo 8, the first crewed spacecraft to leave low Earth orbit and the first human spaceflight to reach the moon. I had an opportunity to do simulation project studies and seminars for all the Apollo astronauts. I became friends with Gene Cernan, Wally Schirra, and all the guys that ended up going to the moon and walking on the moon.

I've had the fortune without the burdens of fame. I haven't been on television much. I'm not a household name. But I am a pioneer in the field.

Earl Nightingale was also a great influence of mine—*Our Changing World* and *The Strangest Secret*. "We become what we think about most of the time." When I gave my POW talk, I carried a little Sony recorder and recorded every talk I gave, in churches, women's clubs, Lions Clubs, Kiwanis International clubs, and Rotary Clubs. I spoke 500 times before anyone would pay me. Having recorded the first 500 speeches, I knew what made people laugh, what didn't, what they liked, and what was a hot button. I got rid of the things that didn't work and kept the things that did. Then one day a little cassette of mine traveled around to somebody and plopped into Earl Nightingale's home recorder.

He listened to it, then called me and said, "Hey, this is Earl Nightingale. I notice you're here in Sarasota, Florida working for Dr. Jonas Salk. I'm calling you because you have a nice voice and I like your stuff. If you're ever in Chicago, go see my partner Lloyd Conant." So, I took my last $500 with me to Chicago. It took me two years to convince them that I had enough in me to record. I watched all the speakers in those days and became close to Robert Schuller, Norman Vincent Peale, Paul Harvey, and Art Linkletter, real influences in my life.

Nightingale-Conant was also responsible for me becoming chairman of psychology for the Olympics. I met the chairman of the sports medicine council for the United States Olympic Committee at a conference. *The Psychology of Winning* album had just hit it big with AT&T, IBM, General Electric, and more companies who were buying it. William Simon, president of the United States Olympic Committee said, "You know, we really need a guy like that to be the one." So, unprepared, never having been a sports psychologist, never having worked in a university in psychology for sports, Bill Simon named me chairman of psychology to enhance the performance of the greatest US athletes for all of America.

My nomination caused a furor. Imagine me going into the Olympic committee of 17 psychiatrists and psychologists, each of whom was also an expert in their sport, figure skating, track and field, fencing, high jumping, all that. They said, "Who do you think you are?"

And I said, "Have you ever heard of the administrator of NASA?"

They said, "No."

I said, "Me neither. I don't know his name. Look at me as that—somebody who's administering the sports psychology programs for the Olympics but who's not going to take any credit. I don't know how to deal with each sport, but you do. You get all the credit. I will help raise the money and work with athletes and teams doing my psychology, but you're the guys."

And they said, "Do you mean you're willing to subordinate your ego to let us do our thing?"

I said, "Absolutely. I couldn't do it anyway. You know that." I learned more from the Olympians than they ever learned from me.

Positively Influencing Others

I have four children, many grandchildren, and now great-grandchildren, some already teenagers. I believe in being a role model, not a critic. If they shouldn't be doing it, neither should you. Values are more likely caught than taught. Be someone worth emulating to your children by setting the example in your life. If you set the example, later on, you'll find that they remembered that they saw. I never got anywhere by preaching. In fact, I remember lecturing my children, and them saying, "Is this your half hour or your 45-minute version of *The Psychology of Winning?*"

Your children are a reflection of how you live. They may misunderstand the advice you give, but there's no misunderstanding how you and your spouse live. Don't tell them about it, show them by your actions. It's much better to walk your talk. A positive role model does more as a parent than any lecturing could possibly do.

I've made every mistake you can make. In other words, I'm a flawed person who's not impressed with himself. My significance comes from my insignificance. I'm an oboe player in the twelfth row of the maestro's orchestra, but I'm not the conductor, and I'm not the guy in front of the cameras.

The older I get, the more I realize it comes down to the few we love, our closest handful of friends, and trying to help young people by passing on everything we've learned. Just like money does you no good when you have it, only when you employ it, if you have knowledge and die with it, it's no good. It's better to pass it on while you're alive.

For me, a widow with a rose garden is as important as a politician, rock star, or superstar athlete. Let's say that you're not interested in entering your roses in the local flower show competition, and the blue ribbon is not important for you; but you love taking care of flowers. The sheer exhilaration of doing something excellent for its own merit—not to prove it to others, not to get the money, and not to get accolades—is its own reward. We all want to be experts in something. We all want to be competitive and beat somebody to make us feel a little better. We all want material things. But the two greatest motivators of all are the sheer exhilaration of doing something excellent, that feels good, and doing it independently without somebody telling us to do it. Those two motivators drive more people to accomplish great things than all the money in the world.

Give More in Value Than You Expect in Payment

One of my philosophies is to always give more in value than you receive in payment. If you give more in value than you receive in payment, you'll always be sought after because you're a bargain. If you're a bargain, they'll be attracted to you. My philosophy has always been to push all your marbles, all your chips, over on the other side. You may not get paid, but still, you pay value first. You don't quid pro quo it in life. Give it all away. Every time, upfront. It will come back to you, probably more than you ever dreamed.

I never got good at making money. I happened to make a lot of money, but I'd never thought about it. I still don't think about money at all. In fact, I have somebody that does that. I don't pay any bills myself or know how much I have beyond a general idea. I do know who I give it to. With my grandchildren, I have a passion project. I ask each of my grandchildren to come to me with their passion. It has to be something that they're so magnificently obsessed with doing that they bring me kind of a business plan. I help them fund their passion so they can get really into it. That's one of the things I'm doing with my estate. I don't want to give people money after I'm dead. What I want to do is make money be useful while I'm alive.

I don't do things because of how expensive they are or put on a show. I used to come in close contact with many people like that. They would take me on a tour, showing me all the things they'd accumulated because that was important to them. Status is not important to me. What is important to me is human interaction, nature, and love.

Doing Something that Benefits Life

I wake up happy and ask myself, "What are you going to do with this day? How can you make life breathe easier as a result of your actions today?" Every day, I try to do something that benefits life. I'm much more in tune with nature, flowers, trees, and the animals these days. I also still have this longing inside to help people, younger people especially, to not be a Redwood tree in a flowerpot. I don't want them to be root bound.

The digital era creates speed and creates the ability to communicate everywhere, but it is the enemy of intimacy. It allows you a virtual smell, but not the real fragrance of the rose. It allows you to have a romance without the love and to go places where you don't get your feet muddy or sand in your shoes. It's the most marvelous tool for communication and the most dangerous thing.

I want younger people to take time. Take time to listen. Take time to look. Take time to smell a rose along the way. Take a hike. Smell the ocean. But don't be so engaged in getting from one place to another that you miss everything along the way.

To learn more about Denis Waitley and his speaking, books, courses, and teachings, please visit www.deniswaitley.com. Follow Denis on Facebook @OfficialDenisWaitley and Instagram @theDenisWaitley

Tweetable: I believe in being a role model, not a critic. If they shouldn't be doing it, neither should you. Values are more likely caught than taught. Be someone worth emulating to your children by setting the example in your life.

WRITING COACH AND EDITOR

Takara Sights is the editor of *Bringing Value, Solving Problems and Leaving a Legacy* and has been publishing inspirational and motivational books with Kyle Wilson since 2015. She works tirelessly to ensure grammar, spelling, and punctuation are correct and she works individually with every author to help them develop and tell their story. As project manager, she is also key in supporting the logistics of communication with each book's many elite authors and the intricate steps of independently publishing a book.

Takara loves contributing to the creation of stunning works and having a hand in helping others tell great stories.

From Takara:

Thank you to my girlfriend, my dog, my parents, and my sister for your unending and immeasurable support over the years. If it weren't for you, my role in these books would not be possible!

Thank you to Kyle Wilson for the opportunity to work with you and learn from you. You are the man!

ADDITIONAL RESOURCES

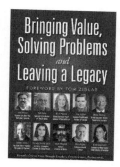

Order in Quantity and SAVE
Mix and Match
Order online KyleWilson.com/books

Printed in Great Britain
by Amazon